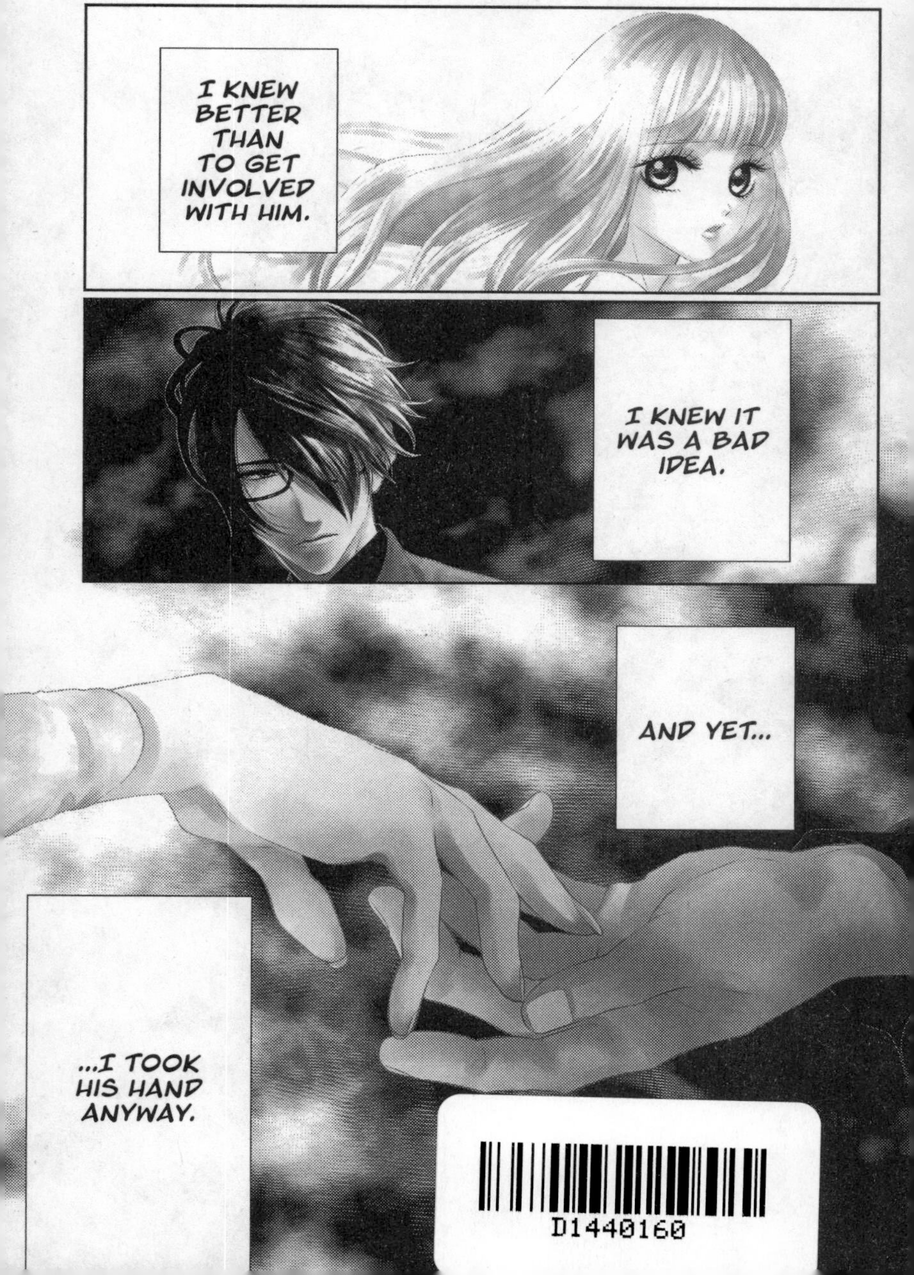
I KNEW BETTER THAN TO GET INVOLVED WITH HIM.
I KNEW IT WAS A BAD IDEA.
AND YET...
...I TOOK HIS HAND ANYWAY.

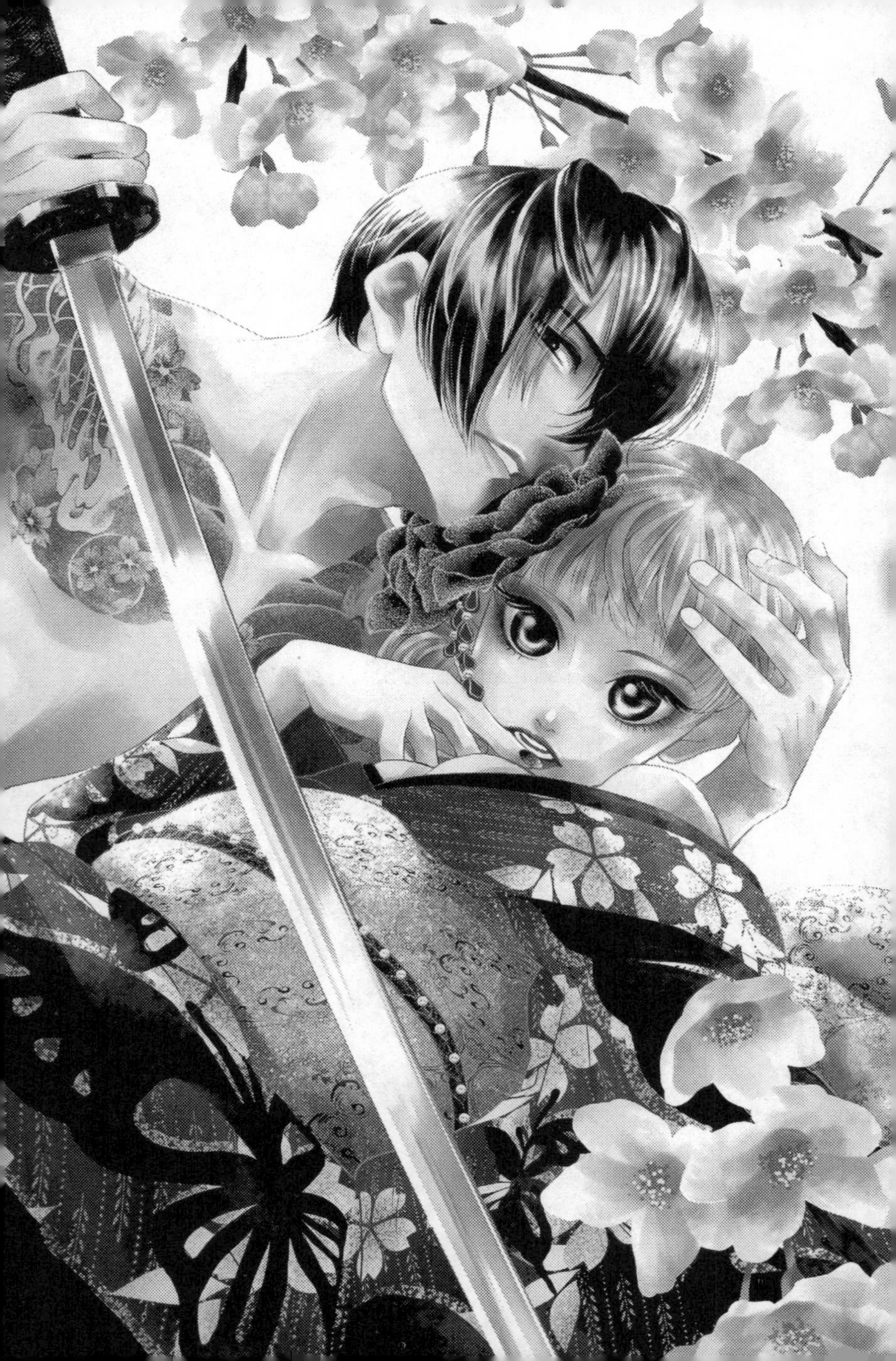

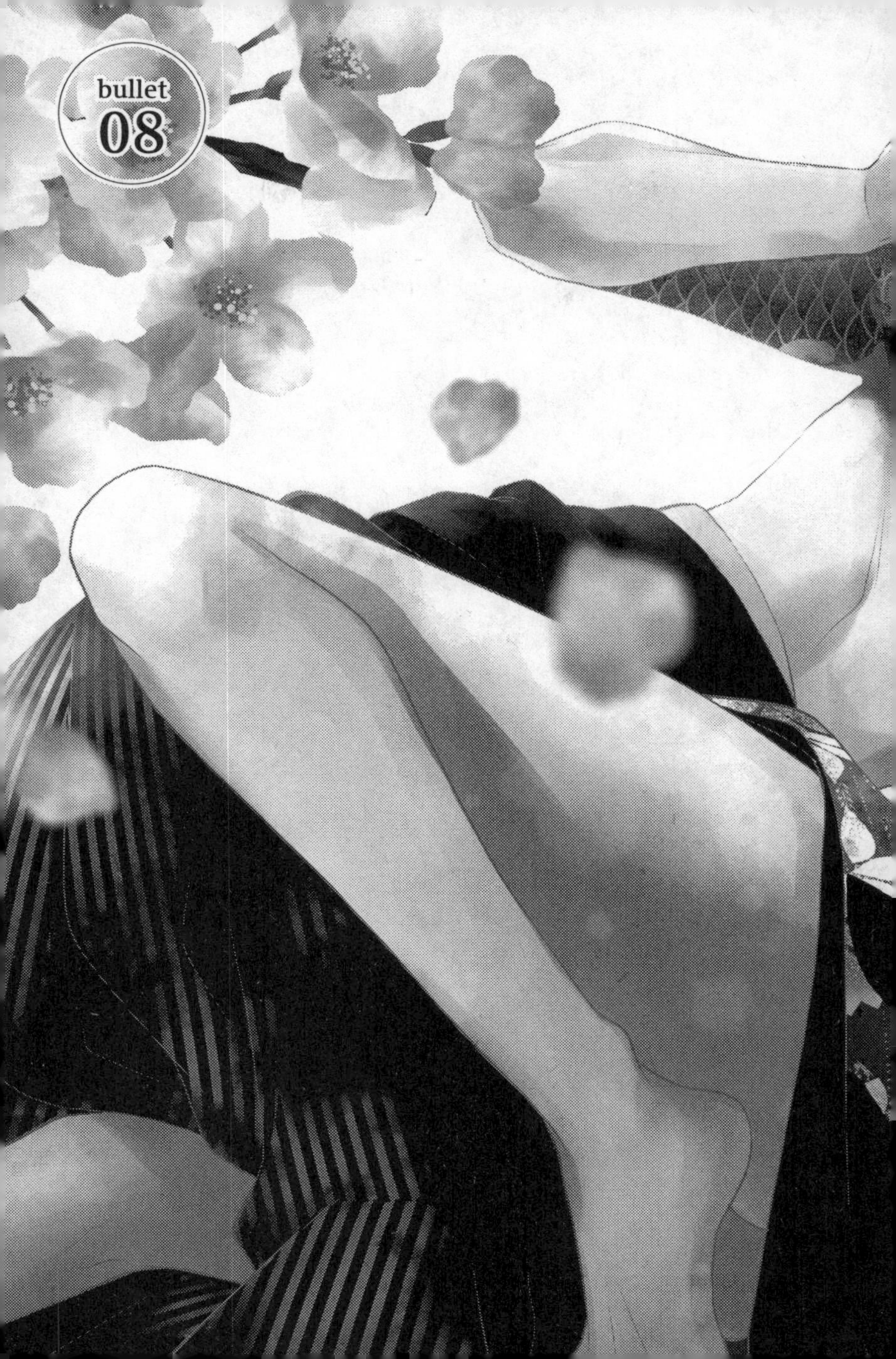
bullet
08

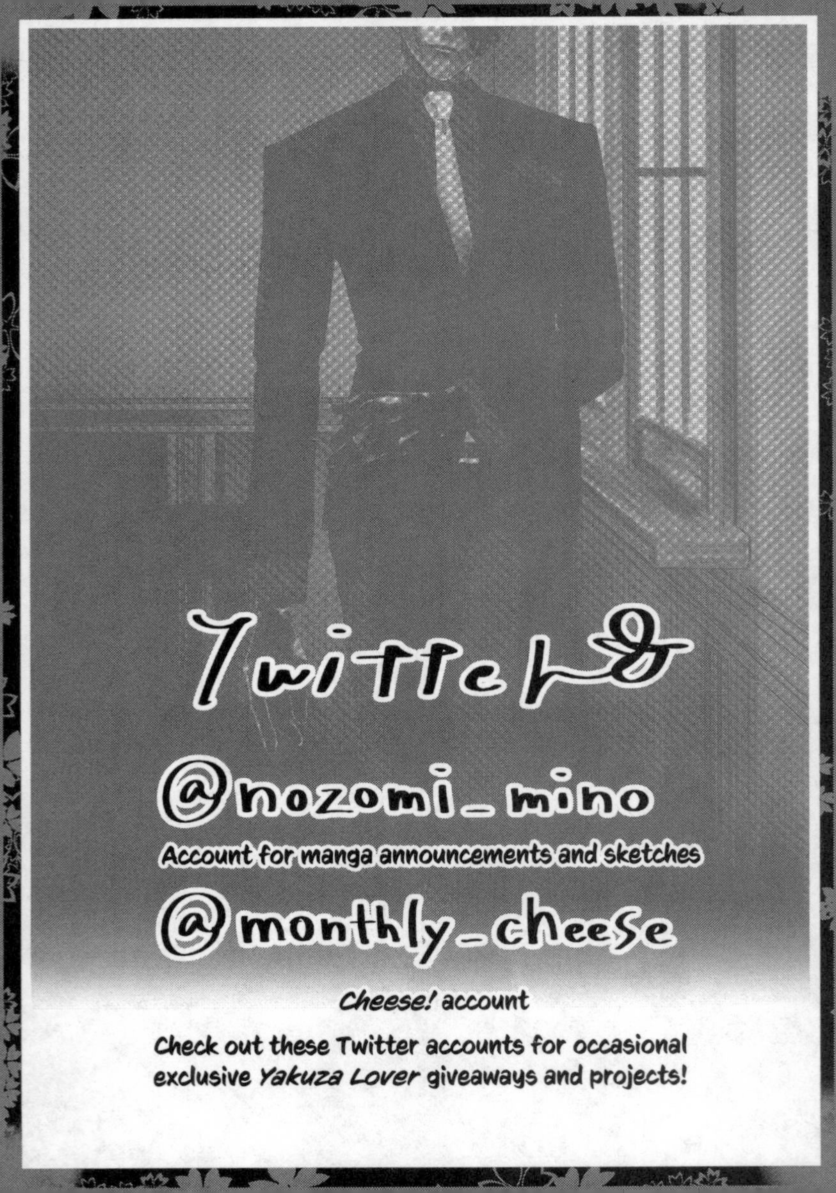
Twitter
@nozomi_mino
Account for manga announcements and sketches
@monthly_cheese
Cheese! account
Check out these Twitter accounts for occasional exclusive *Yakuza Lover* giveaways and projects!

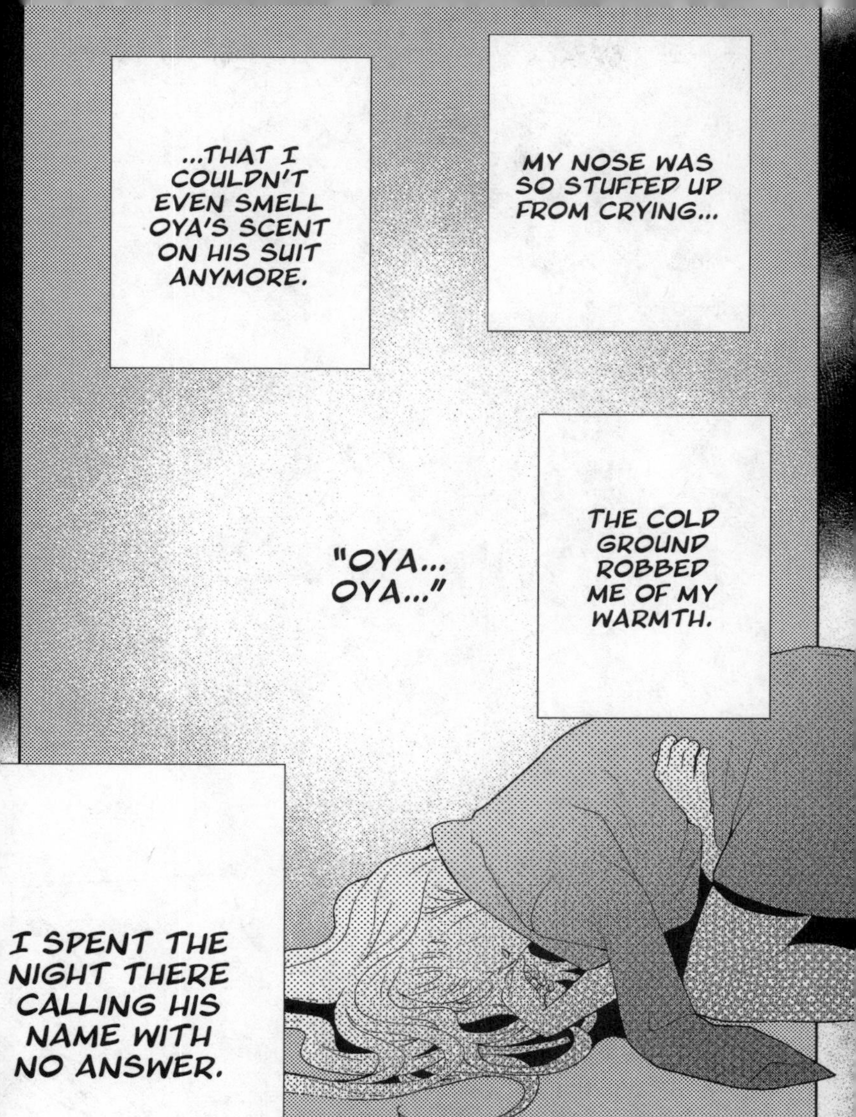
MY NOSE WAS SO STUFFED UP FROM CRYING...
...THAT I COULDN'T EVEN SMELL OYA'S SCENT ON HIS SUIT ANYMORE.
THE COLD GROUND ROBBED ME OF MY WARMTH.
"OYA... OYA..."
I SPENT THE NIGHT THERE CALLING HIS NAME WITH NO ANSWER.

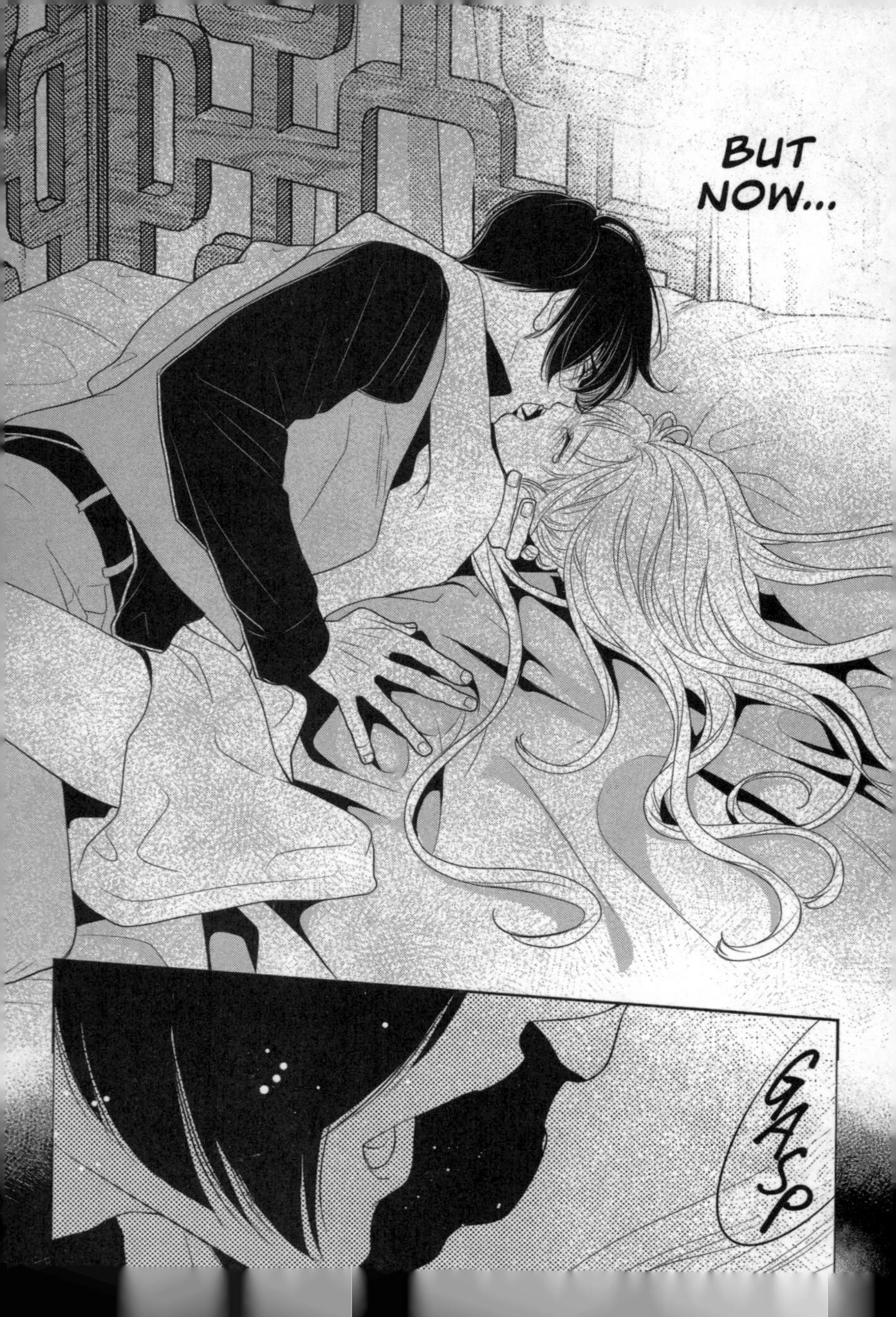
BUT NOW...
GASP

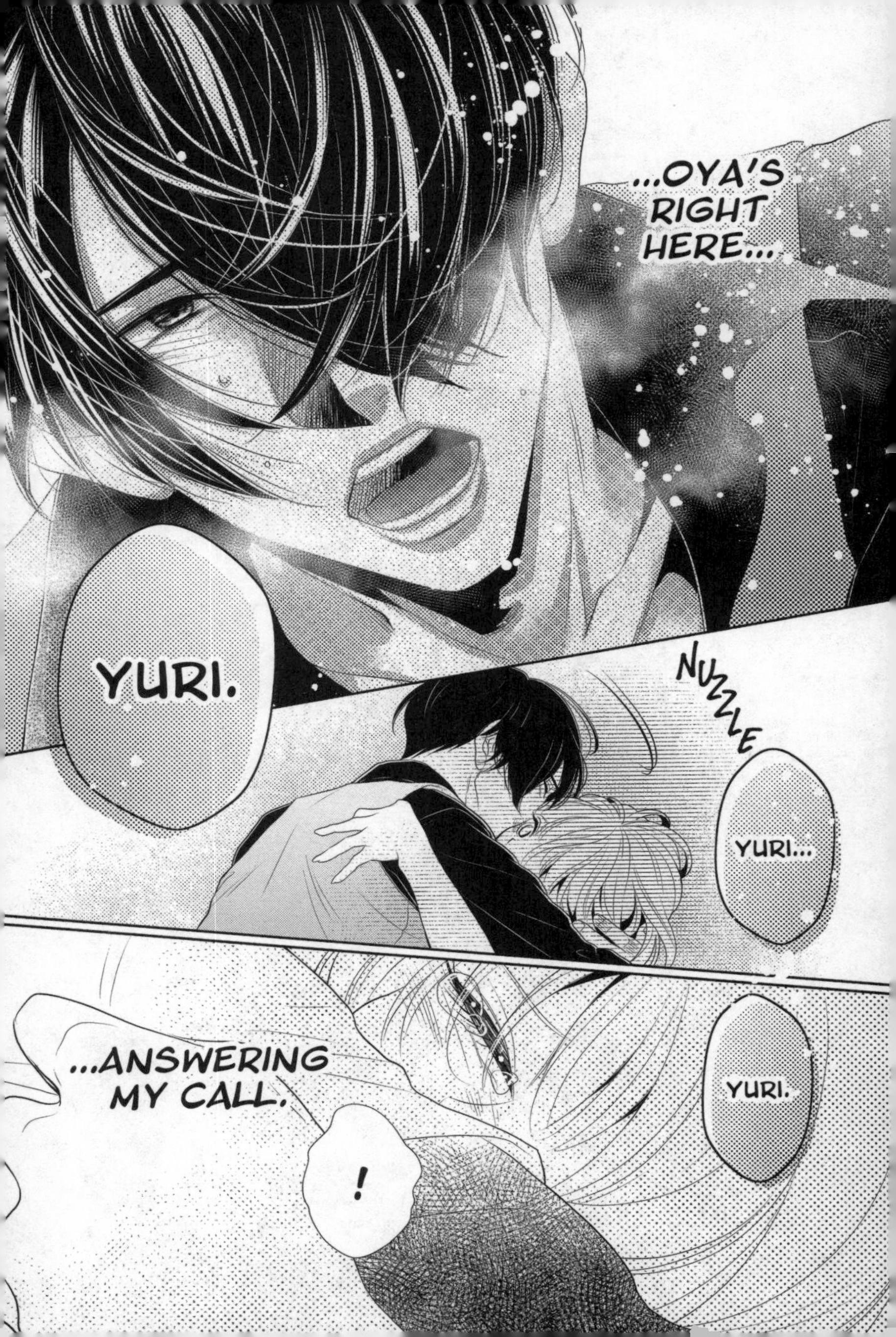
...OYA'S RIGHT HERE...
YURI.
NUZZLE
YURI...
YURI.
...ANSWERING MY CALL.
!

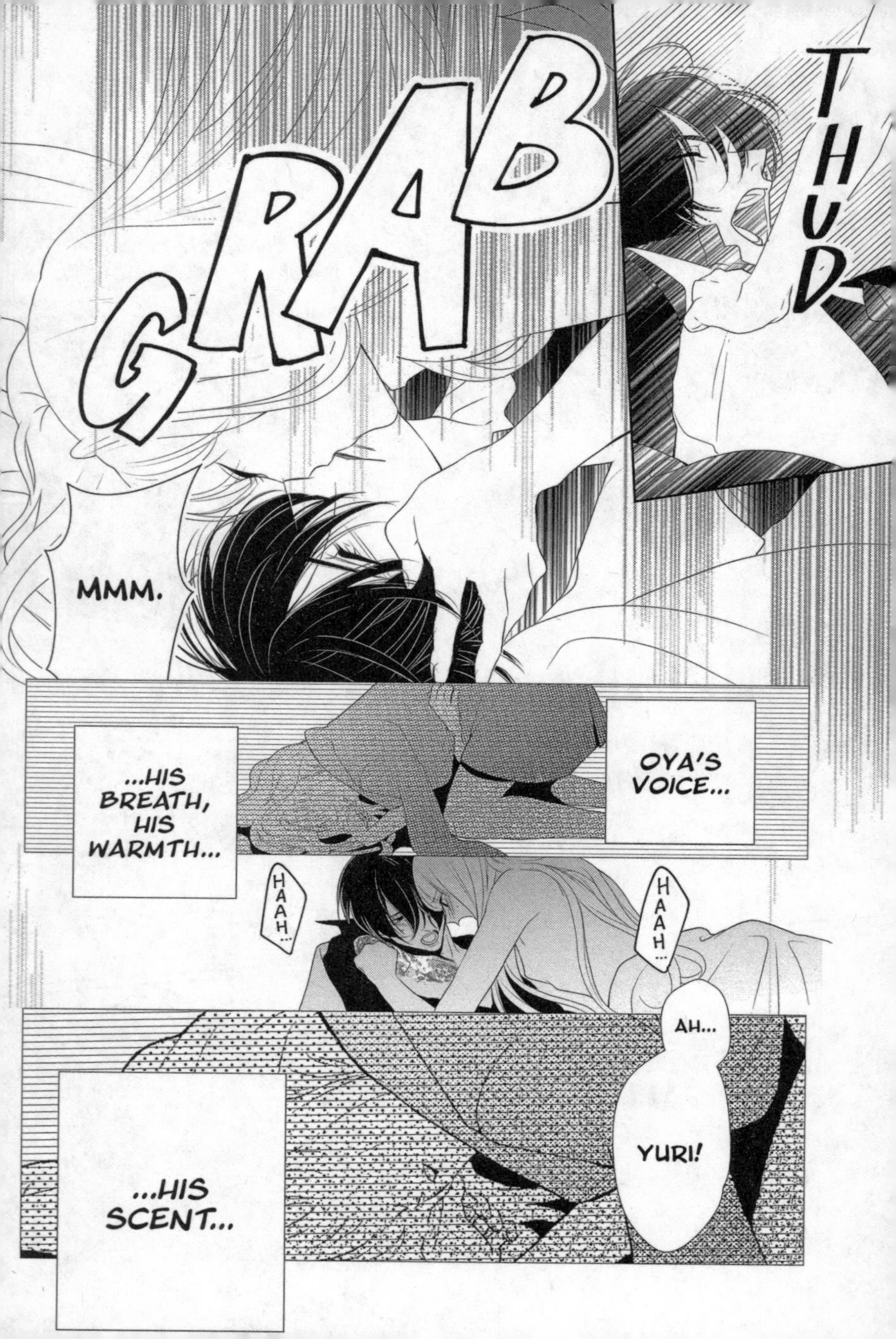
THUD
GRAB
MMM.
OYA'S VOICE...
...HIS BREATH, HIS WARMTH...
HAAH...
HAAH...
AH...
YURI!
...HIS SCENT...

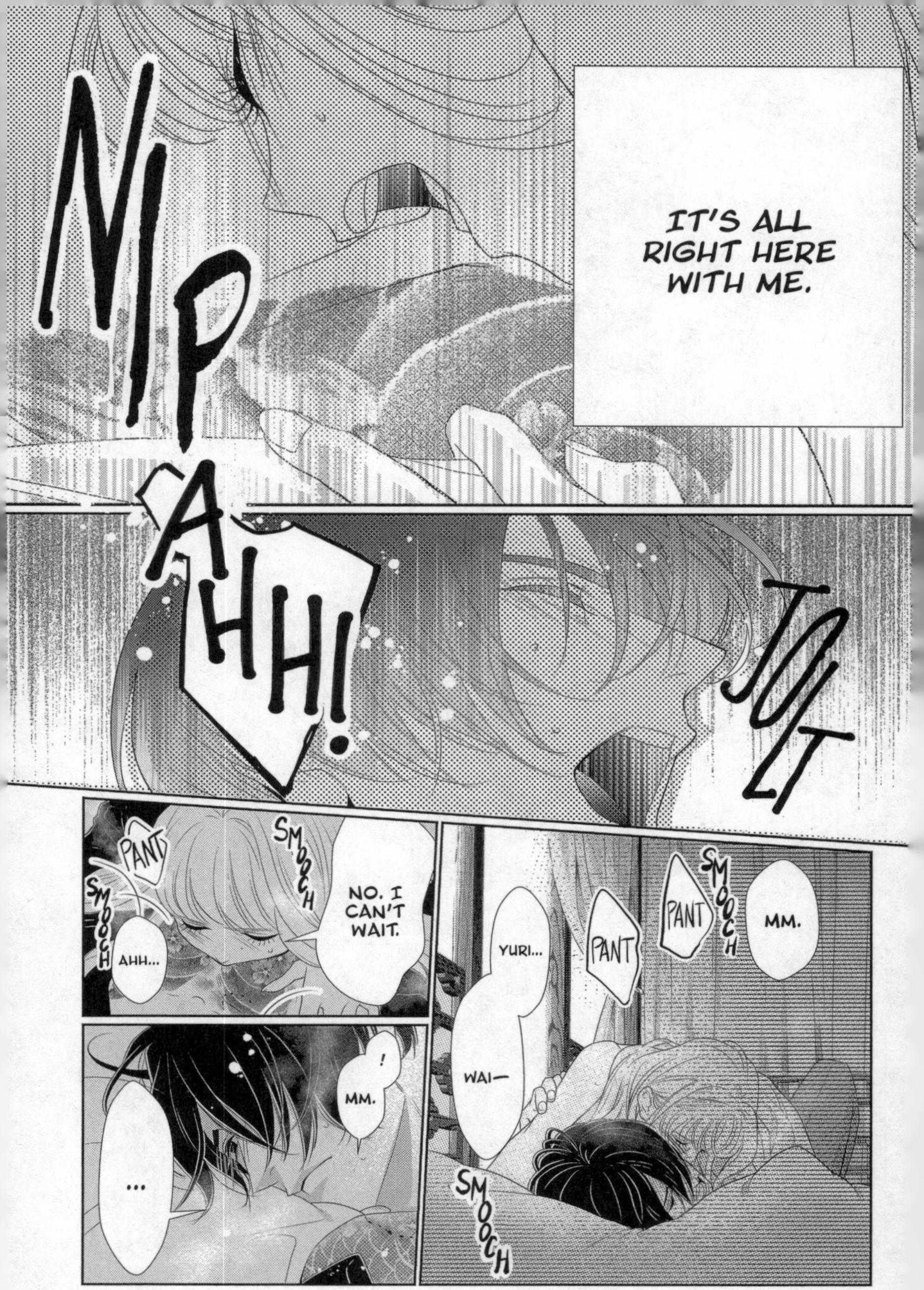
IT'S ALL RIGHT HERE WITH ME.
NIP
JOLT
AHHH!
MM.
SMOOCH
PANT
PANT
YURI...
WAI—
SMOOCH
NO. I CAN'T WAIT.
SMOOCH
PANT
SMOOCH
AHH...
!
MM.
...

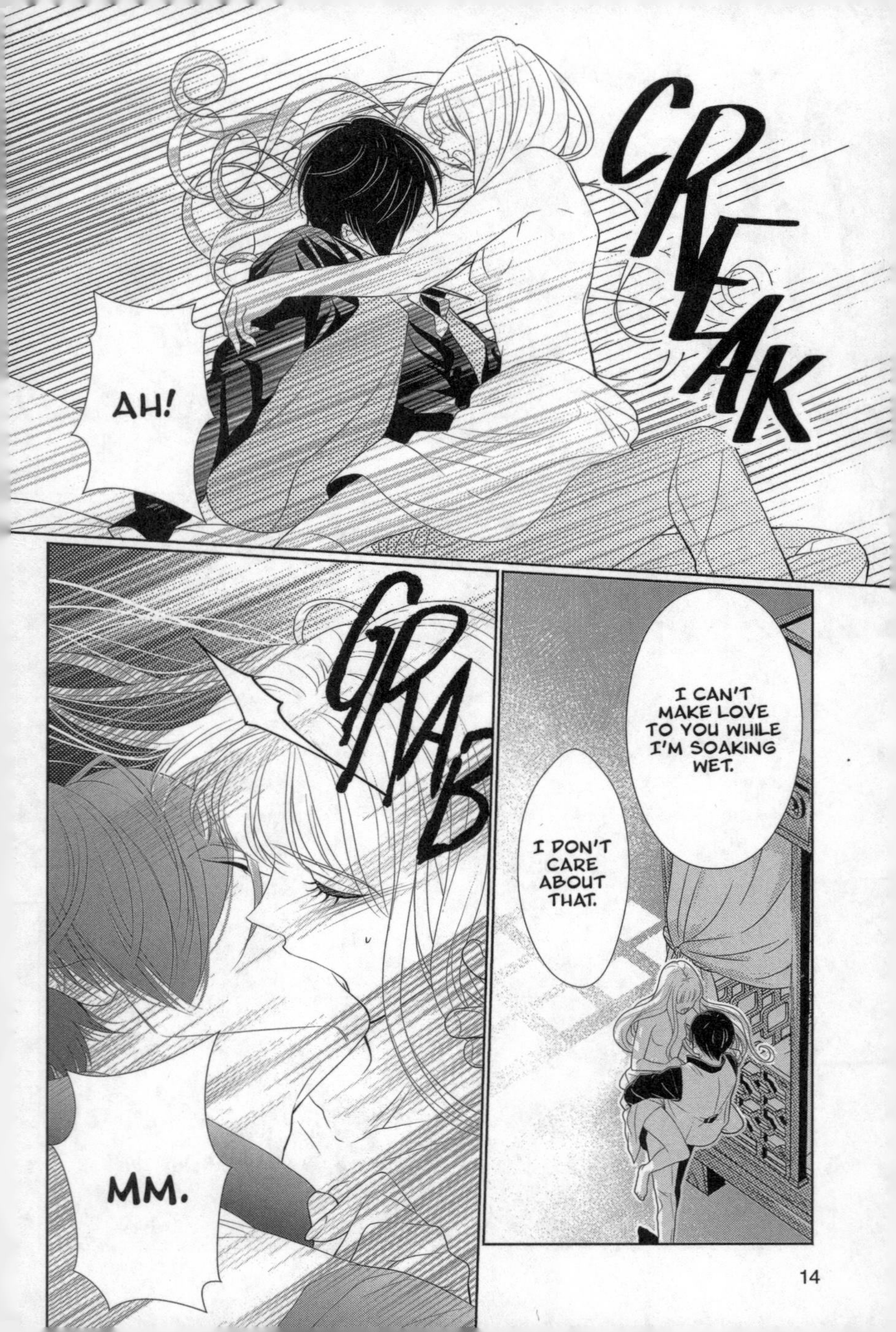
CREAK
AH!
I CAN'T MAKE LOVE TO YOU WHILE I'M SOAKING WET.
I DON'T CARE ABOUT THAT.
GRAB
MM.

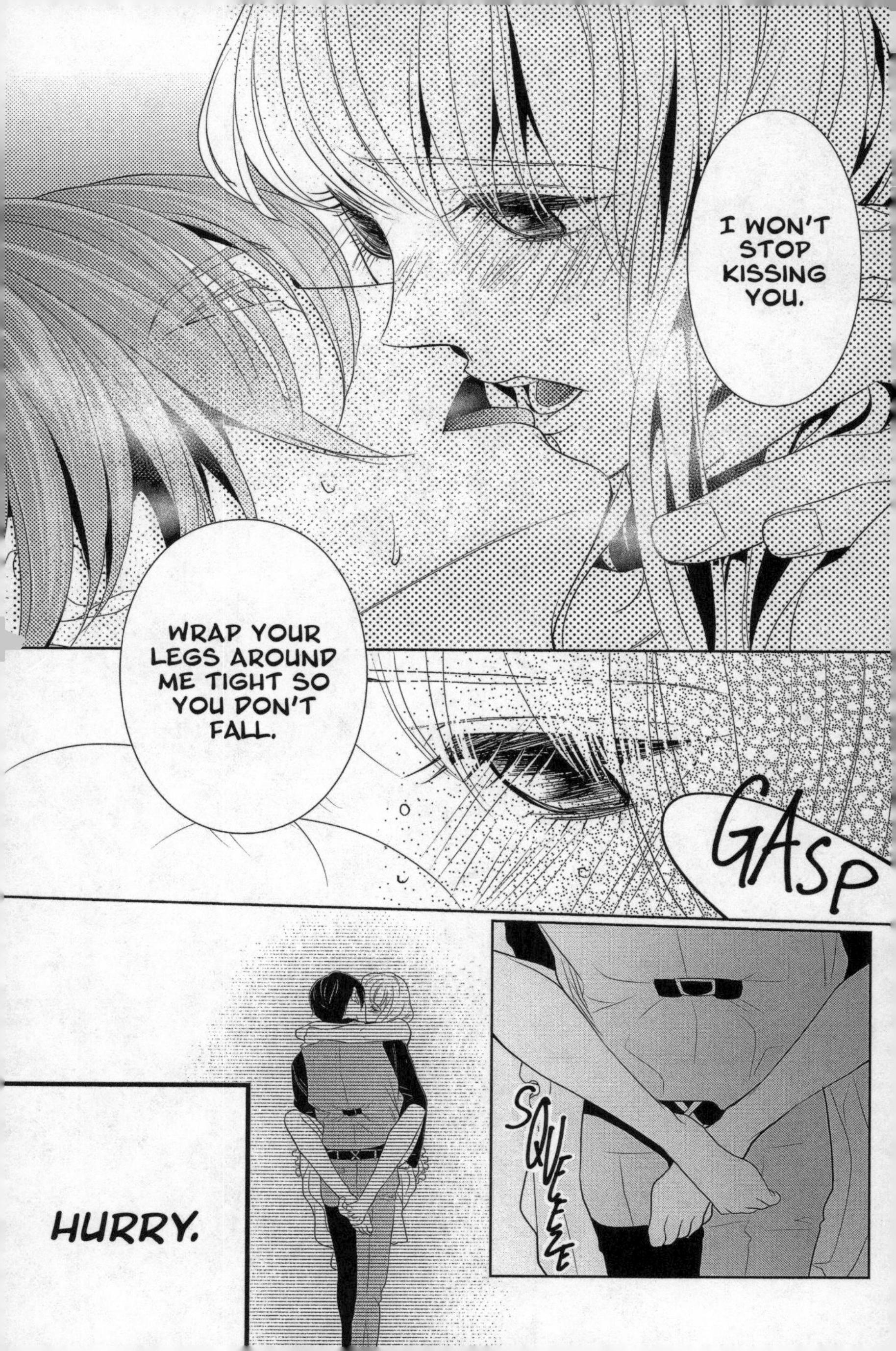
I WON'T STOP KISSING YOU.
WRAP YOUR LEGS AROUND ME TIGHT SO YOU DON'T FALL.
GASP
SQUEEEZE
HURRY.

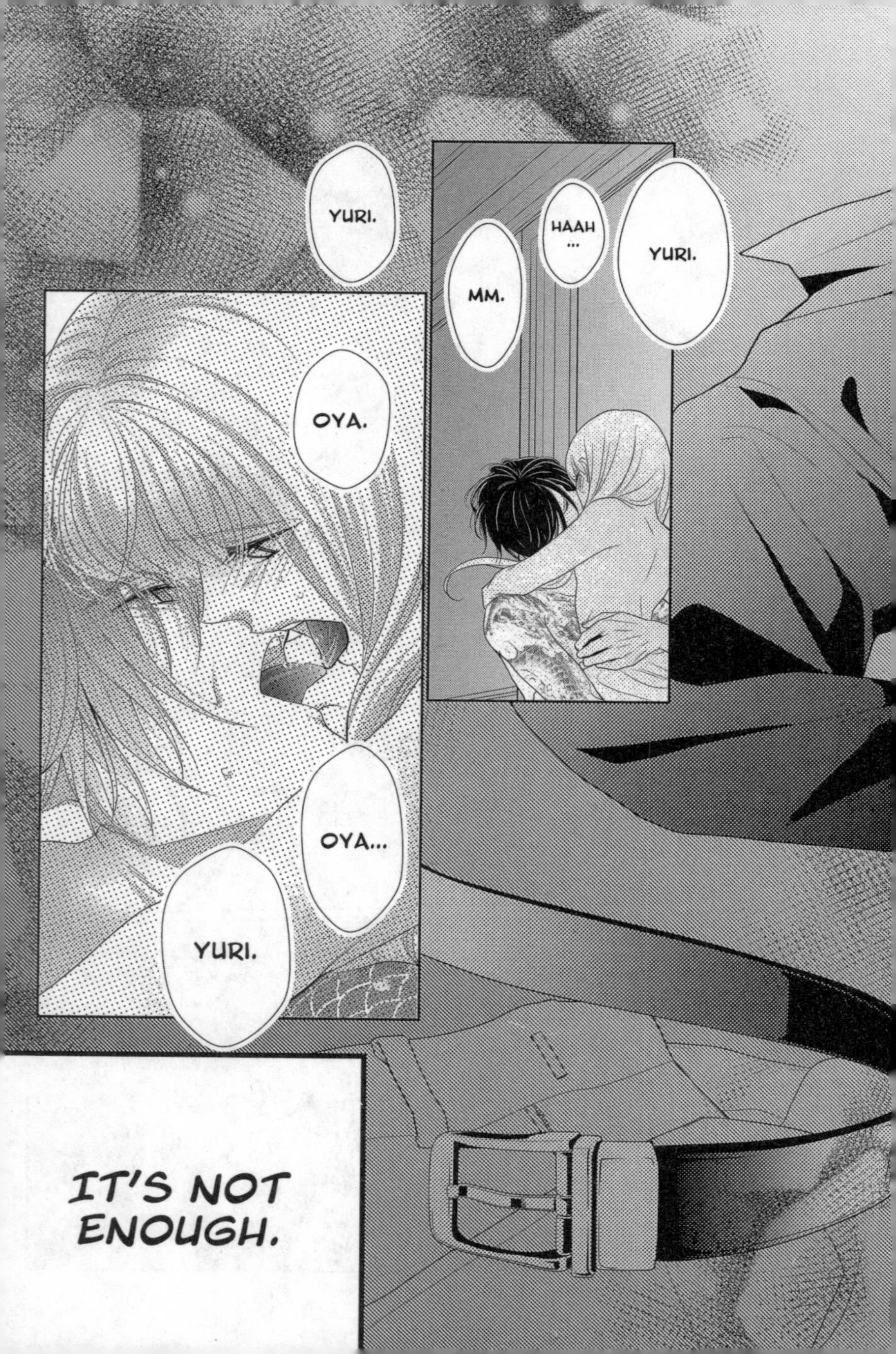
YURI.
HAAH ...
MM.
YURI.
OYA.
OYA...
YURI.
IT'S NOT ENOUGH.

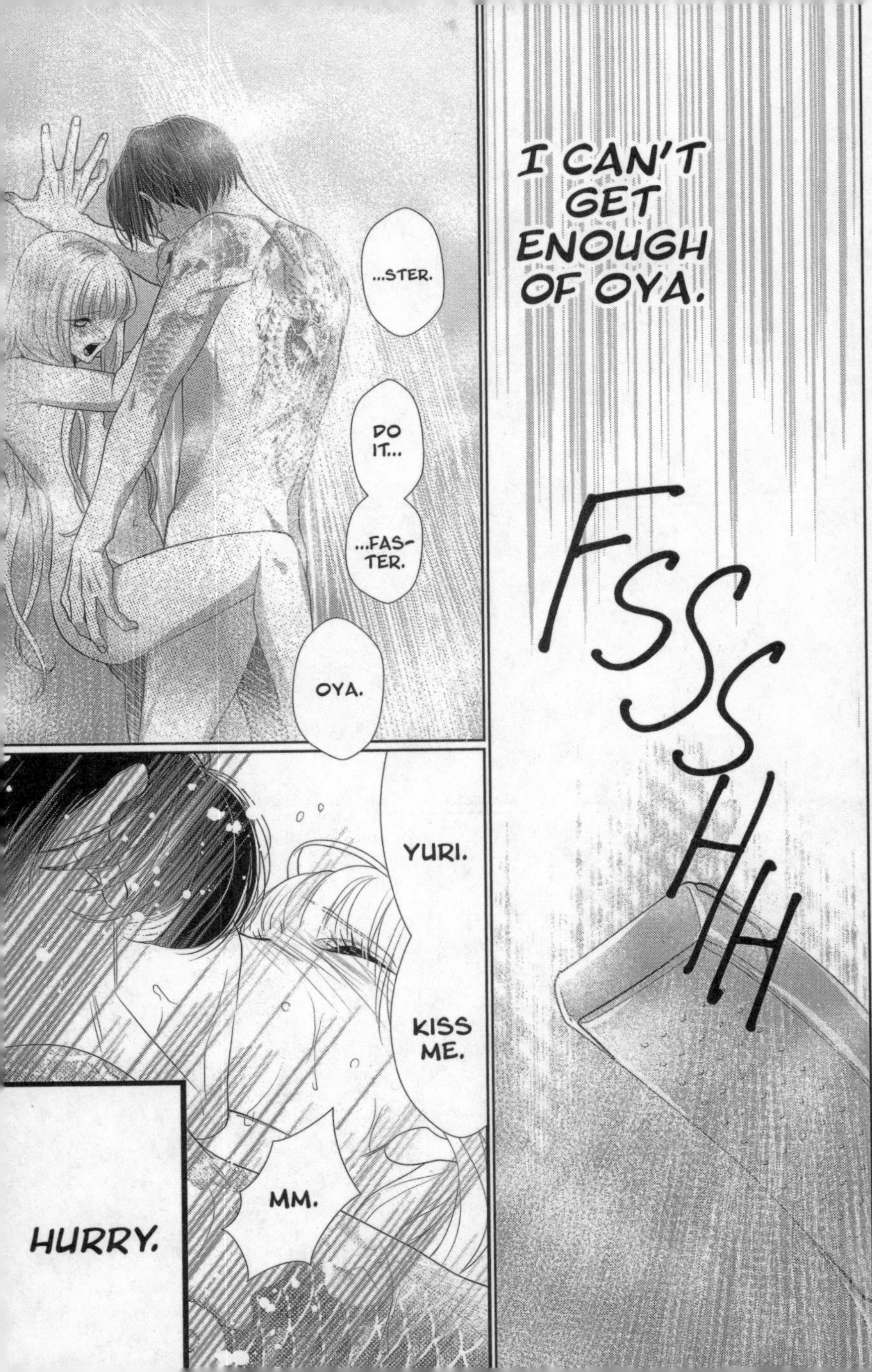
I CAN'T GET ENOUGH OF OYA.
FSSSHHH
...STER.
DO IT...
...FAS-TER.
OYA.
YURI.
KISS ME.
MM.
HURRY.

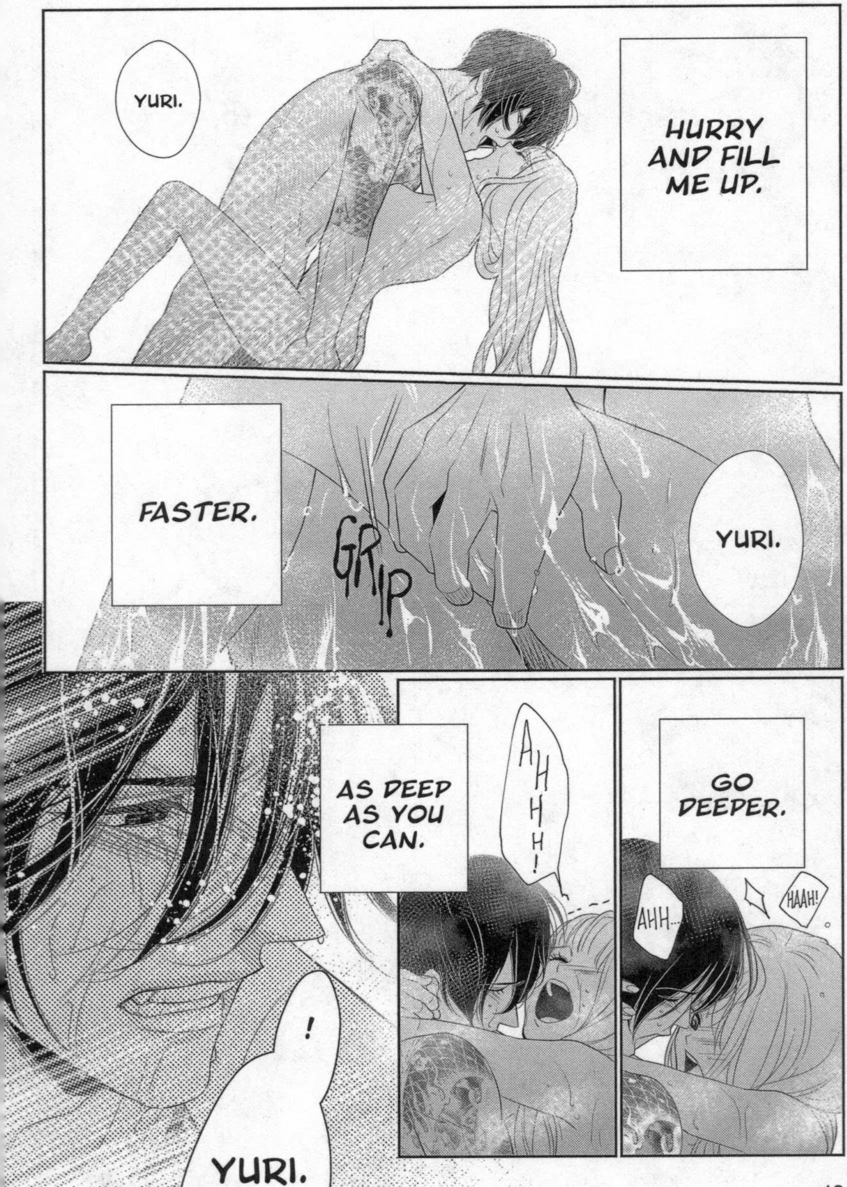
HURRY AND FILL ME UP.
YURI.
YURI.
FASTER.
GRIP
GO DEEPER.
HAAH!
AHH...
AHHH!
AS DEEP AS YOU CAN.
!
YURI.

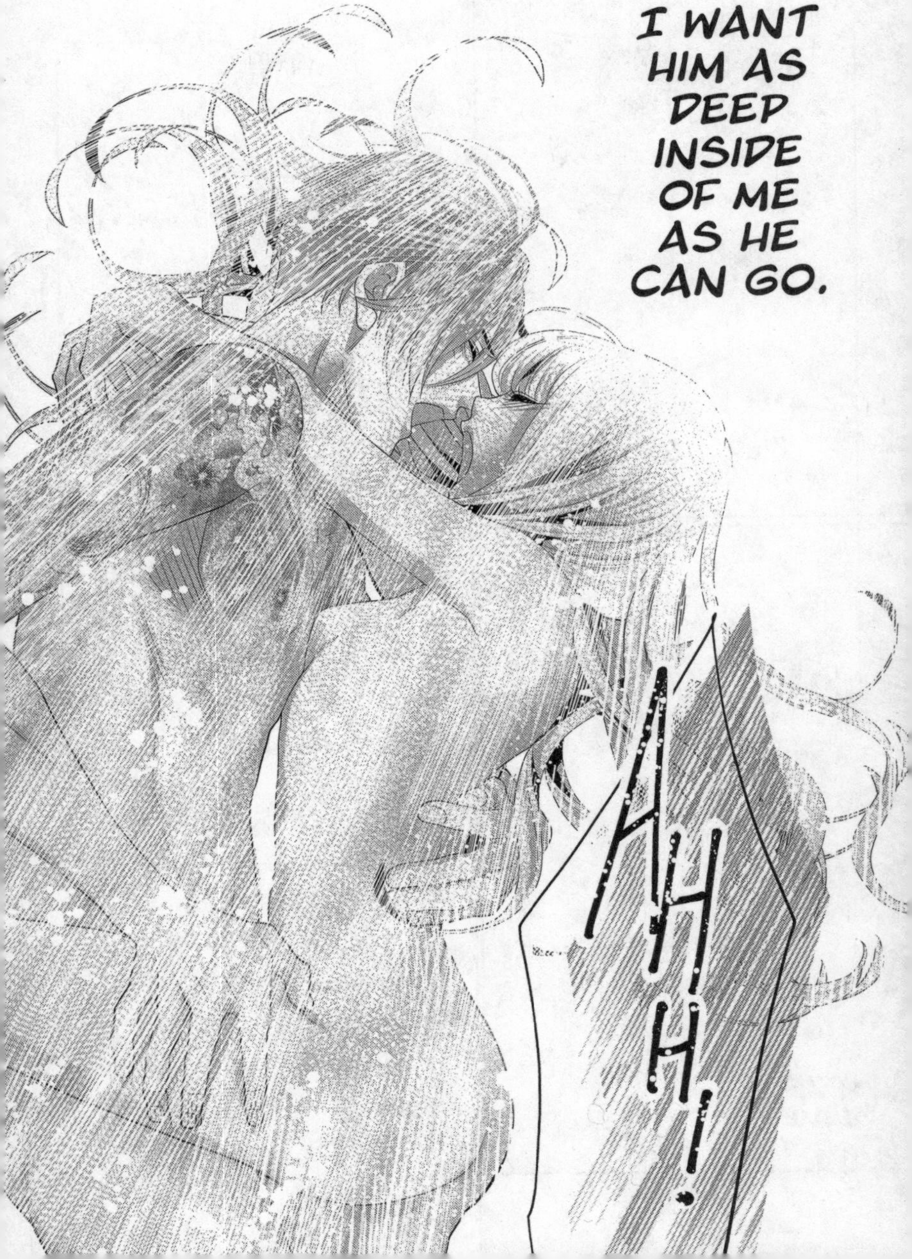
I WANT HIM AS DEEP INSIDE OF ME AS HE CAN GO.
AHHH!

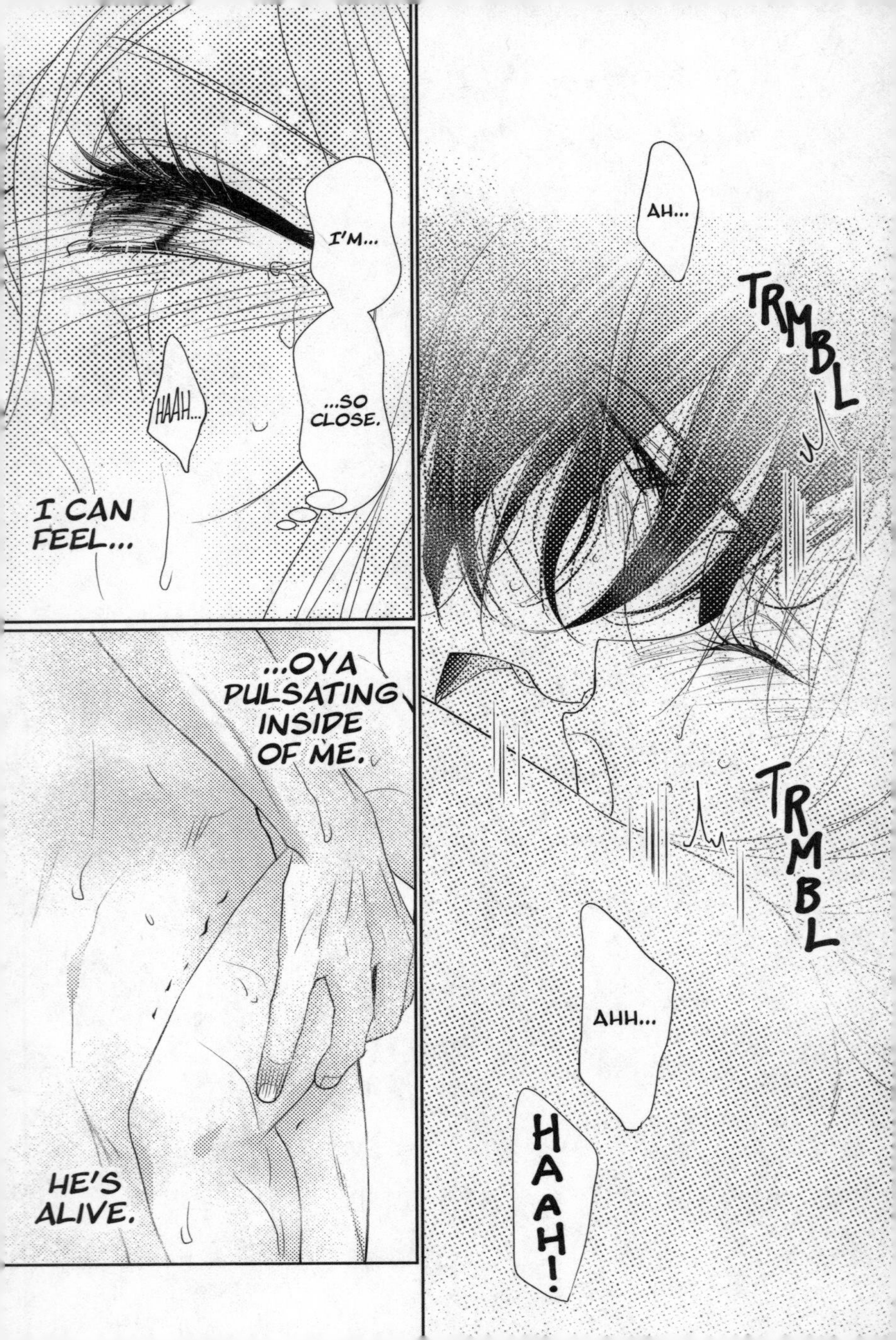
AH...
TRMBL
TRMBL
AHH...
HAAH!
I'M...
...SO CLOSE.
HAAH...
I CAN FEEL...
...OYA PULSATING INSIDE OF ME.
HE'S ALIVE.

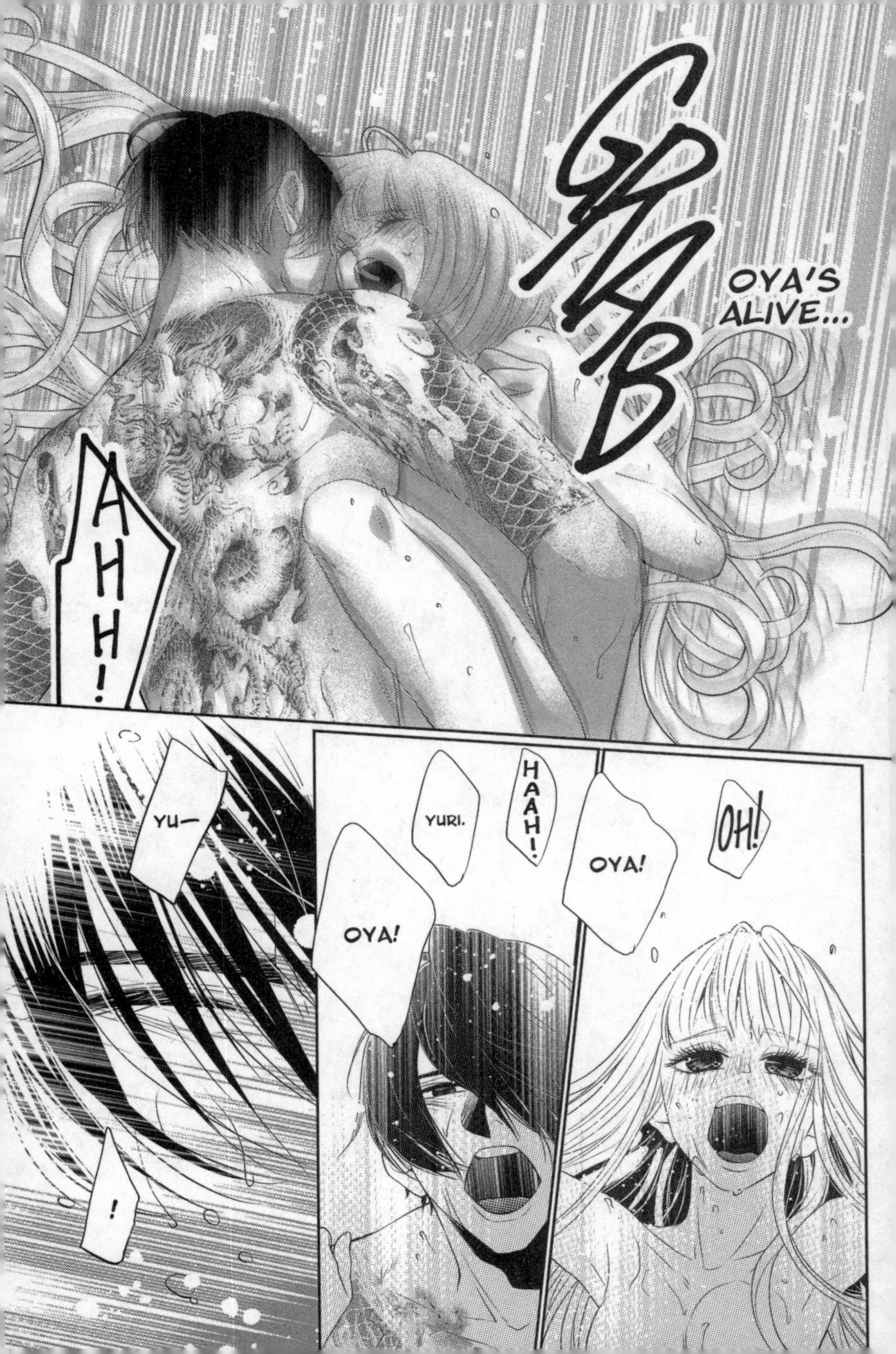
OYA'S ALIVE...
GRAB
AHH!
OH!
OYA!
HAAH!
YURI.
OYA!
YU—
!

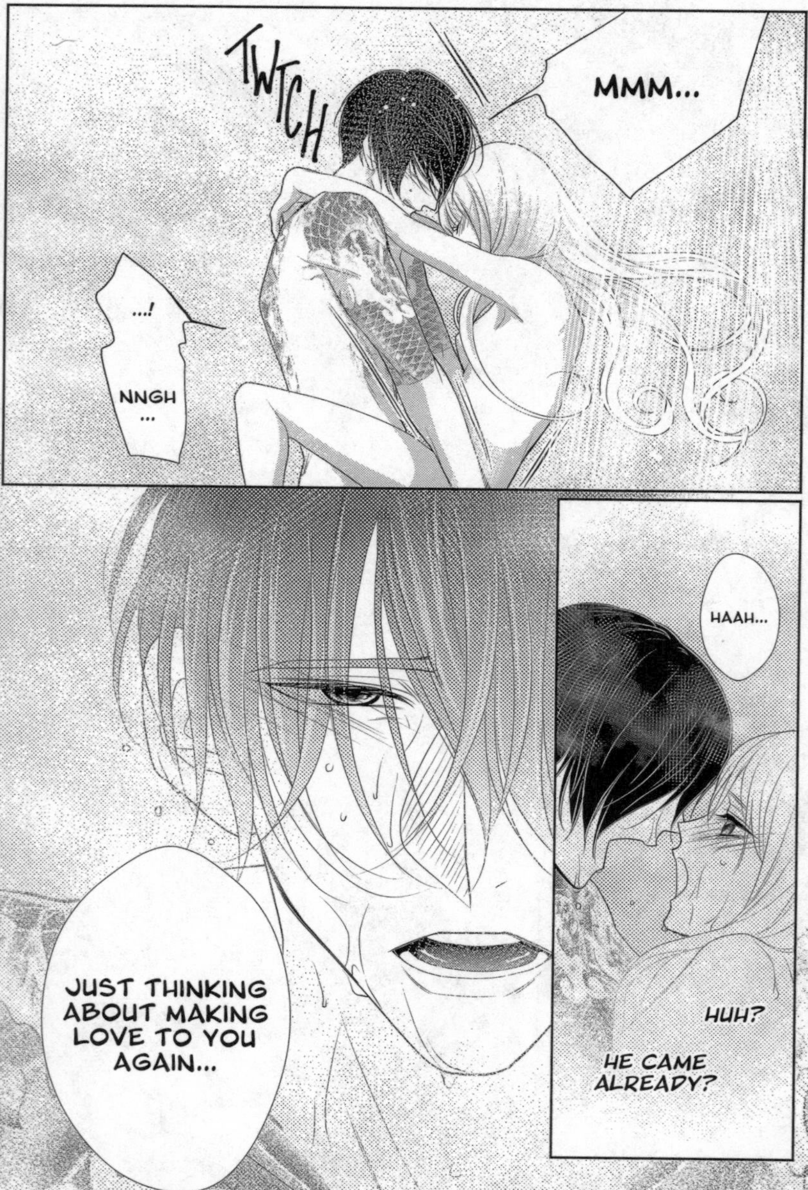
MMM...
TWITCH
...!
NNGH...
HAAH...
HUH?
HE CAME ALREADY?
JUST THINKING ABOUT MAKING LOVE TO YOU AGAIN...

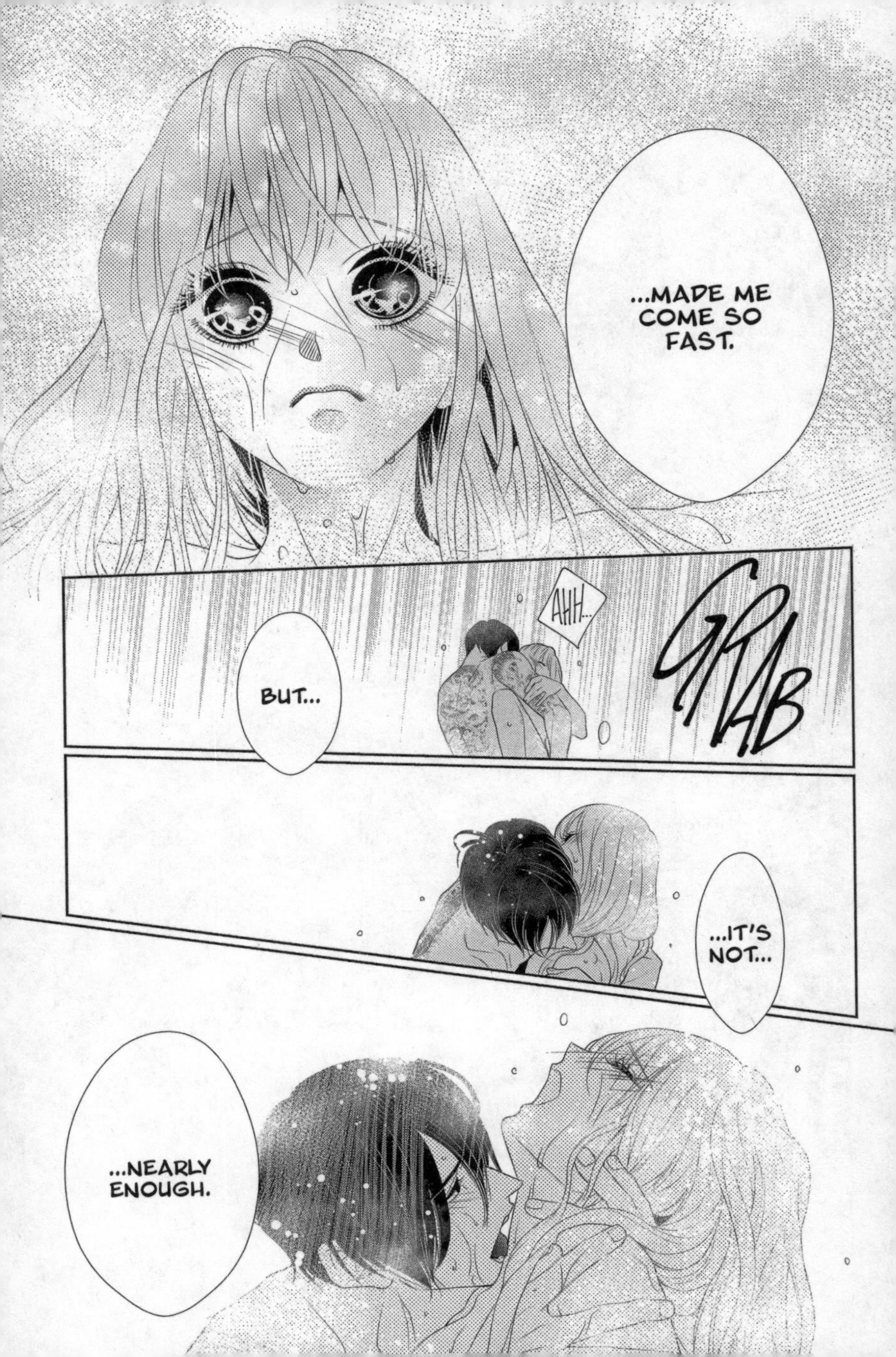
...MADE ME COME SO FAST.
GRAB
AHH...
BUT...
...IT'S NOT...
...NEARLY ENOUGH.

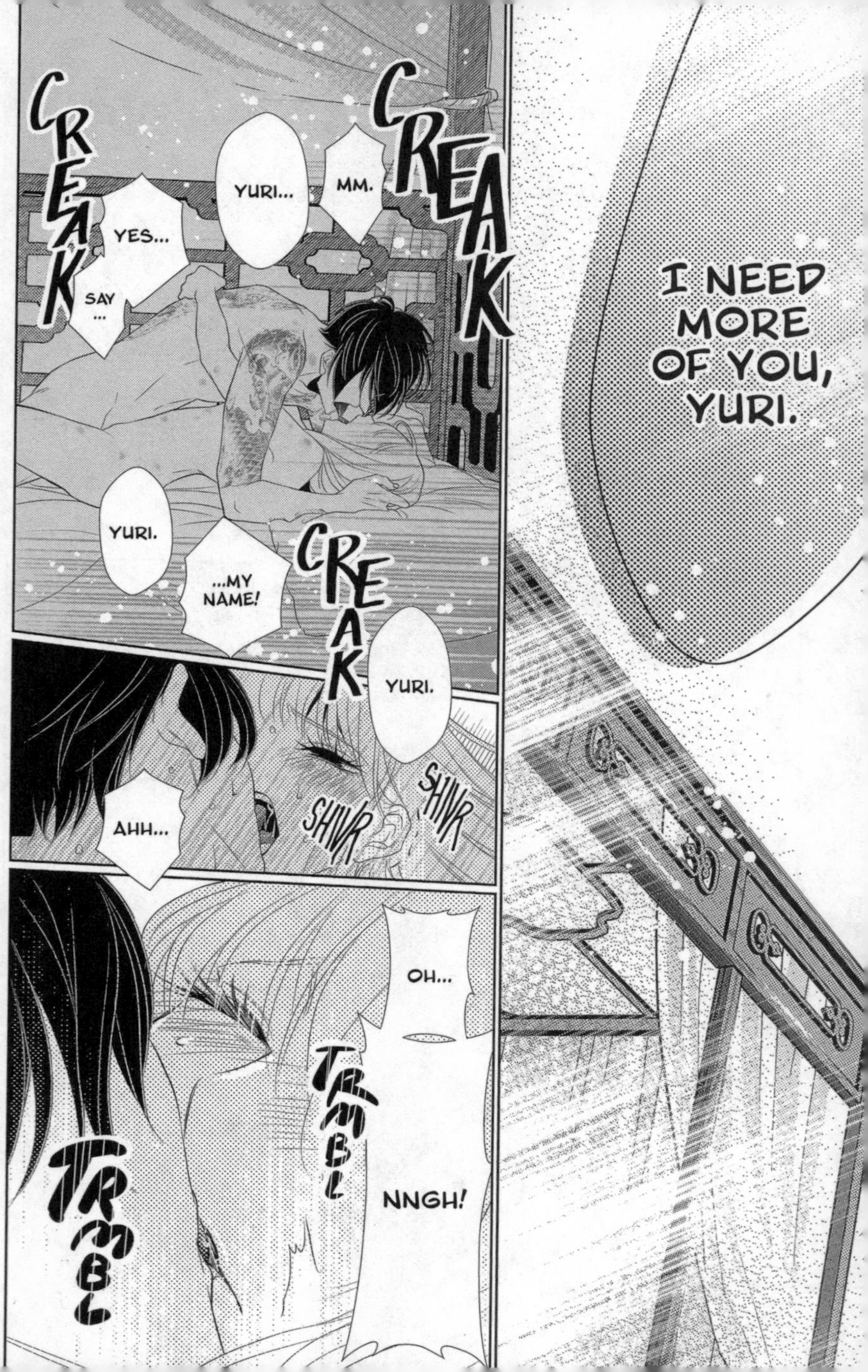
I NEED MORE OF YOU, YURI.
CREAK
MM.
YURI...
CREAK
YES...
SAY...
CREAK
...MY NAME!
YURI.
YURI.
SHIVR
SHIVR
AHH...
OH...
TRMBL
NNGH!
TRMBL

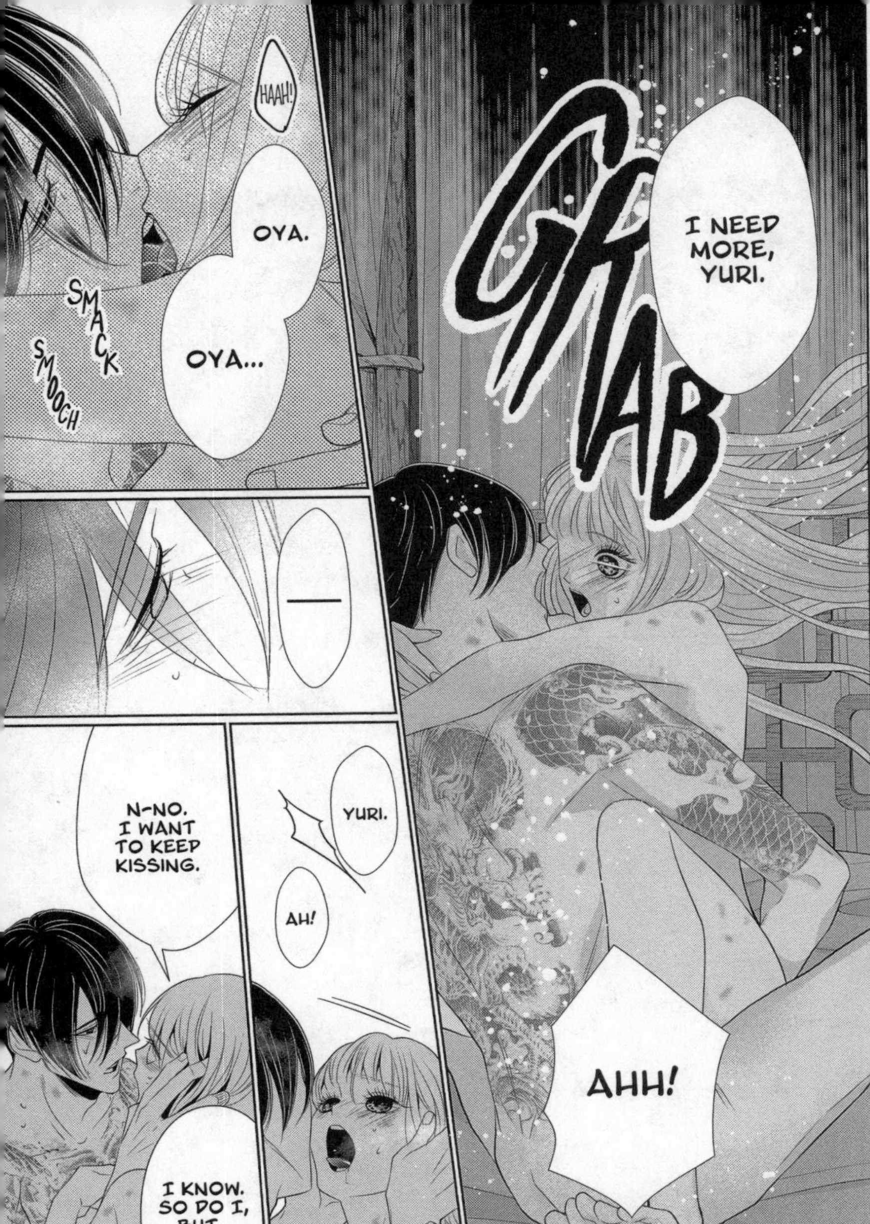
GRAB
I NEED MORE, YURI.
AHH!
HAAH!
OYA.
OYA...
SMACK
SMOOCH
—
YURI.
AH!
N-NO. I WANT TO KEEP KISSING.
I KNOW. SO DO I, BUT...

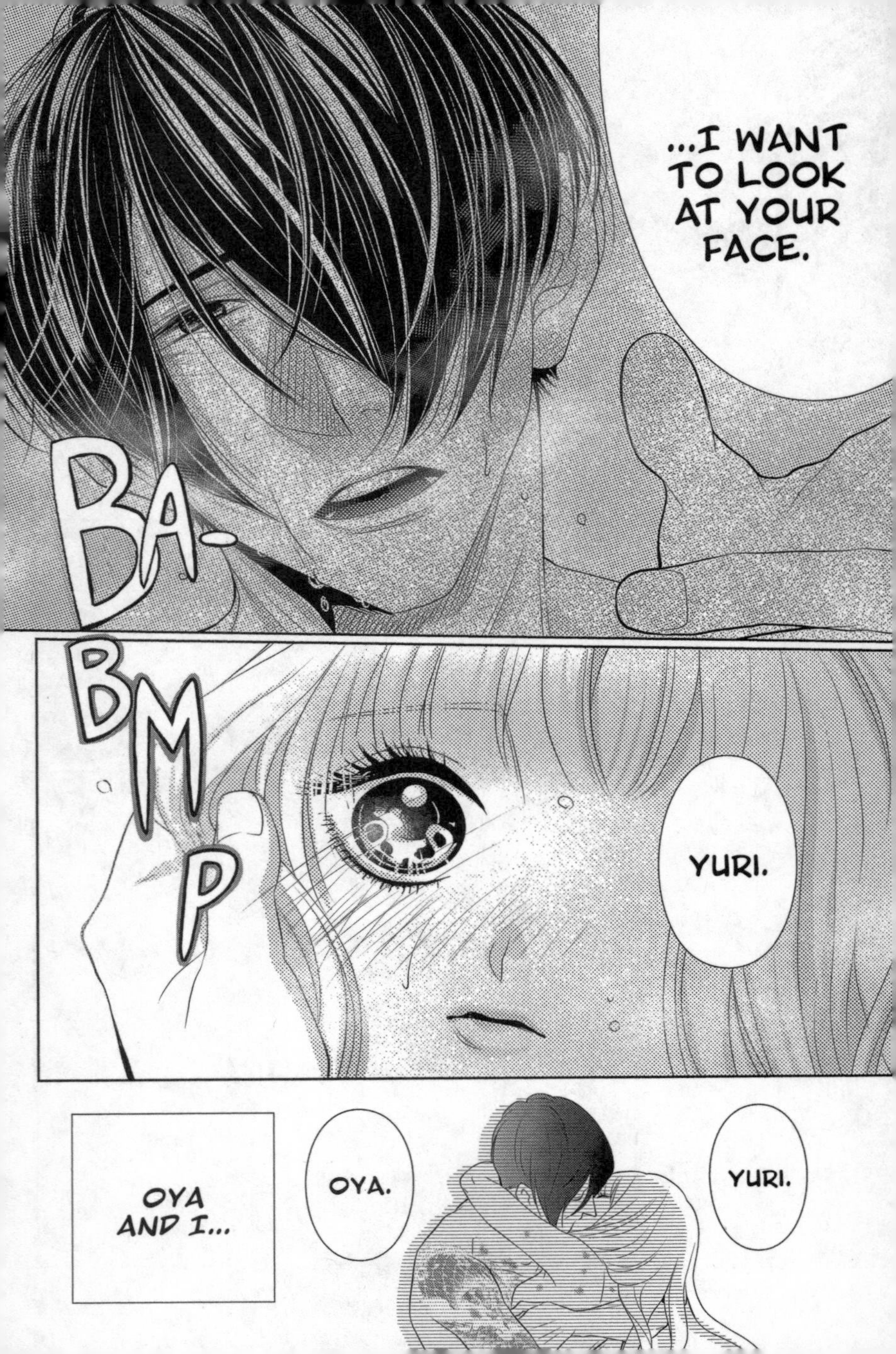
...I WANT TO LOOK AT YOUR FACE.
BA-BMP
YURI.
YURI.
OYA.
OYA AND I...

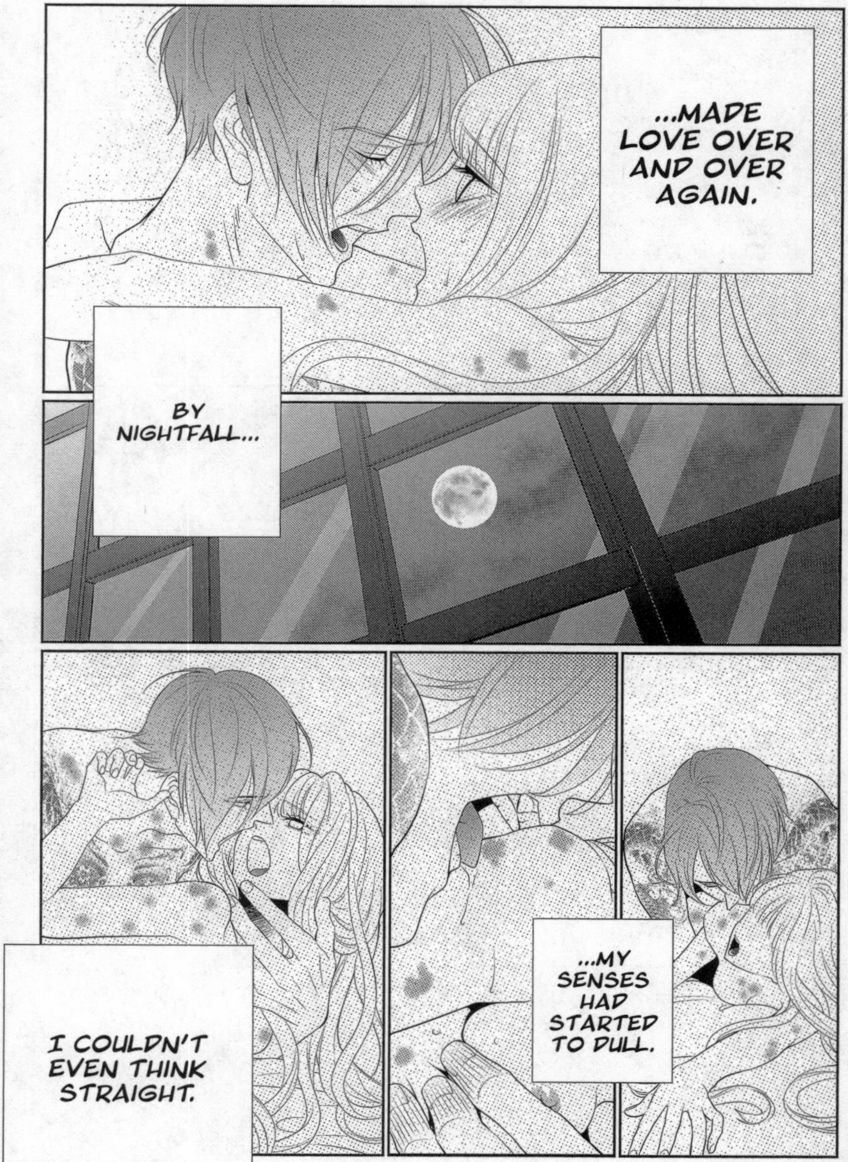
...MADE LOVE OVER AND OVER AGAIN.
BY NIGHTFALL...
...MY SENSES HAD STARTED TO DULL.
I COULDN'T EVEN THINK STRAIGHT.

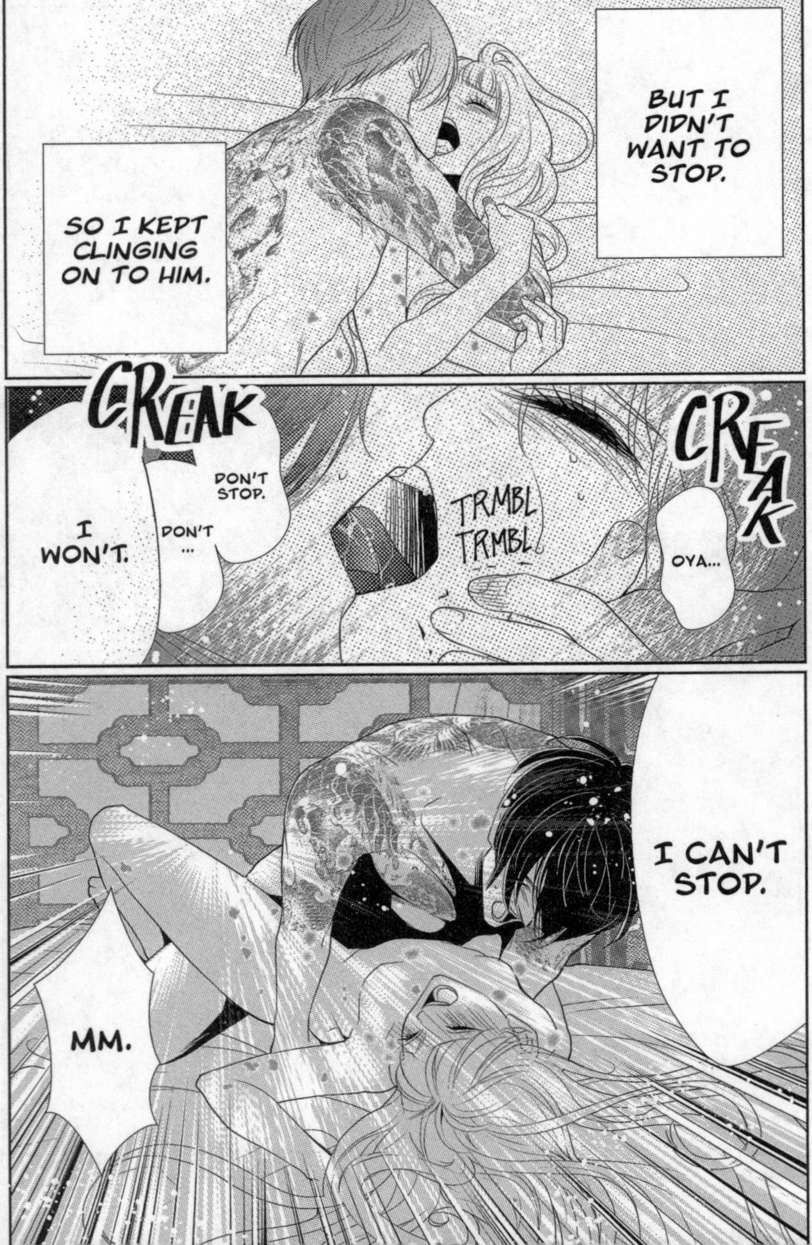
BUT I DIDN'T WANT TO STOP.
SO I KEPT CLINGING ON TO HIM.
CREAK
OYA...
TRMBL TRMBL
CREAK
DON'T STOP.
DON'T ...
I WON'T.
I CAN'T STOP.
MM.

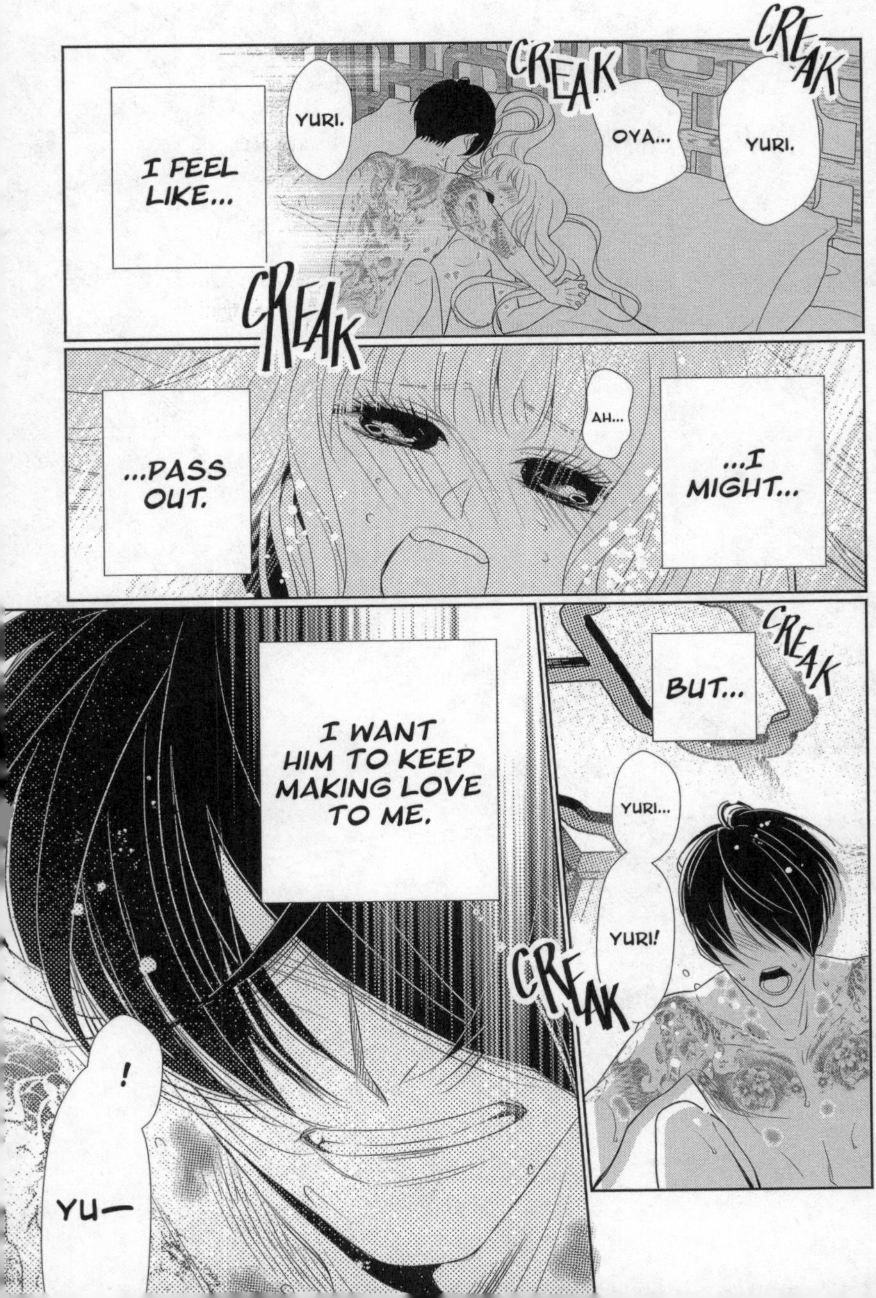
CREAK
YURI.
CREAK
OYA...
YURI.
I FEEL LIKE...
CREAK
...I MIGHT...
AH...
...PASS OUT.
CREAK
BUT...
YURI...
YURI!
CREAK
I WANT HIM TO KEEP MAKING LOVE TO ME.
!
YU—

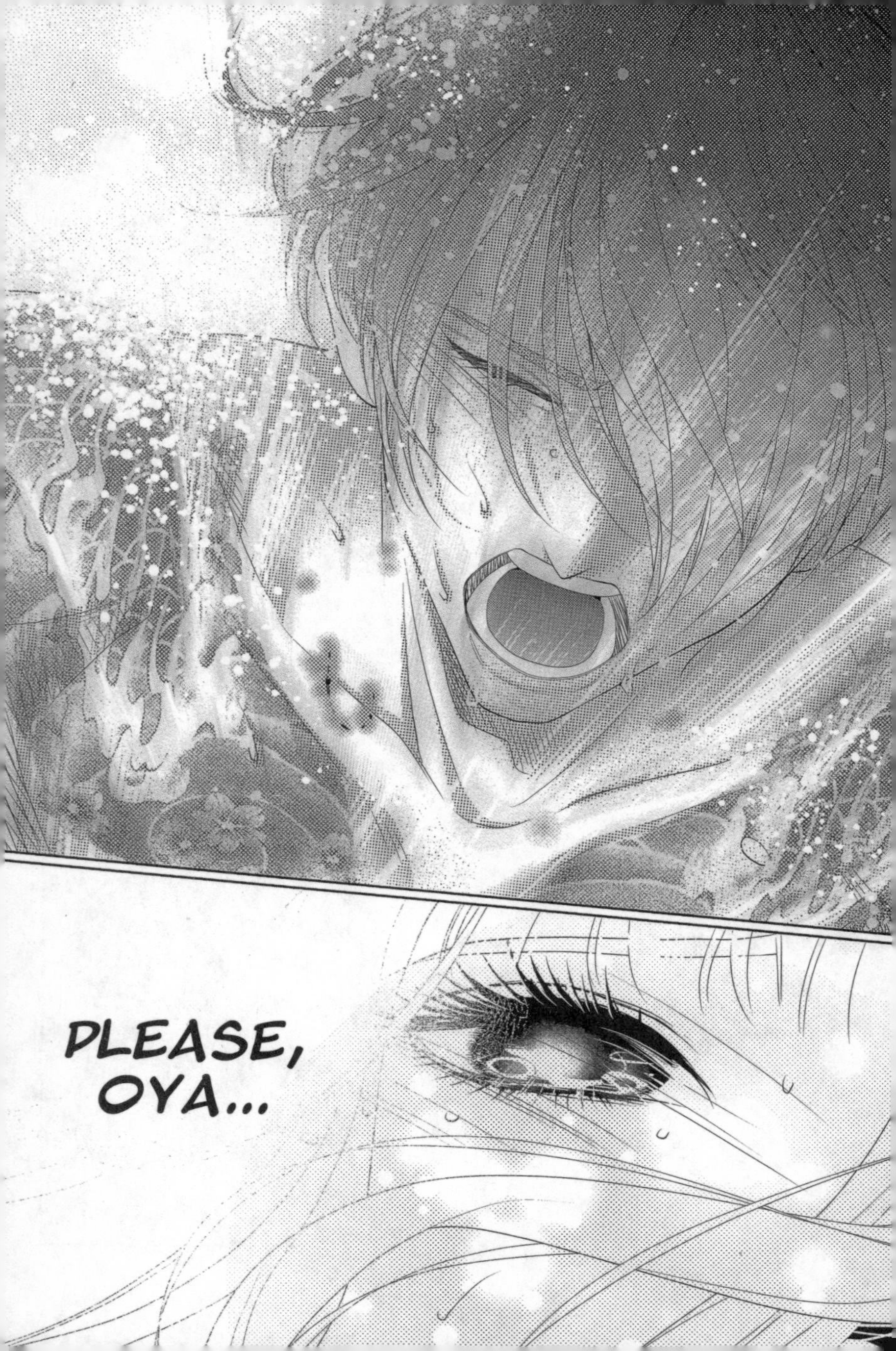
PLEASE, OYA...

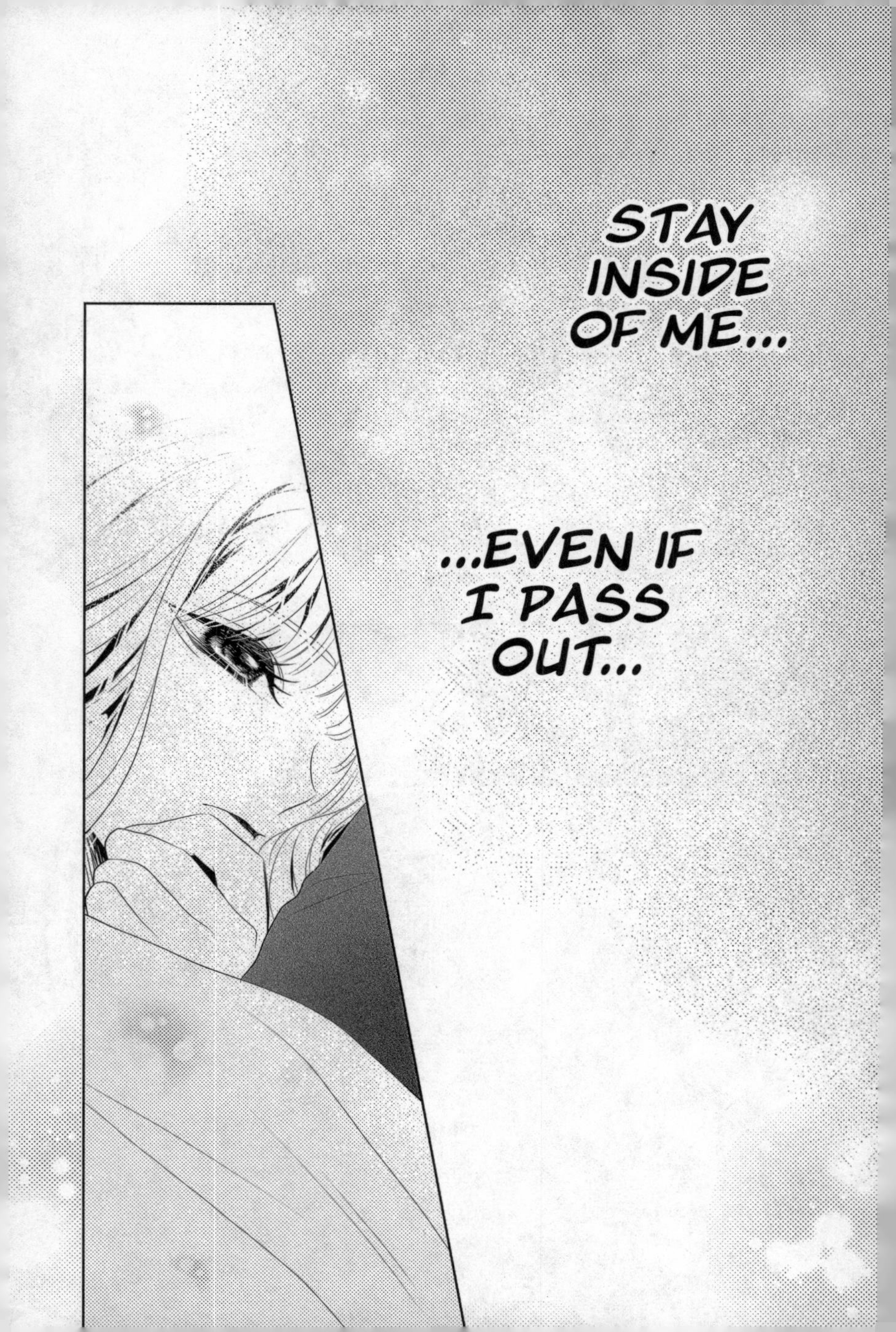
STAY INSIDE OF ME...
...EVEN IF I PASS OUT...

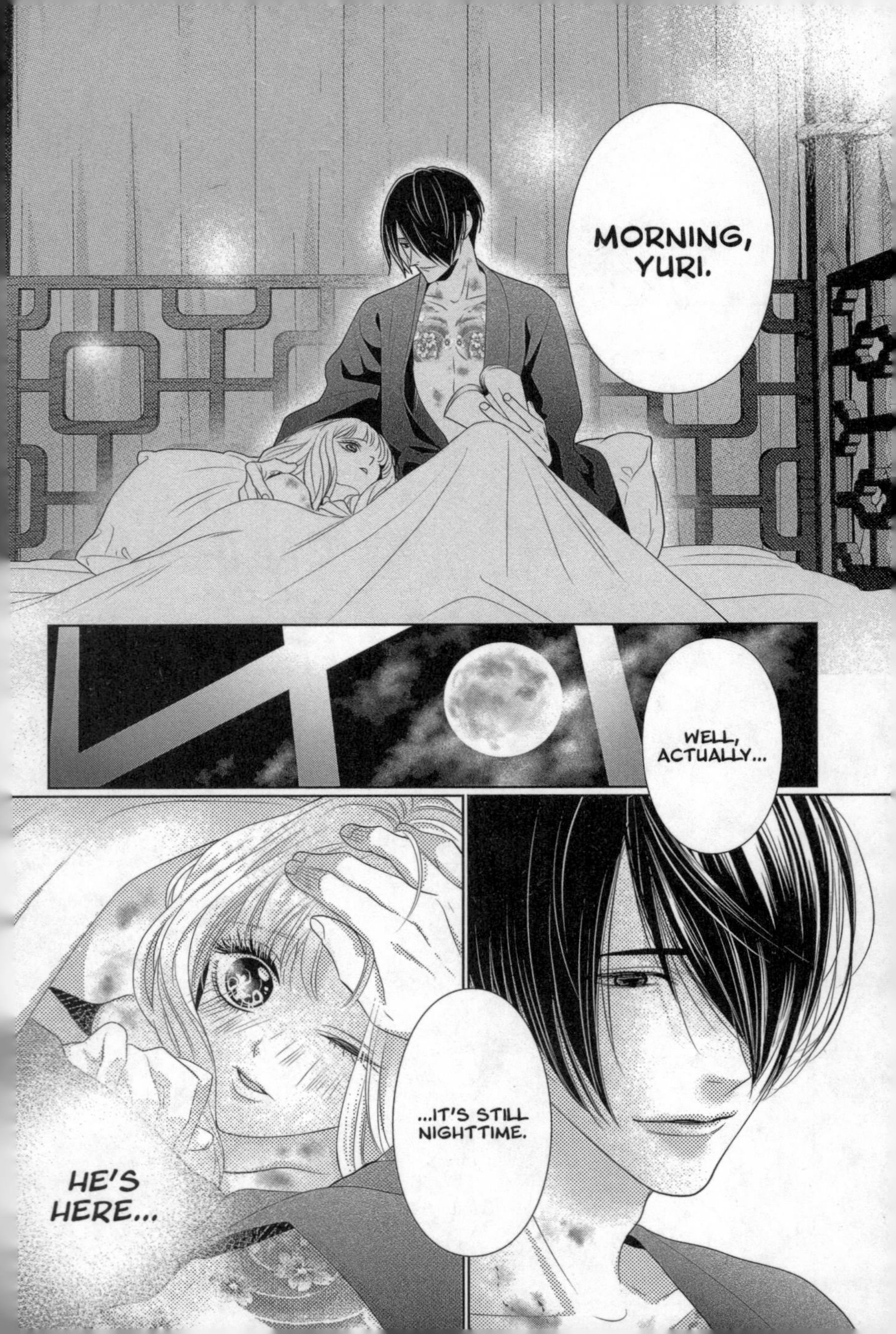
MORNING, YURI.
WELL, ACTUALLY...
...IT'S STILL NIGHTTIME.
HE'S HERE...

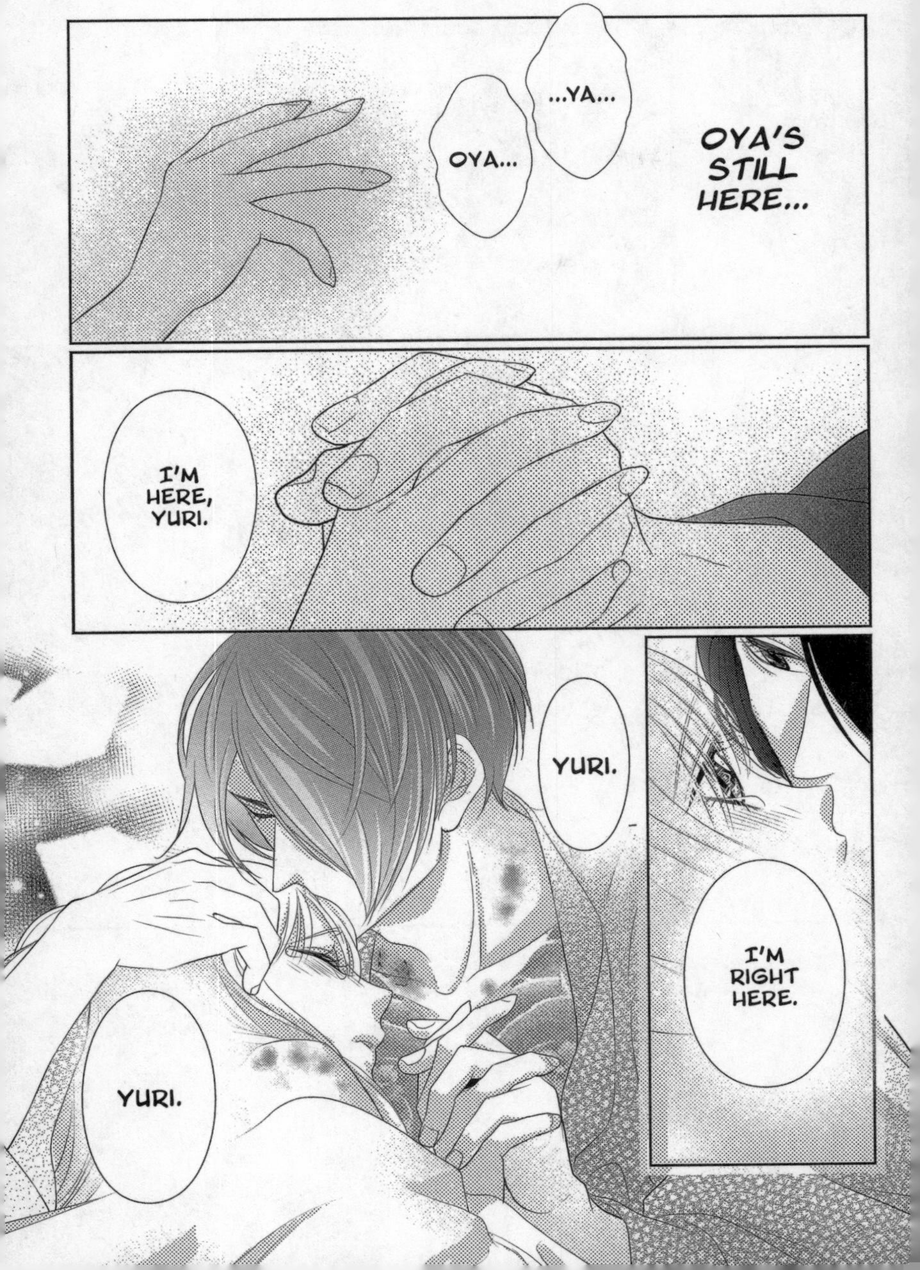
OYA'S STILL HERE...
...YA...
OYA...
I'M HERE, YURI.
I'M RIGHT HERE.
YURI.
YURI.

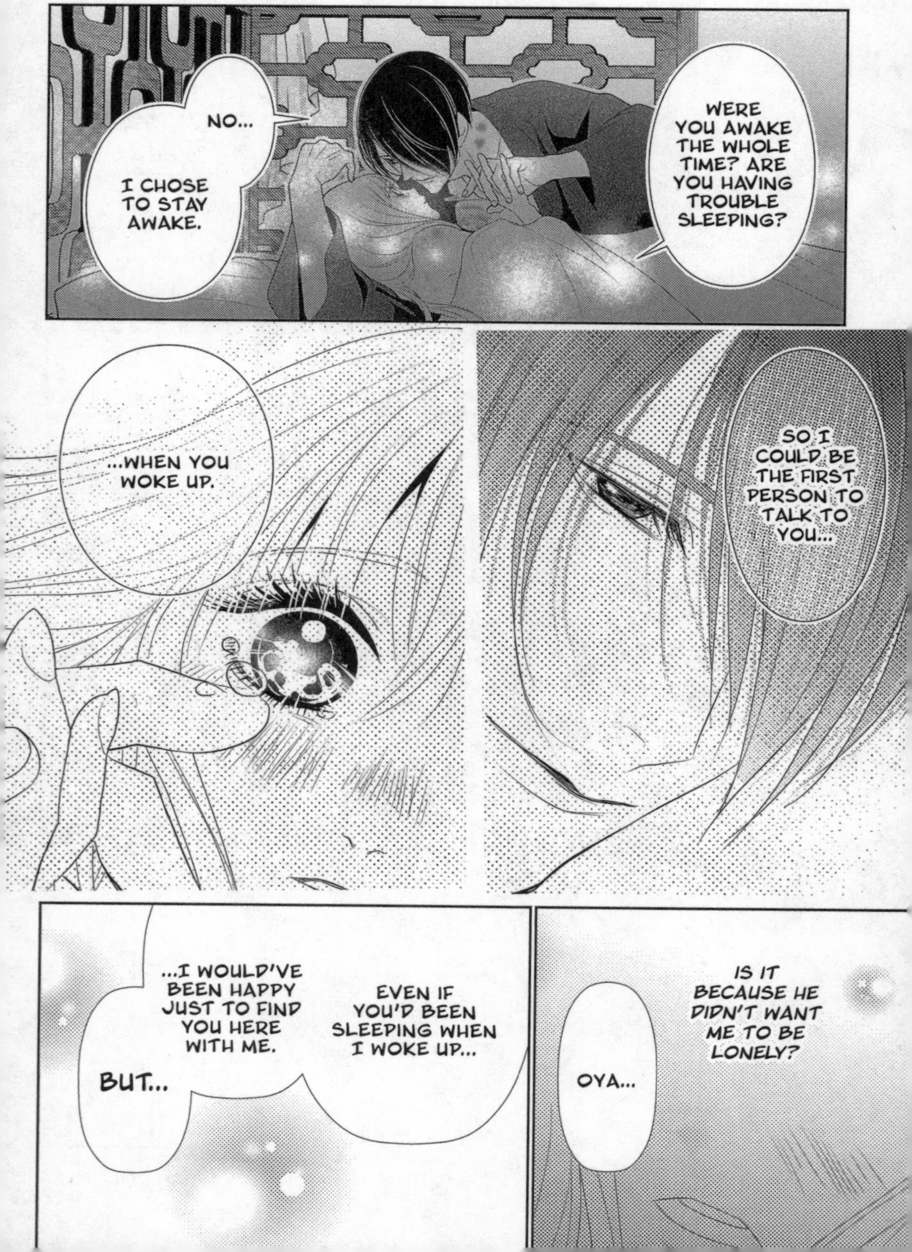
WERE YOU AWAKE THE WHOLE TIME? ARE YOU HAVING TROUBLE SLEEPING?
NO...
I CHOSE TO STAY AWAKE.
SO I COULD BE THE FIRST PERSON TO TALK TO YOU...
...WHEN YOU WOKE UP.
IS IT BECAUSE HE DIDN'T WANT ME TO BE LONELY?
OYA...
EVEN IF YOU'D BEEN SLEEPING WHEN I WOKE UP...
...I WOULD'VE BEEN HAPPY JUST TO FIND YOU HERE WITH ME.
BUT...

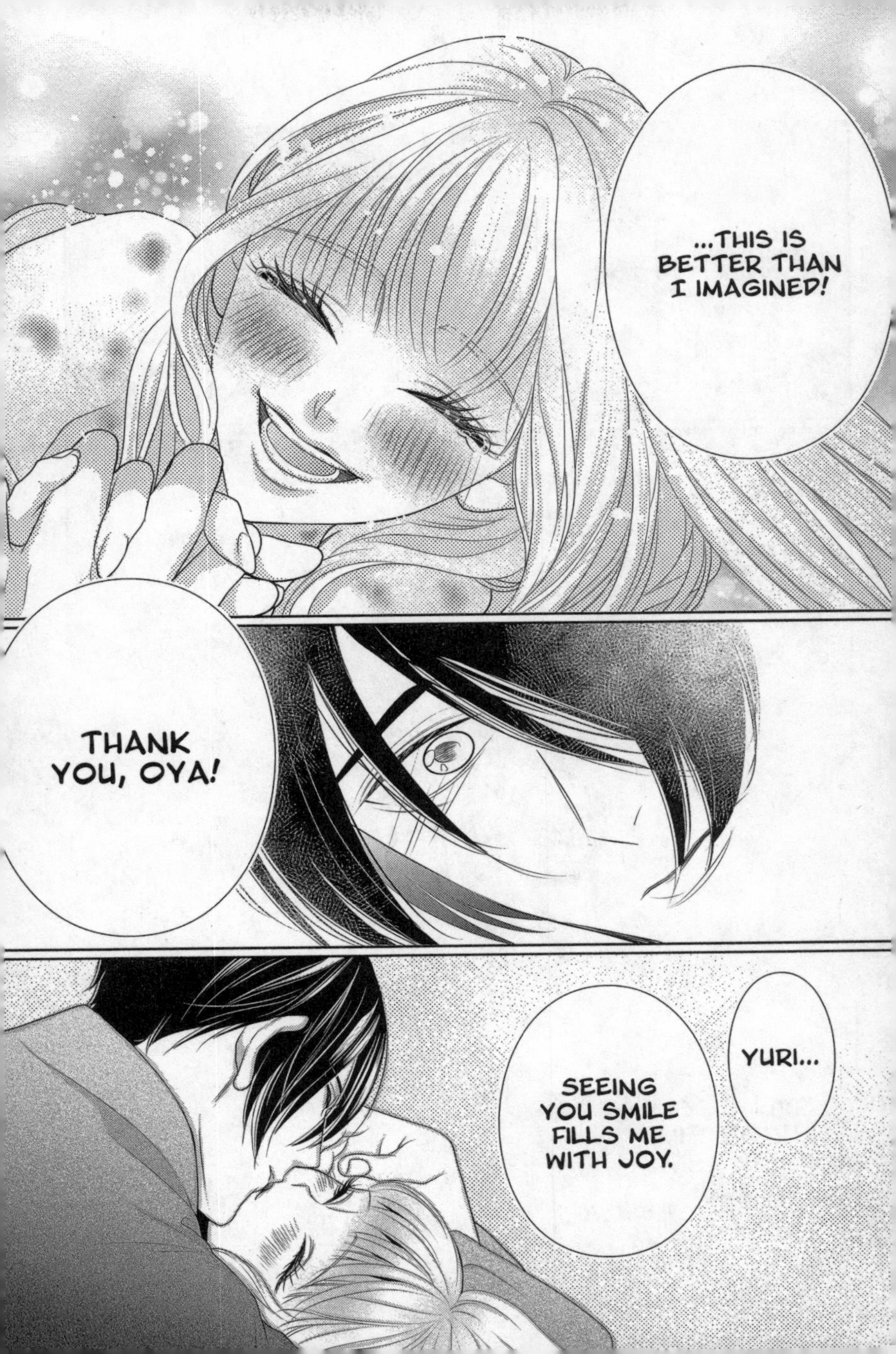
...THIS IS BETTER THAN I IMAGINED!
THANK YOU, OYA!
YURI...
SEEING YOU SMILE FILLS ME WITH JOY.

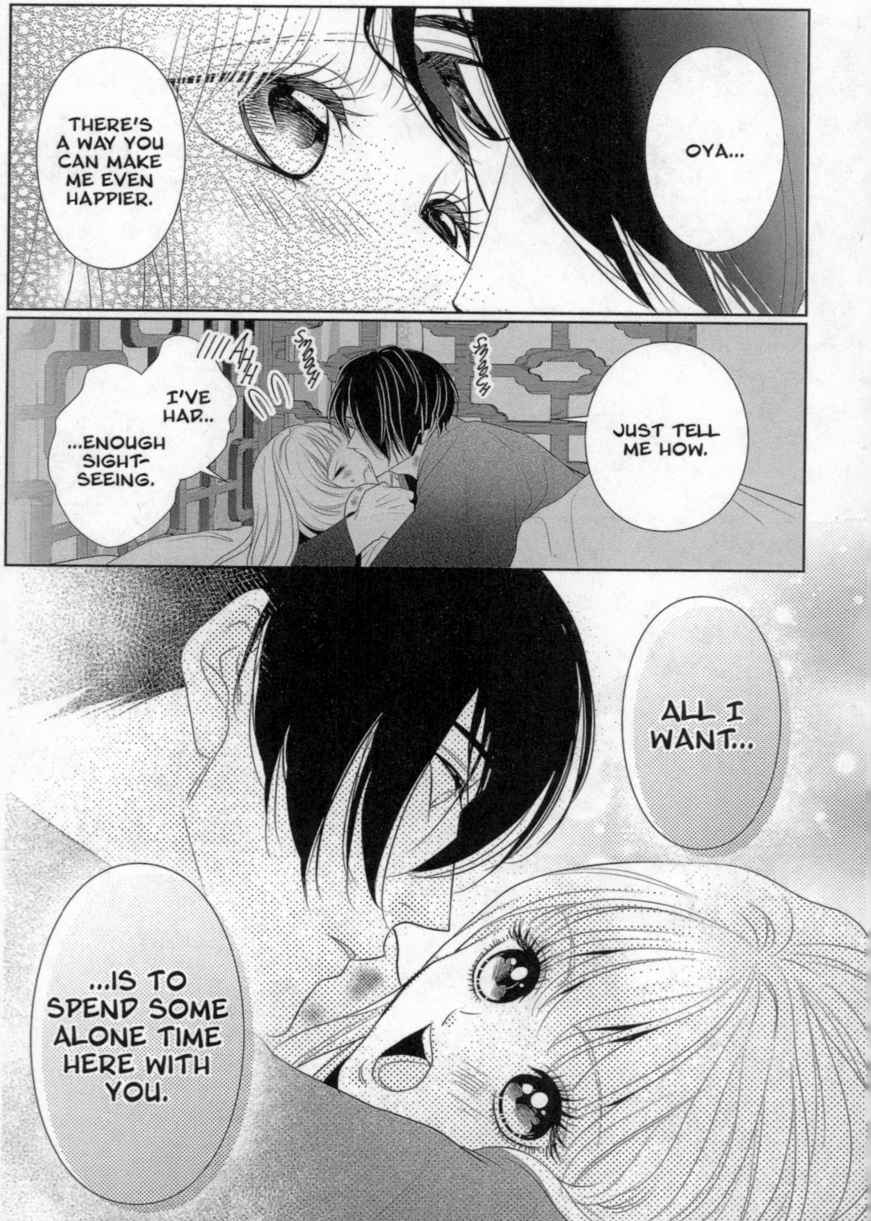
OYA...
THERE'S A WAY YOU CAN MAKE ME EVEN HAPPIER.
JUST TELL ME HOW.
SMOOCH
SMOOCH
AHH
I'VE HAD...
...ENOUGH SIGHT-SEEING.
ALL I WANT...
...IS TO SPEND SOME ALONE TIME HERE WITH YOU.

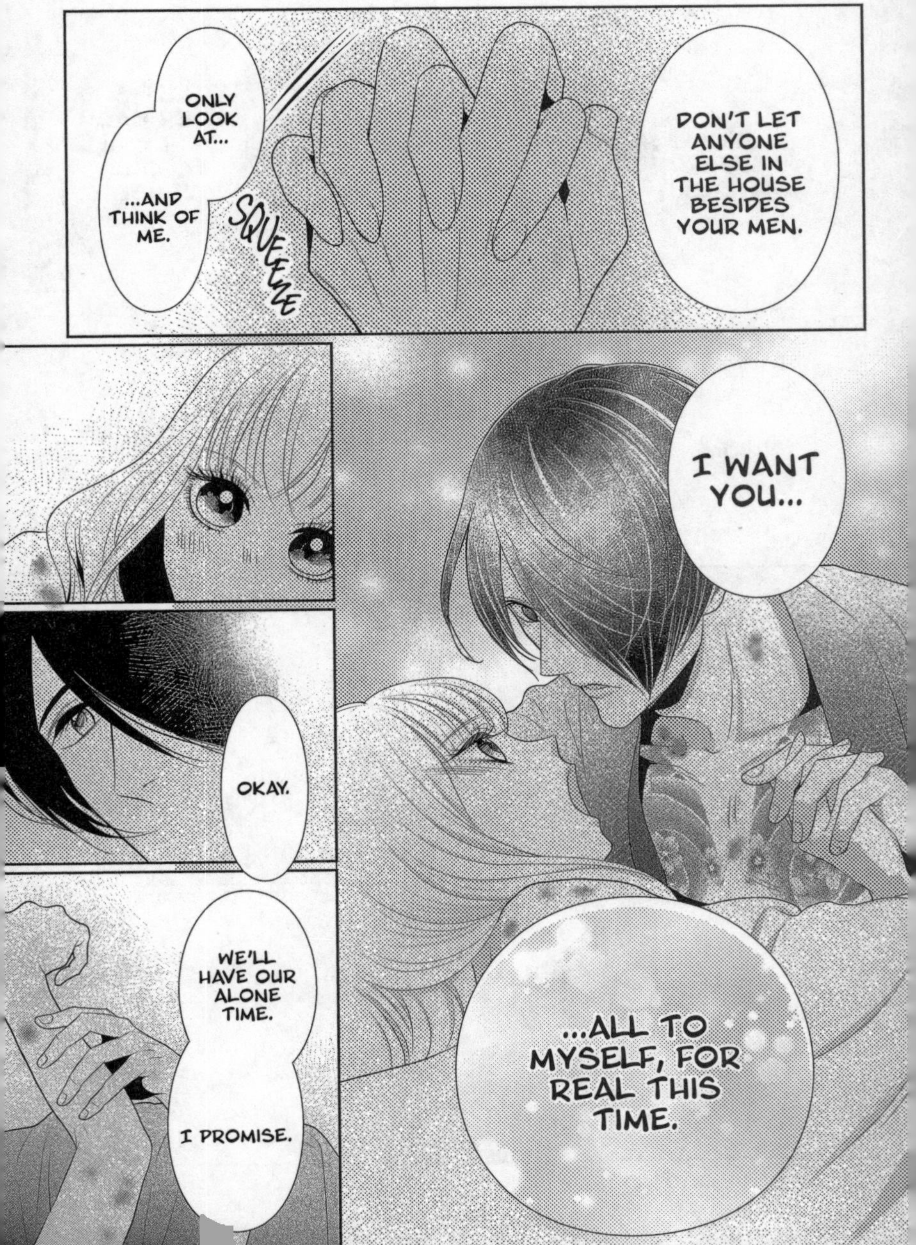
DON'T LET ANYONE ELSE IN THE HOUSE BESIDES YOUR MEN.
ONLY LOOK AT...
...AND THINK OF ME.
SQUEEZE
I WANT YOU...
...ALL TO MYSELF, FOR REAL THIS TIME.
OKAY.
WE'LL HAVE OUR ALONE TIME.
I PROMISE.

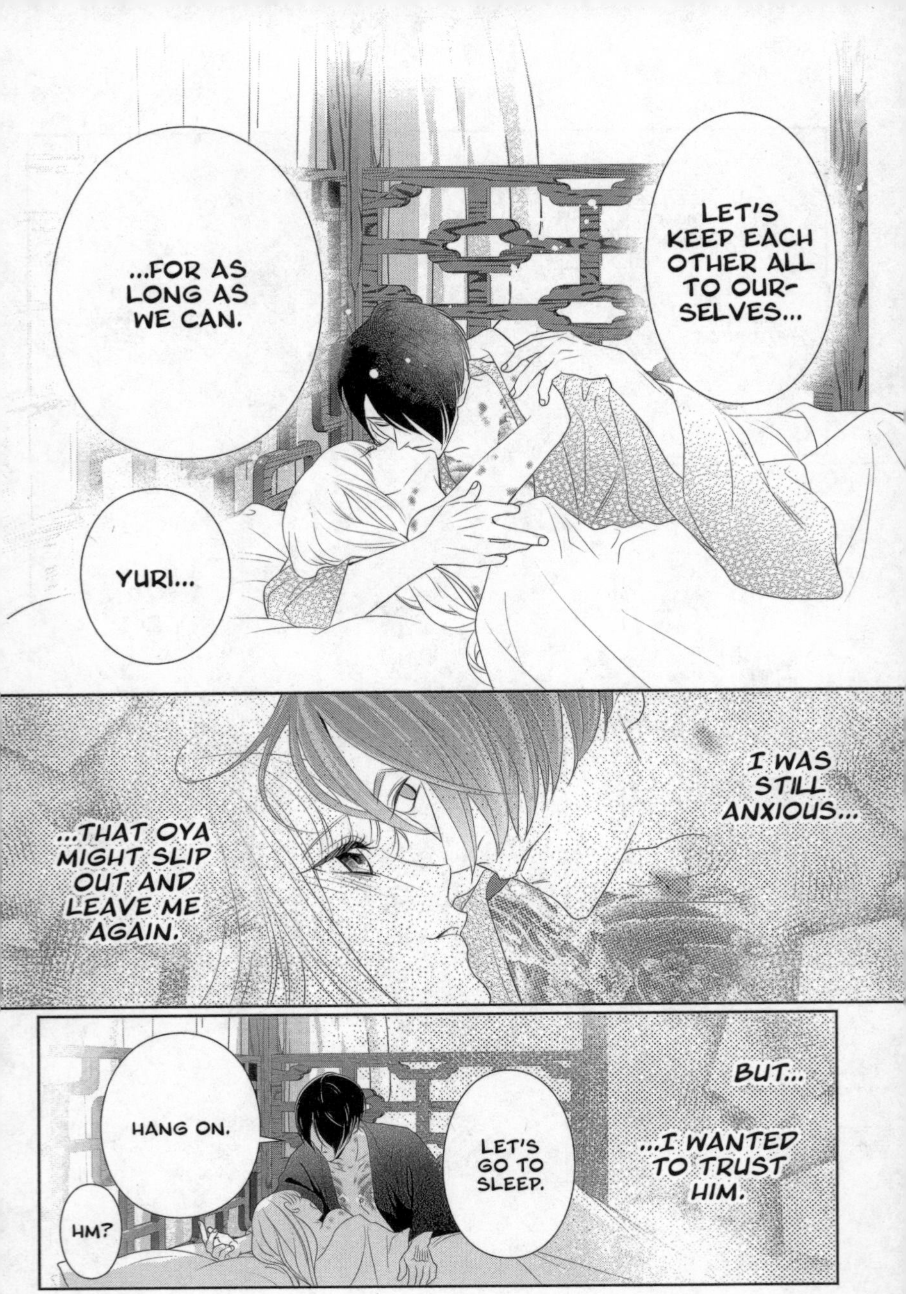
LET'S KEEP EACH OTHER ALL TO OUR-SELVES...
...FOR AS LONG AS WE CAN.
YURI...
I WAS STILL ANXIOUS...
...THAT OYA MIGHT SLIP OUT AND LEAVE ME AGAIN.
BUT...
...I WANTED TO TRUST HIM.
LET'S GO TO SLEEP.
HANG ON.
HM?

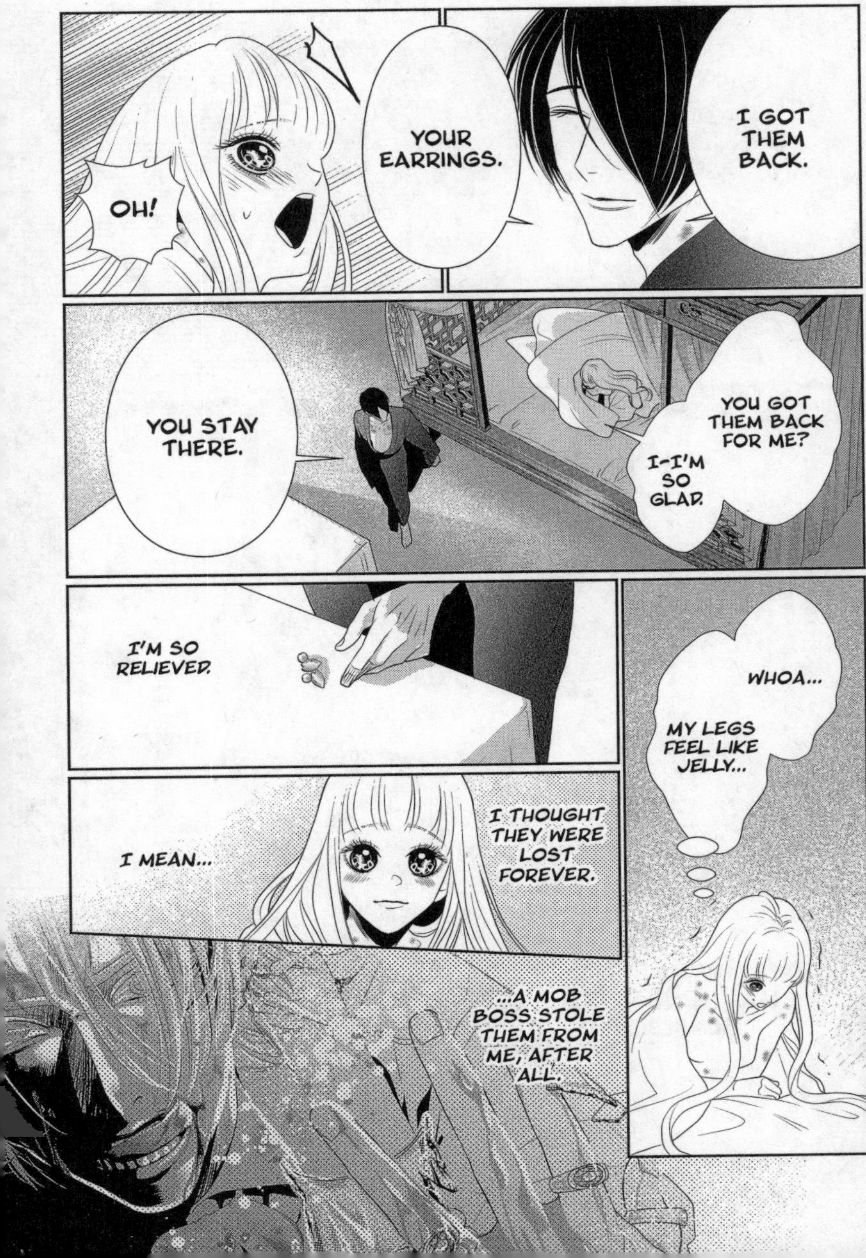
I GOT THEM BACK.
YOUR EARRINGS.
OH!
YOU GOT THEM BACK FOR ME?
I-I'M SO GLAD.
YOU STAY THERE.
WHOA...
MY LEGS FEEL LIKE JELLY...
I'M SO RELIEVED.
I THOUGHT THEY WERE LOST FOREVER.
I MEAN...
...A MOB BOSS STOLE THEM FROM ME, AFTER ALL.

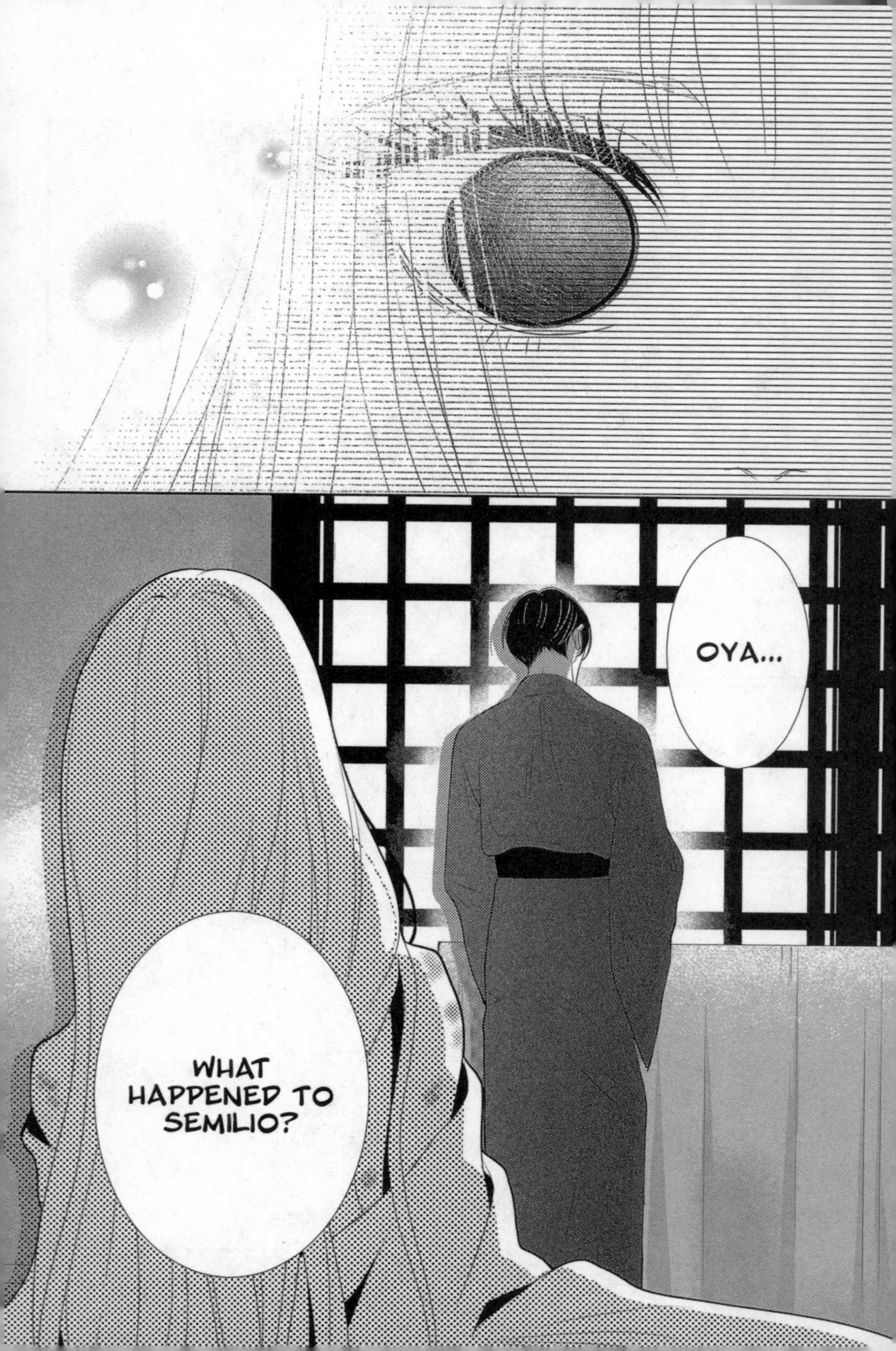
OYA...
WHAT HAPPENED TO SEMILIO?

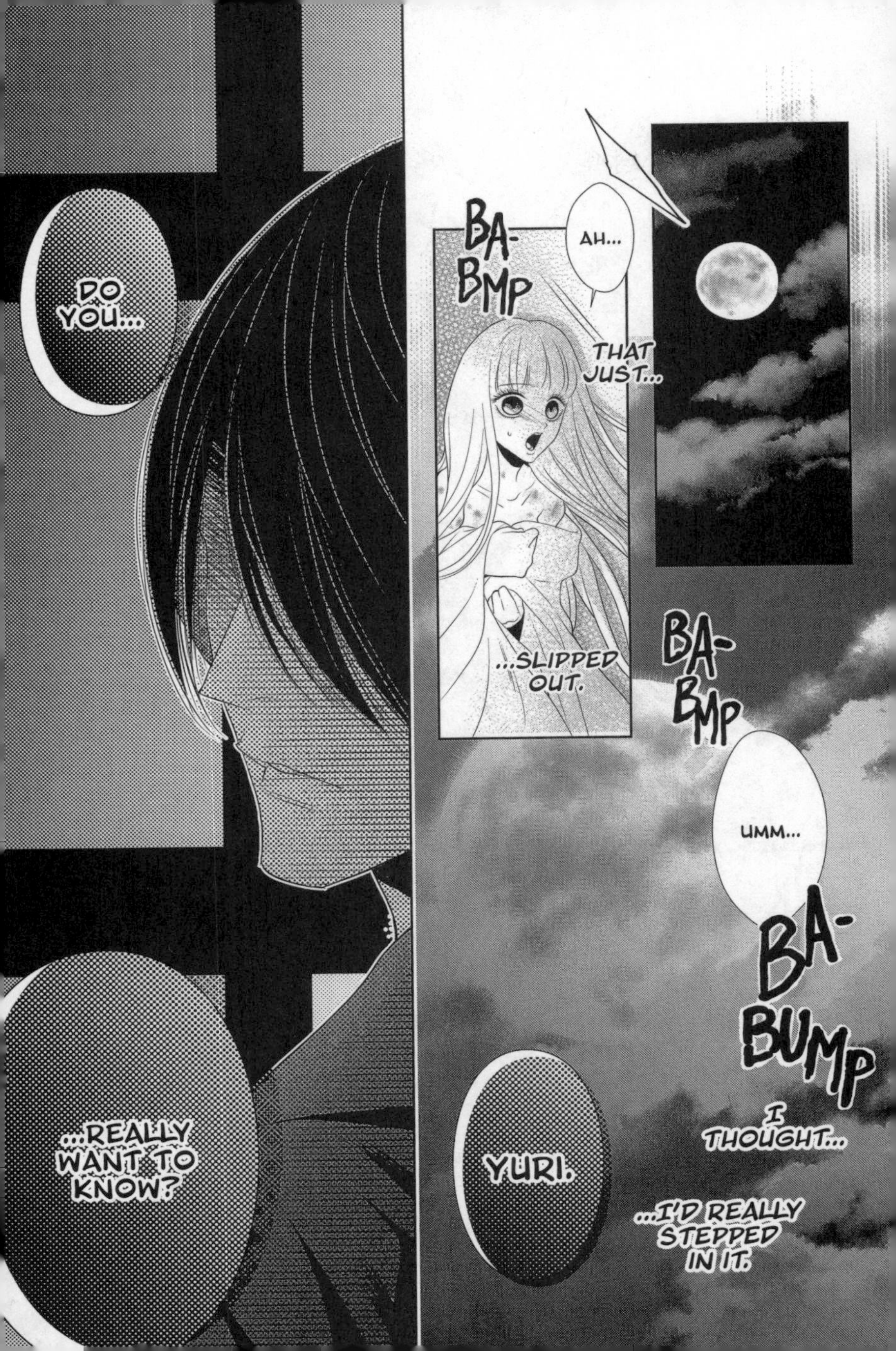
AH...
BA-BMP
THAT JUST...
...SLIPPED OUT.
BA-BMP
UMM...
BA-BUMP
I THOUGHT...
...I'D REALLY STEPPED IN IT.
YURI.
DO YOU...
...REALLY WANT TO KNOW?

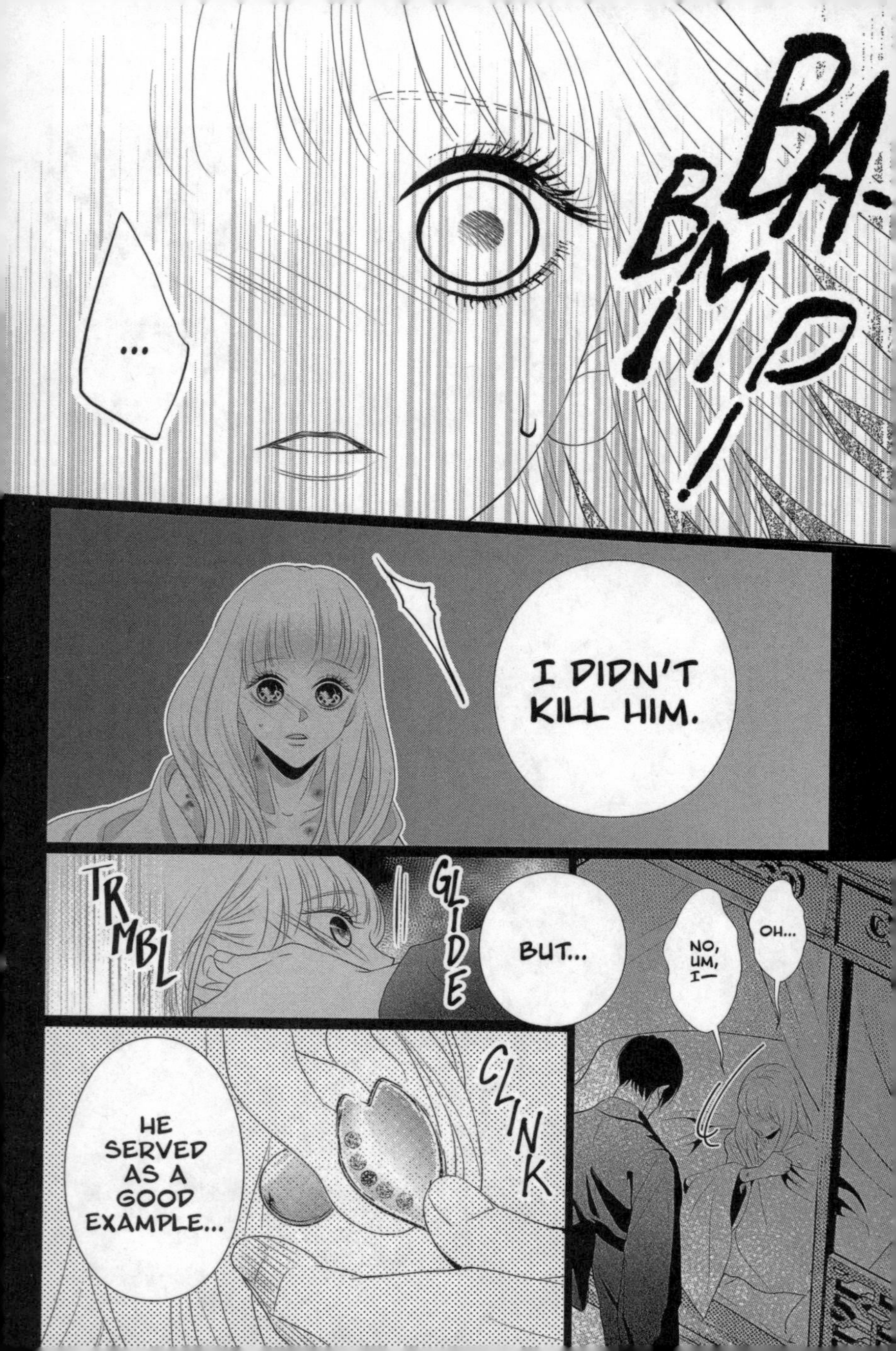
BA-BMP!
...
I DIDN'T KILL HIM.
OH...
NO, UM, I—
BUT...
GLIDE
TRMBL
CLINK
HE SERVED AS A GOOD EXAMPLE...

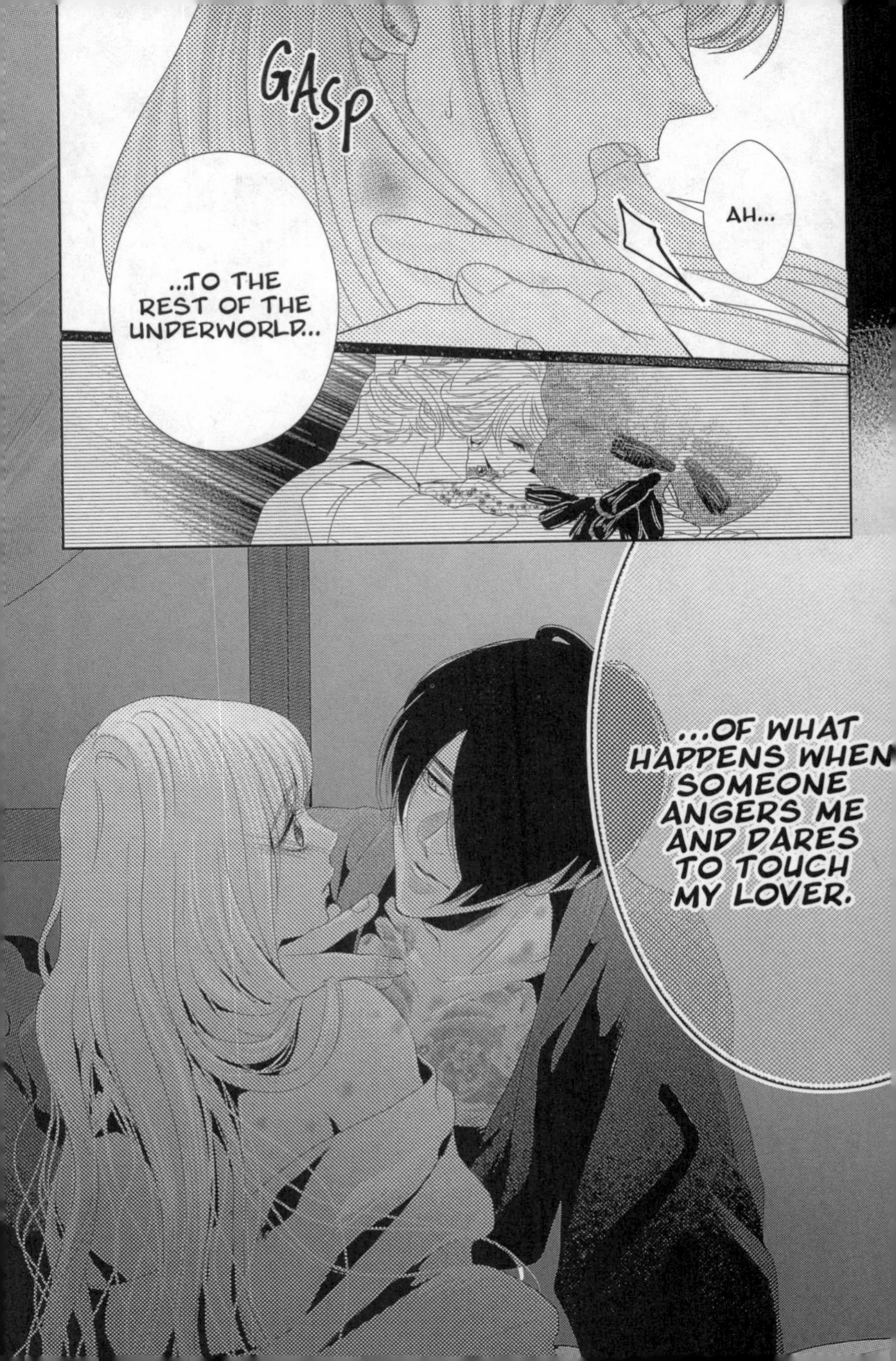
AH...
GASP
...TO THE REST OF THE UNDERWORLD...
...OF WHAT HAPPENS WHEN SOMEONE ANGERS ME AND DARES TO TOUCH MY LOVER.

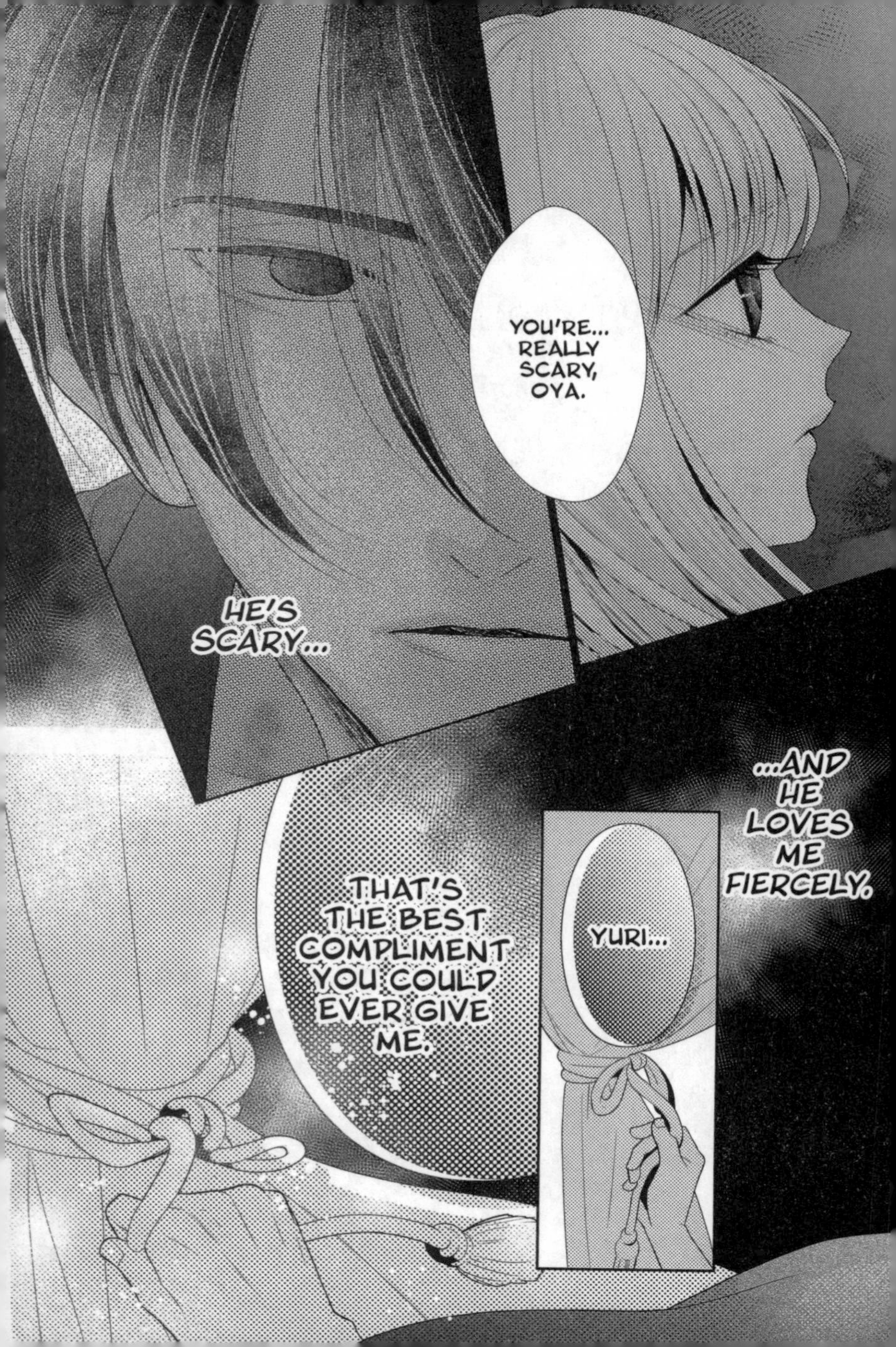
YOU'RE... REALLY SCARY, OYA.
HE'S SCARY...
...AND HE LOVES ME FIERCELY.
YURI...
THAT'S THE BEST COMPLIMENT YOU COULD EVER GIVE ME.

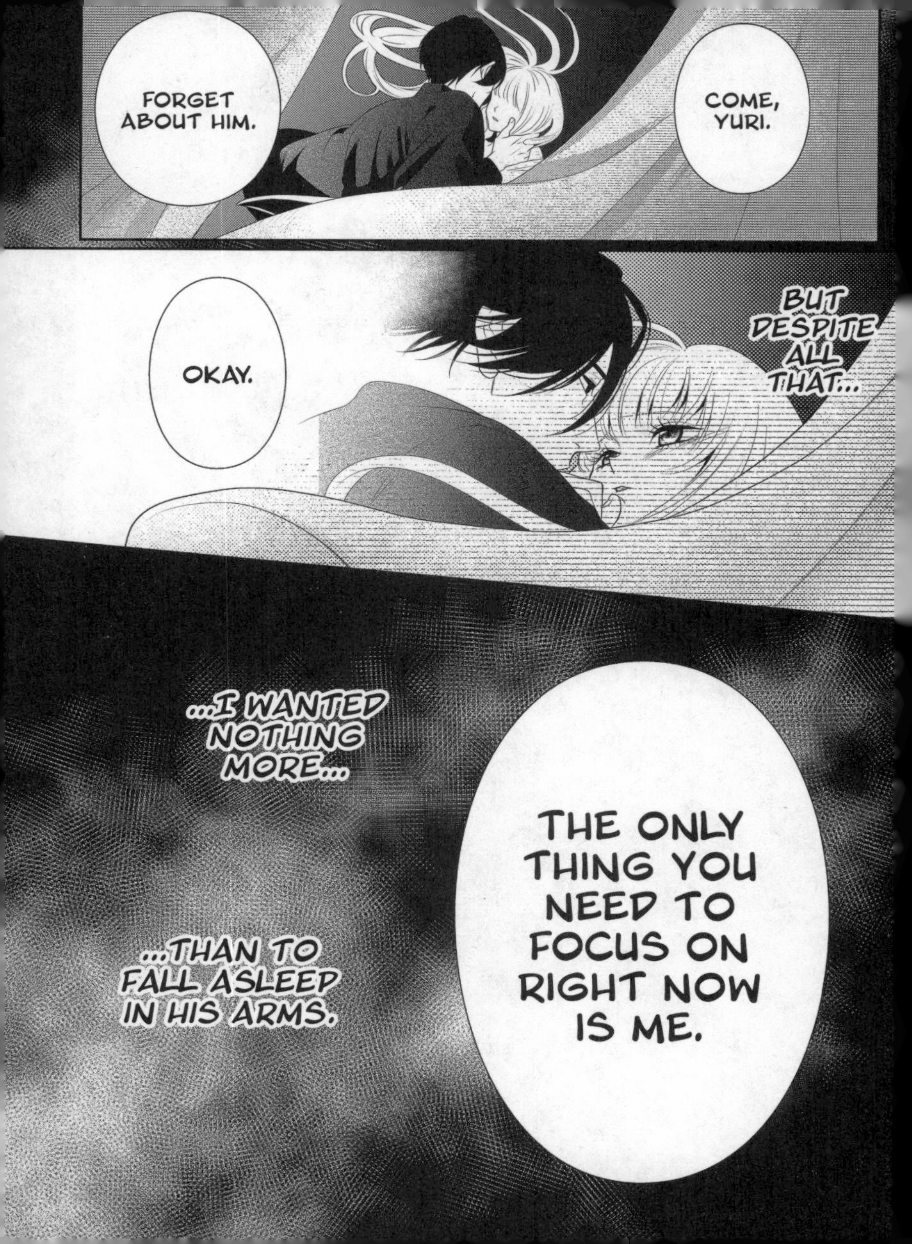
COME, YURI.
FORGET ABOUT HIM.
BUT DESPITE ALL THAT...
OKAY.
THE ONLY THING YOU NEED TO FOCUS ON RIGHT NOW IS ME.
...I WANTED NOTHING MORE...
...THAN TO FALL ASLEEP IN HIS ARMS.

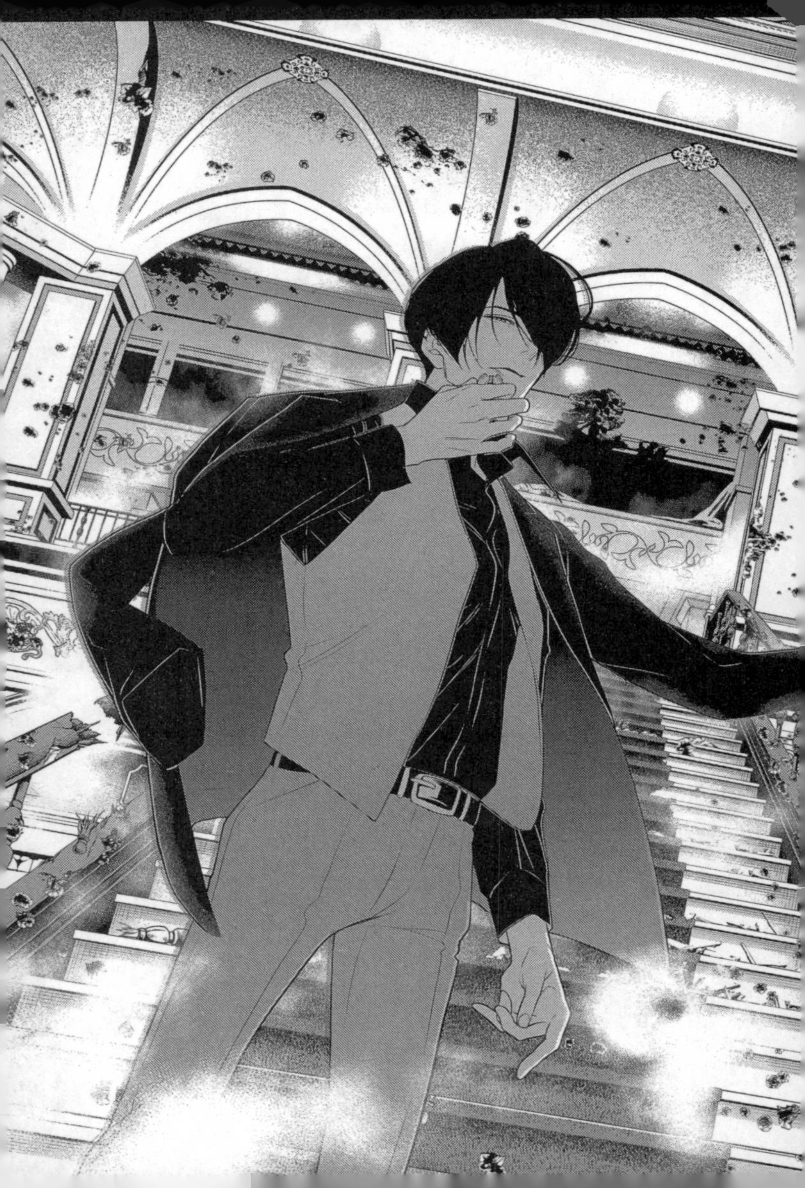

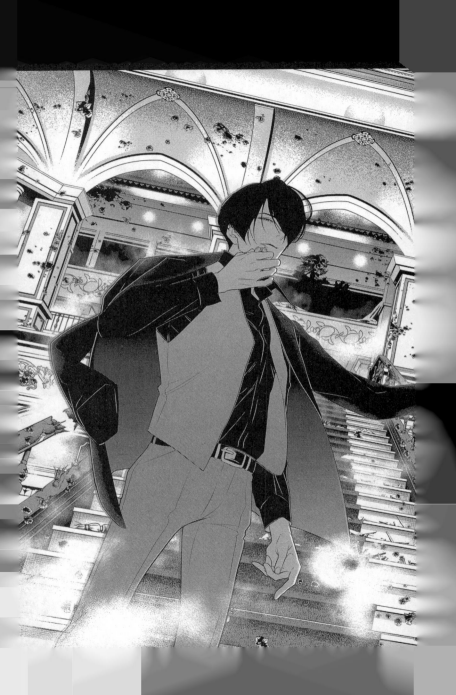

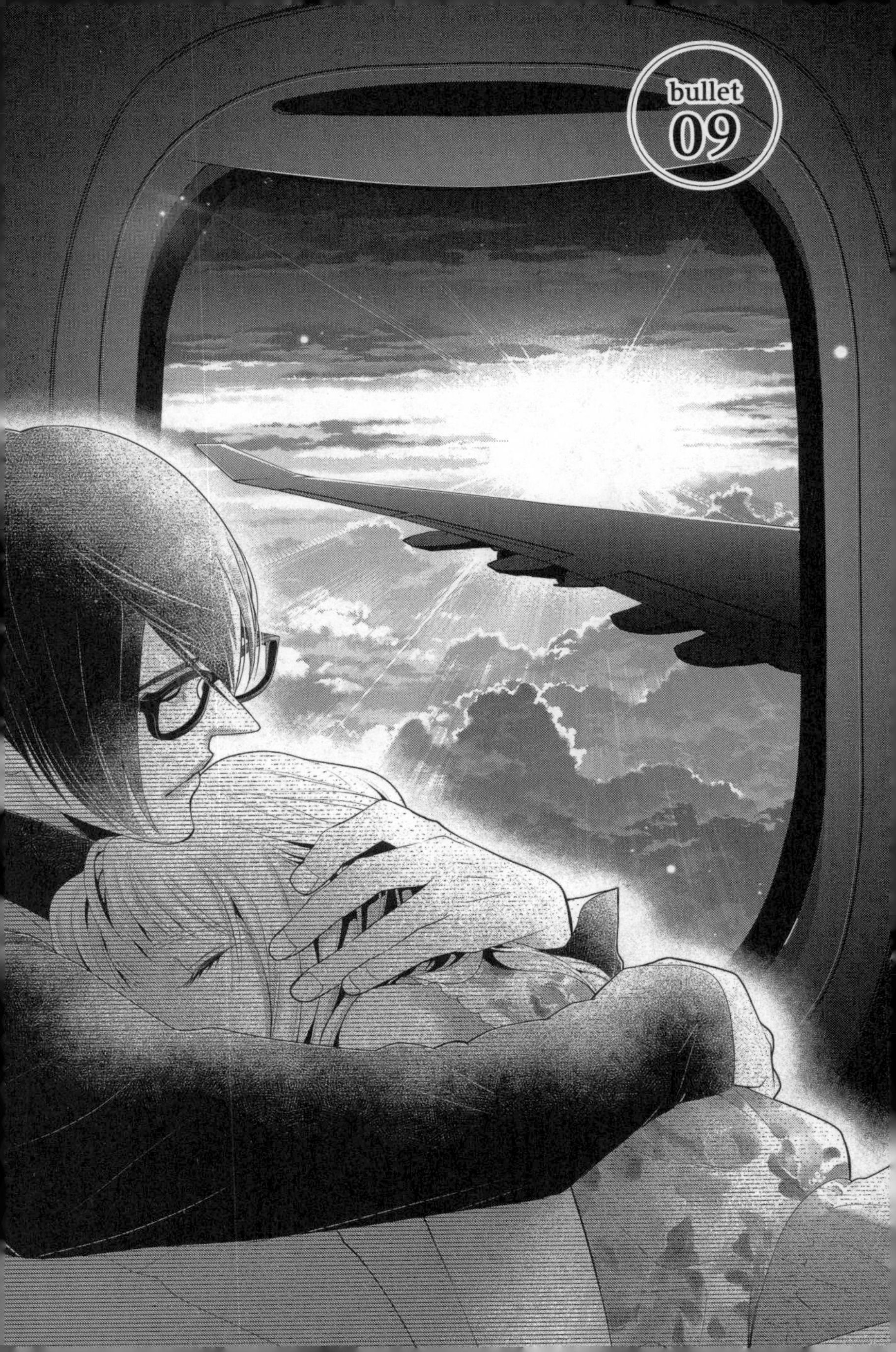
bullet
09

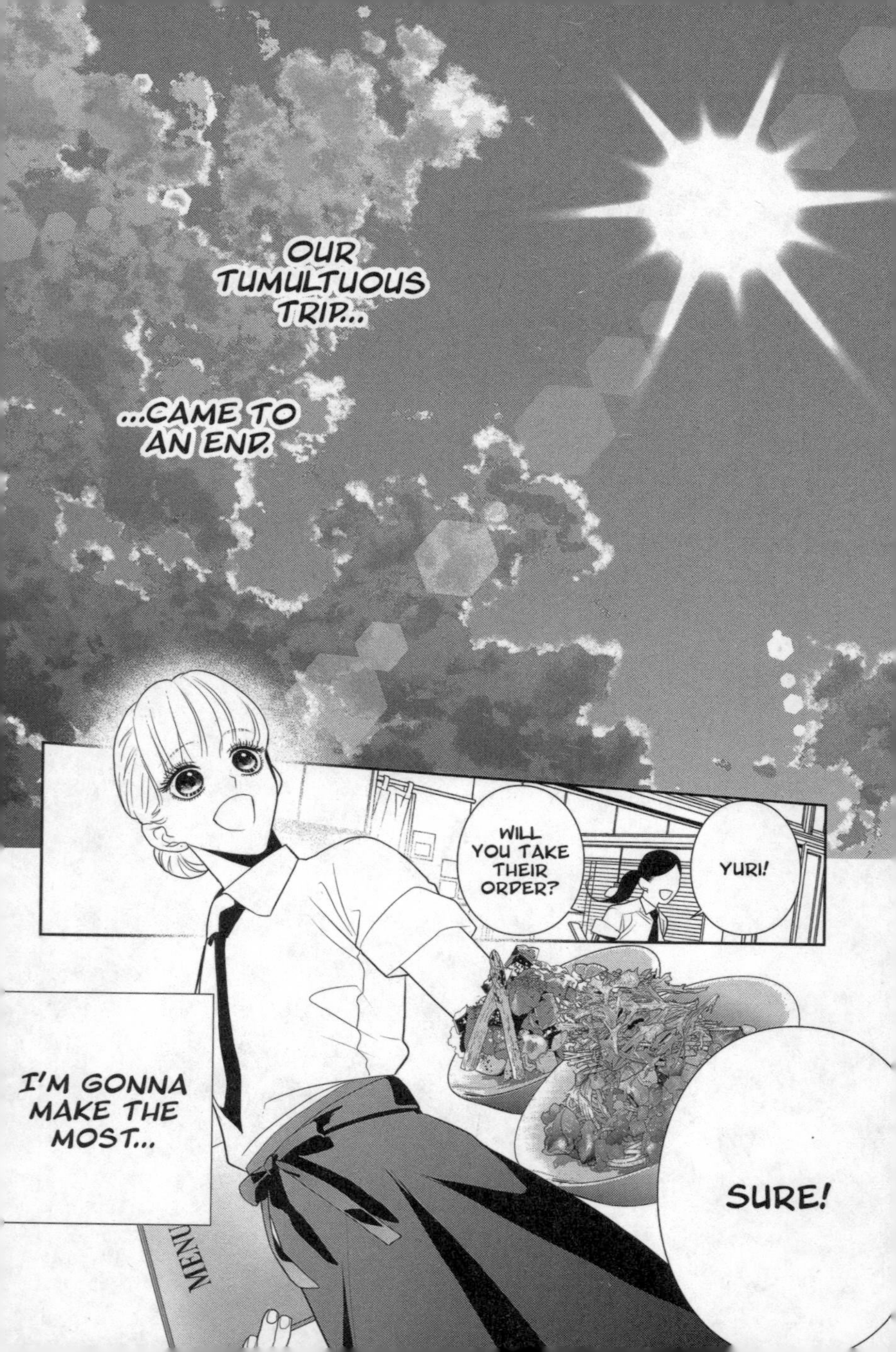
OUR TUMULTUOUS TRIP...
...CAME TO AN END.
YURI!
WILL YOU TAKE THEIR ORDER?
SURE!
I'M GONNA MAKE THE MOST...
MENU

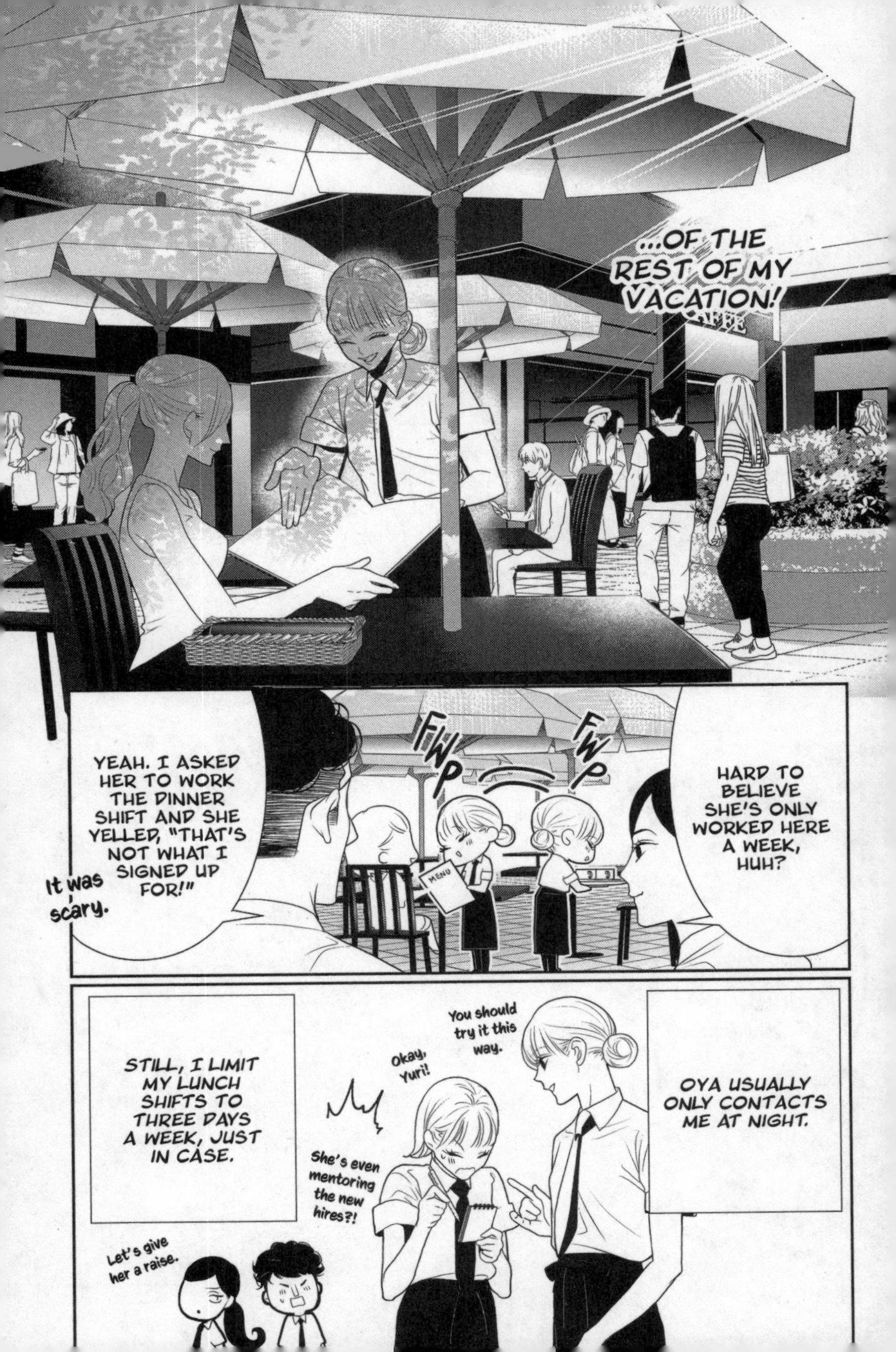

...OF THE REST OF MY VACATION!
HARD TO BELIEVE SHE'S ONLY WORKED HERE A WEEK, HUH?
FWP
FWP
YEAH. I ASKED HER TO WORK THE DINNER SHIFT AND SHE YELLED, "THAT'S NOT WHAT I SIGNED UP FOR!"
It was scary.
MENU
OYA USUALLY ONLY CONTACTS ME AT NIGHT.
You should try it this way.
Okay, Yuri!
She's even mentoring the new hires?!
STILL, I LIMIT MY LUNCH SHIFTS TO THREE DAYS A WEEK, JUST IN CASE.
Let's give her a raise.

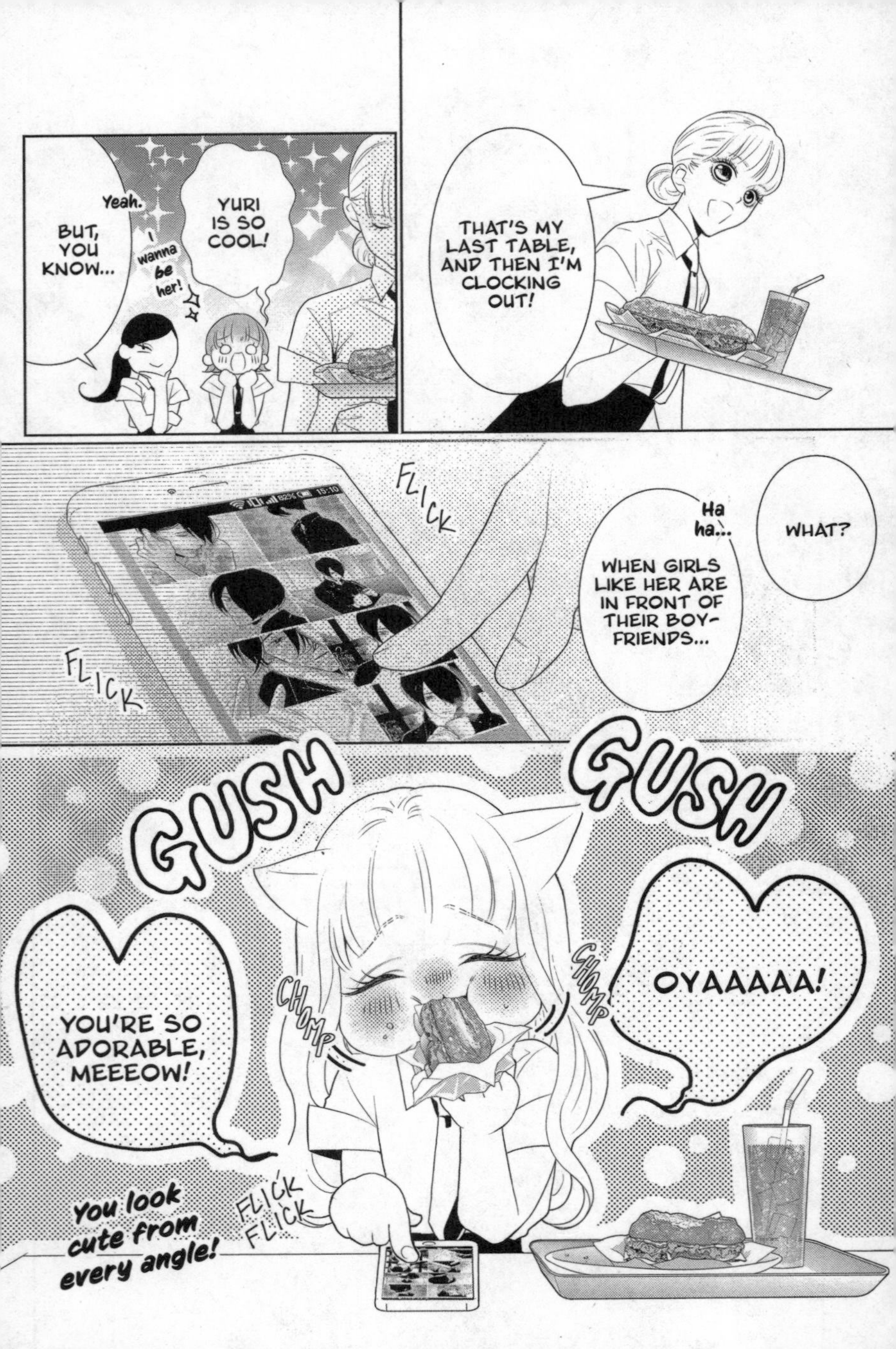
THAT'S MY LAST TABLE, AND THEN I'M CLOCKING OUT!
YURI IS SO COOL!
I wanna be her!
Yeah.
BUT, YOU KNOW...
WHAT?
Ha ha...
WHEN GIRLS LIKE HER ARE IN FRONT OF THEIR BOY-FRIENDS...
FLICK
FLICK
GUSH
GUSH
OYAAAAA!
CHOMP
CHOMP
YOU'RE SO ADORABLE, MEEEOW!
FLICK FLICK
You look cute from every angle!

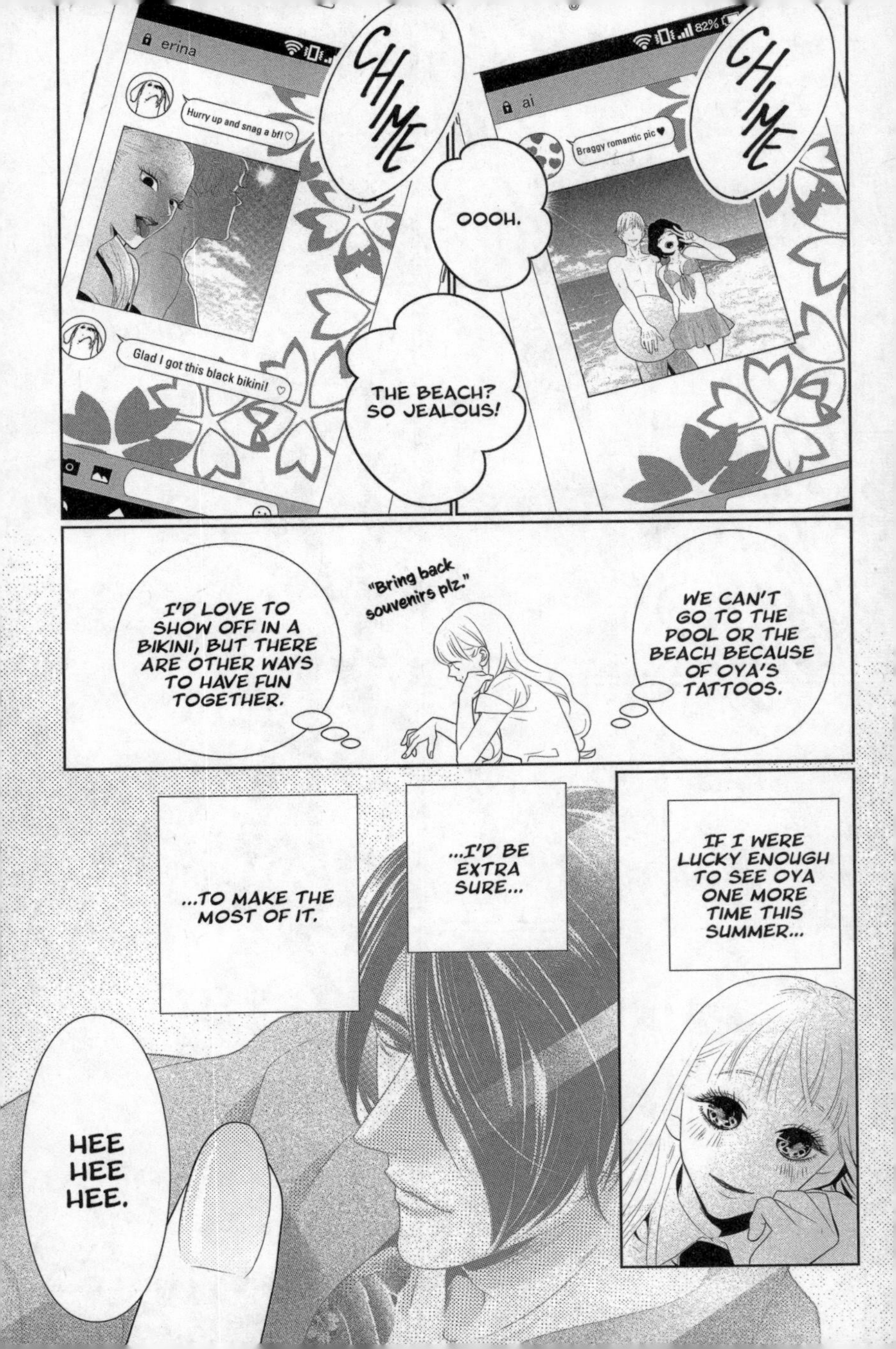
CHIME
82%
ai
Braggy romantic pic♥
CHIME
OOOH.
erina
Hurry up and snag a bf!♡
THE BEACH? SO JEALOUS!
Glad I got this black bikini!♡
WE CAN'T GO TO THE POOL OR THE BEACH BECAUSE OF OYA'S TATTOOS.
"Bring back souvenirs plz."
I'D LOVE TO SHOW OFF IN A BIKINI, BUT THERE ARE OTHER WAYS TO HAVE FUN TOGETHER.
IF I WERE LUCKY ENOUGH TO SEE OYA ONE MORE TIME THIS SUMMER...
...I'D BE EXTRA SURE...
...TO MAKE THE MOST OF IT.
HEE HEE HEE.

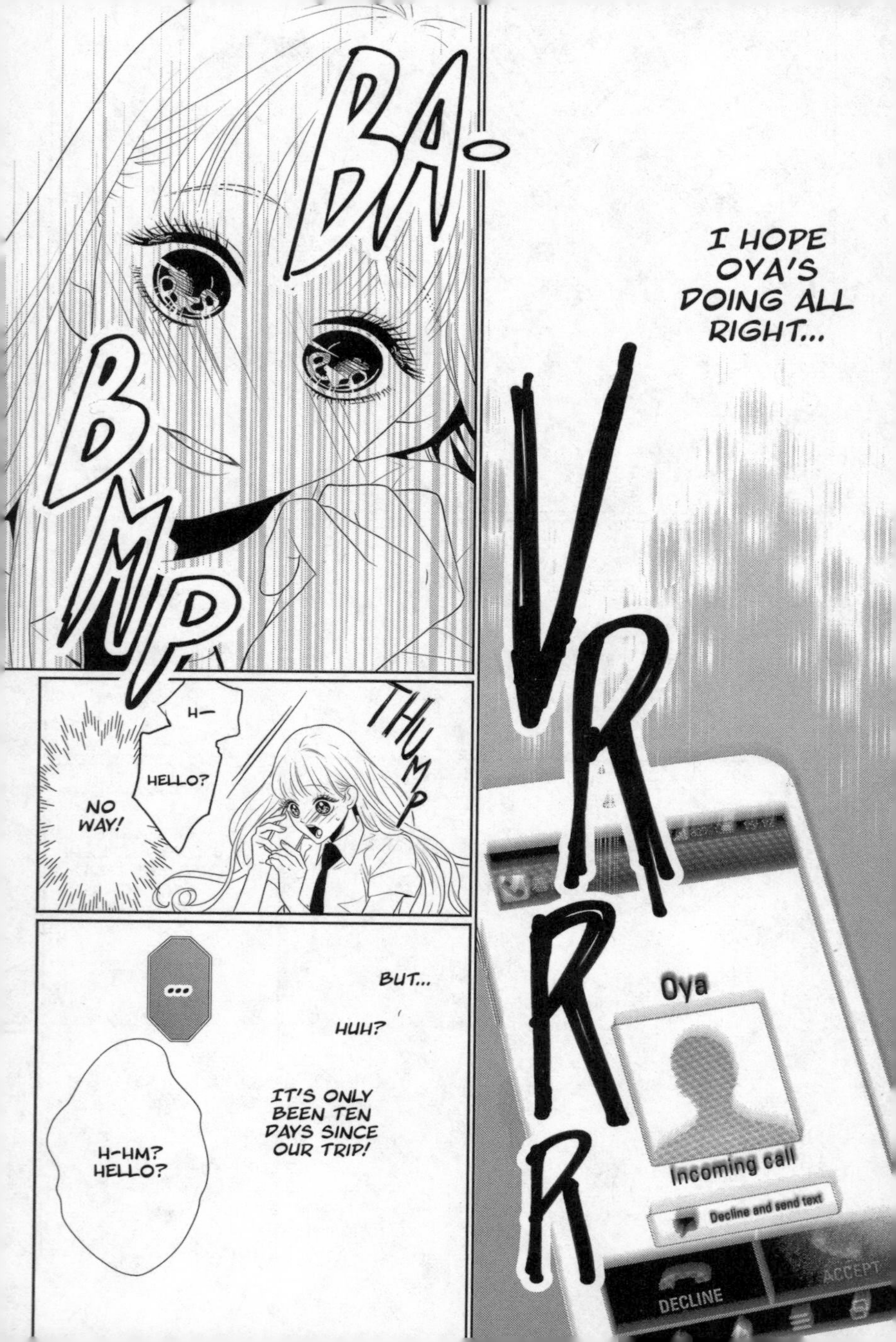
I HOPE OYA'S DOING ALL RIGHT...
VRRRR
Oya
Incoming call
Decline and send text
DECLINE
ACCEPT
BA-DA-
BUMP
THUMP
H—
HELLO?
NO WAY!
BUT...
...
HUH?
IT'S ONLY BEEN TEN DAYS SINCE OUR TRIP!
H-HM? HELLO?

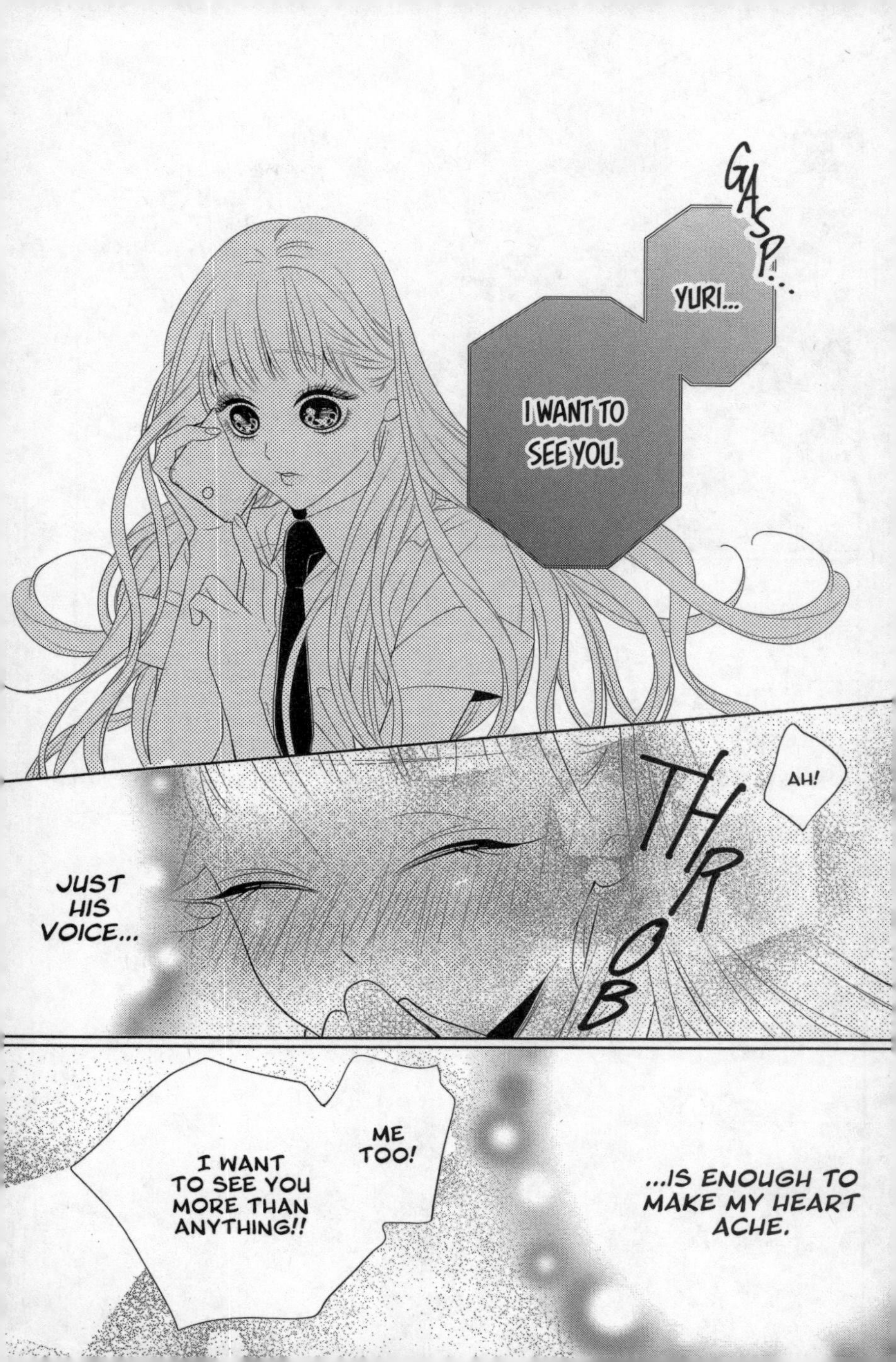
GASP...
YURI...
I WANT TO SEE YOU.
AH!
THROB
JUST HIS VOICE...
...IS ENOUGH TO MAKE MY HEART ACHE.
ME TOO!
I WANT TO SEE YOU MORE THAN ANYTHING!!

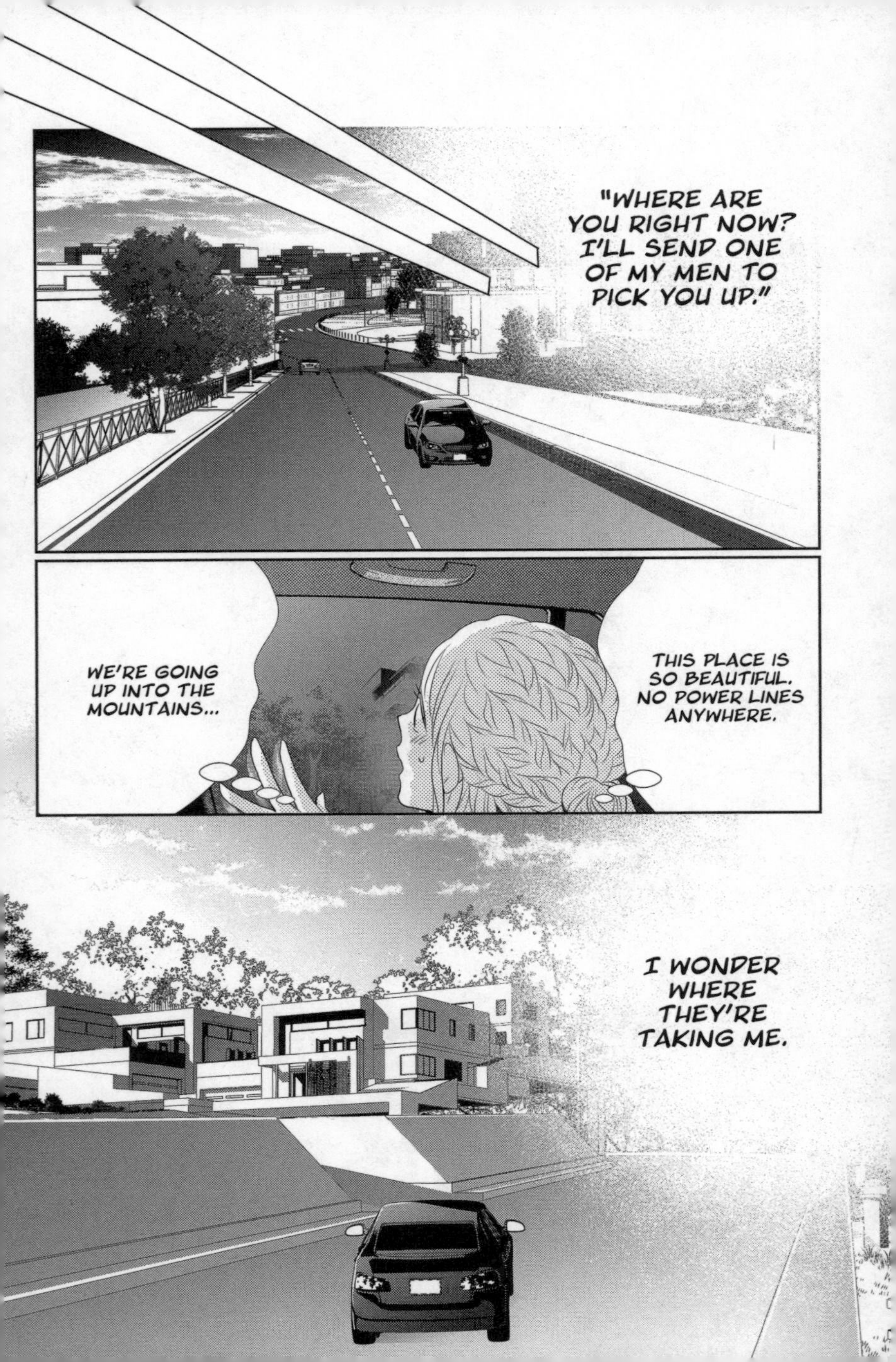
"WHERE ARE YOU RIGHT NOW? I'LL SEND ONE OF MY MEN TO PICK YOU UP."
THIS PLACE IS SO BEAUTIFUL. NO POWER LINES ANYWHERE.
WE'RE GOING UP INTO THE MOUNTAINS...
I WONDER WHERE THEY'RE TAKING ME.

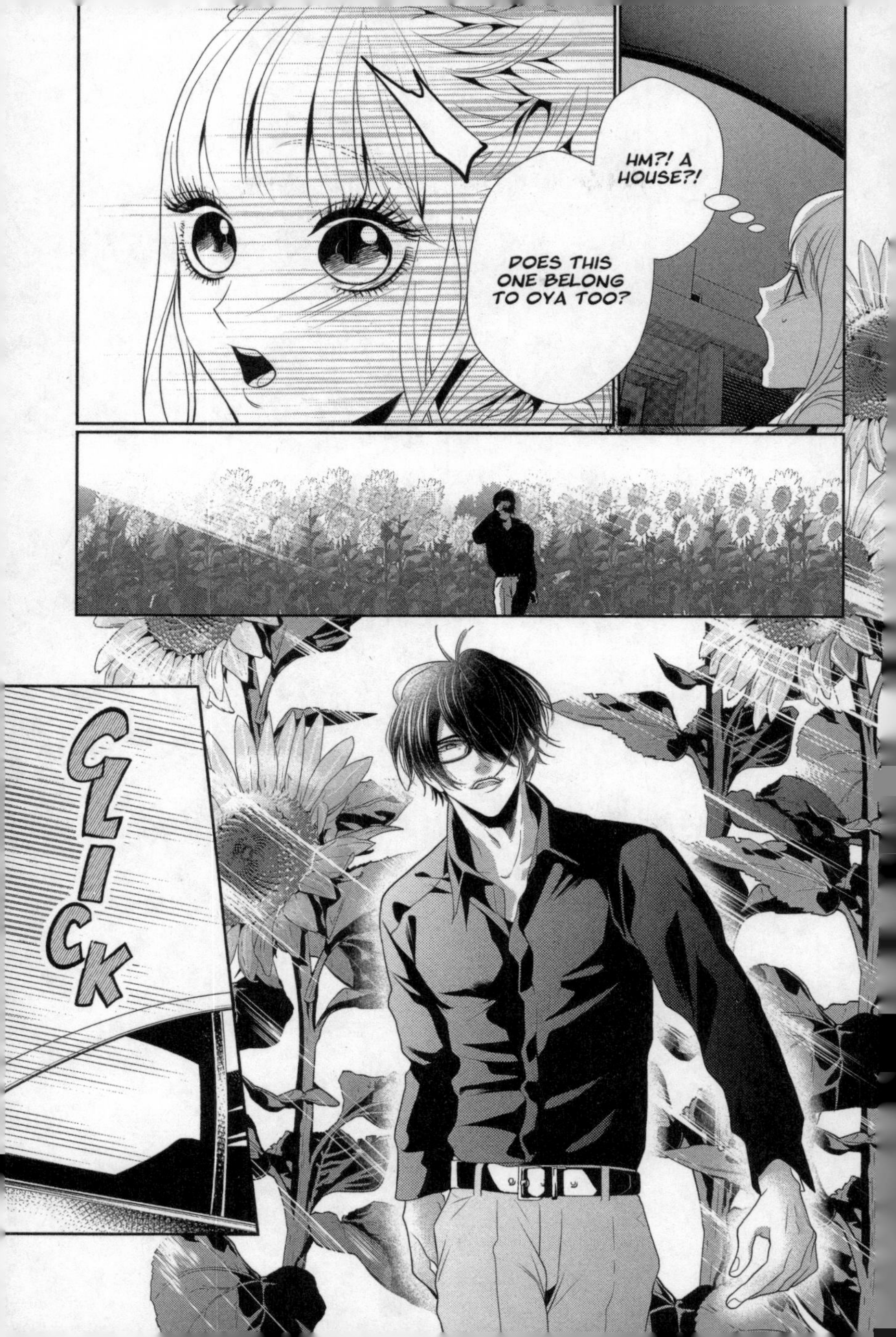
HM?! A HOUSE?!
DOES THIS ONE BELONG TO OYA TOO?
CLICK

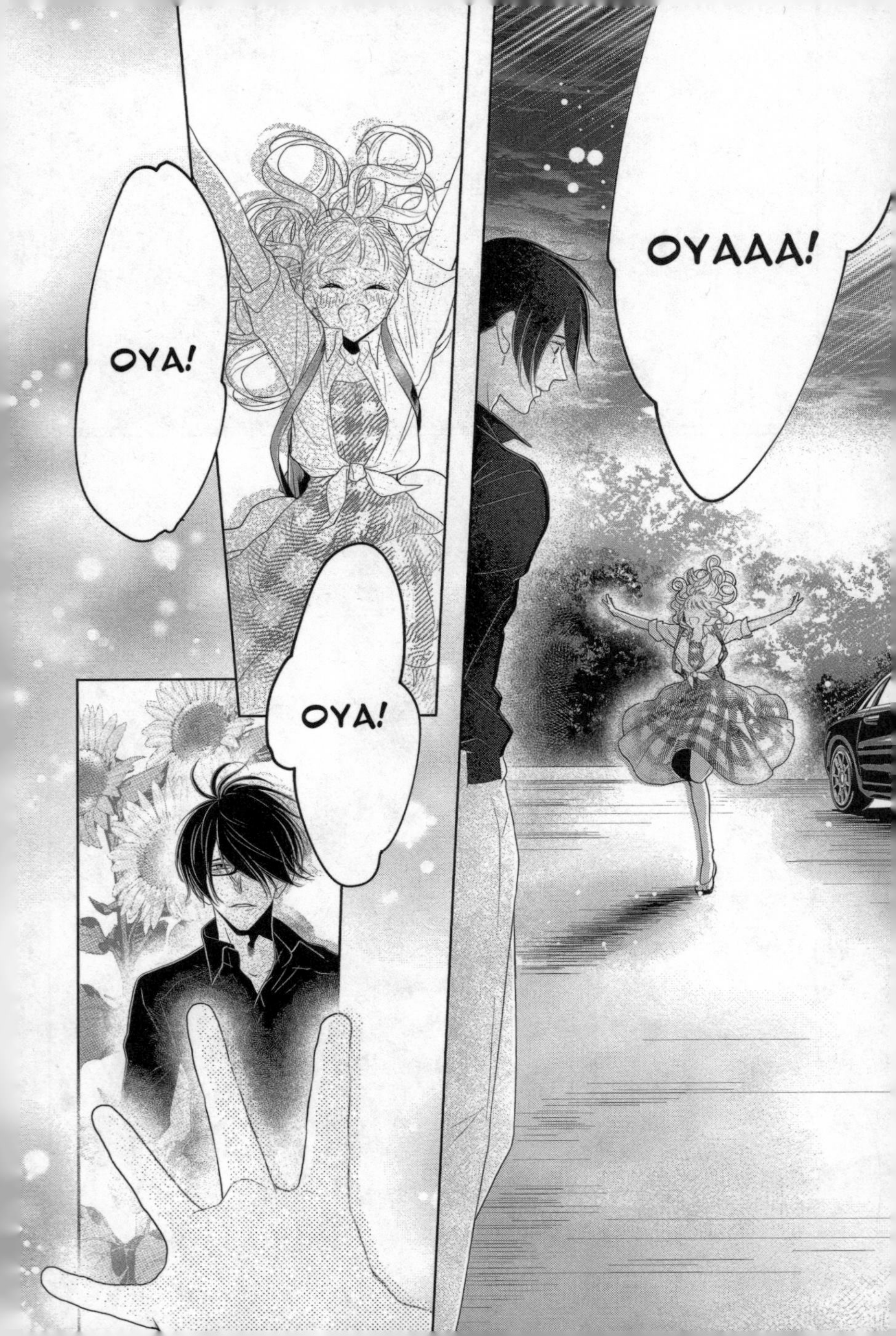
OYAAA!
OYA!
OYA!

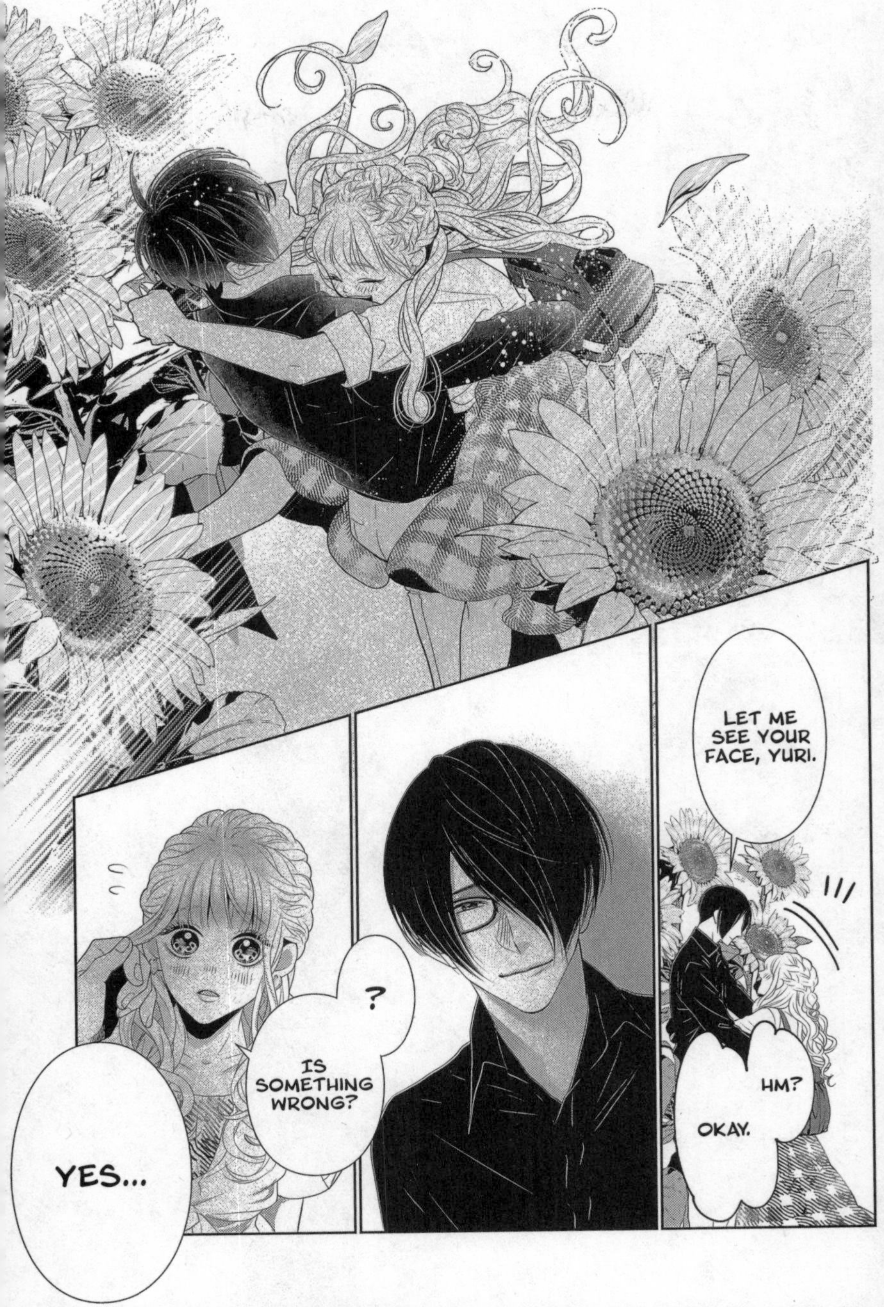

LET ME SEE YOUR FACE, YURI.
HM?
OKAY.
IS SOMETHING WRONG?
?
YES...

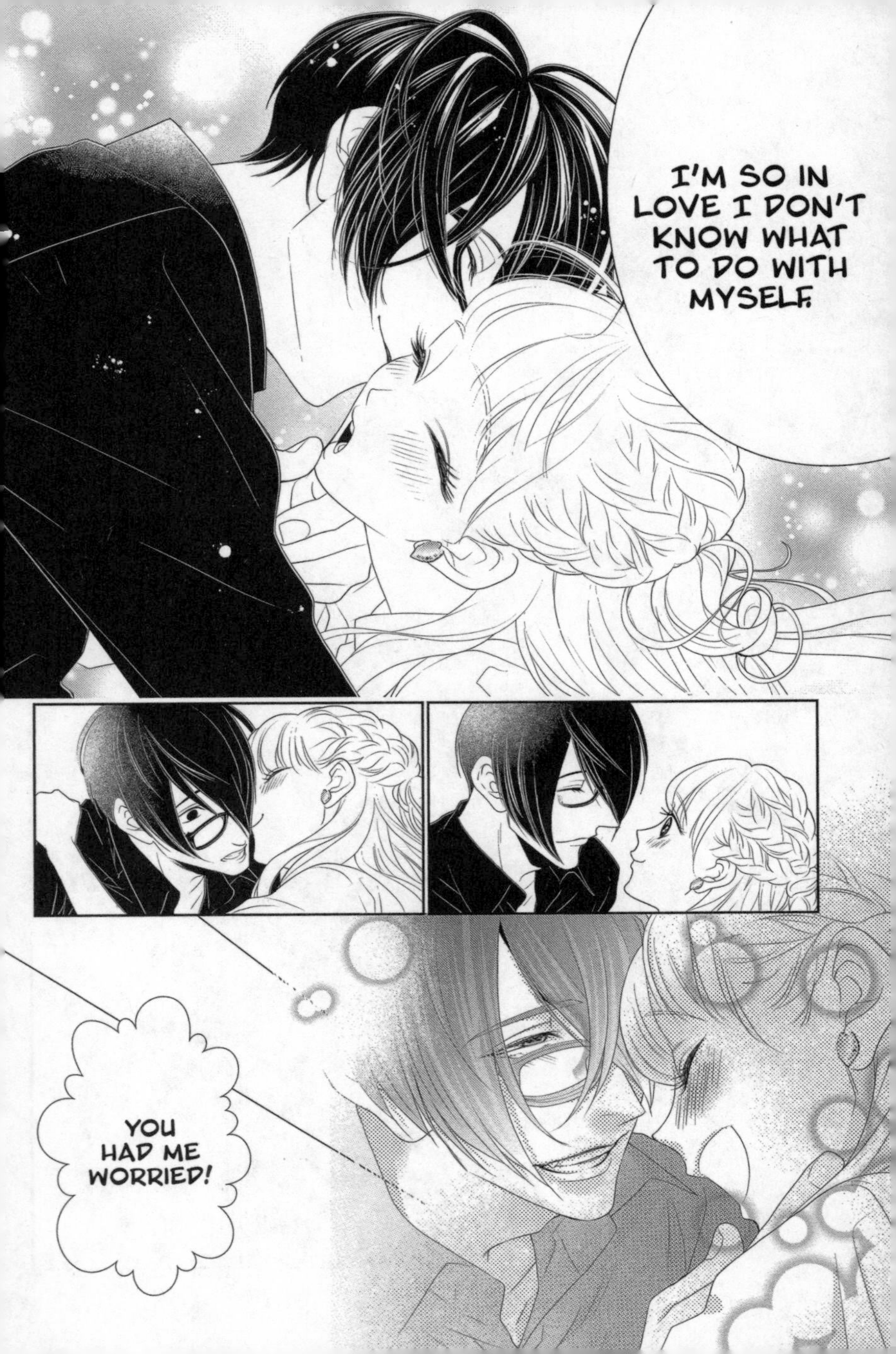
I'M SO IN LOVE I DON'T KNOW WHAT TO DO WITH MYSELF.
YOU HAD ME WORRIED!

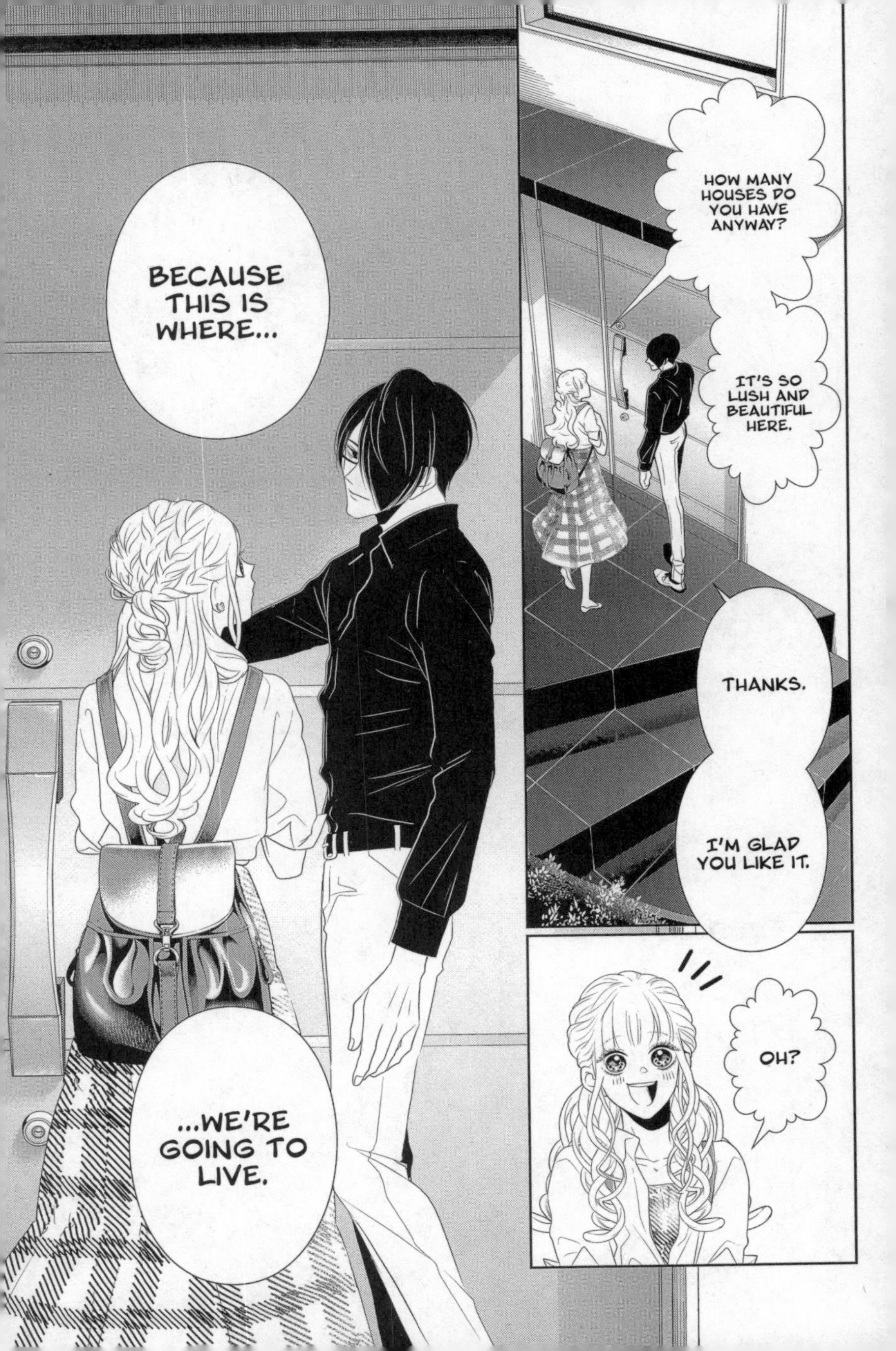
HOW MANY HOUSES DO YOU HAVE ANYWAY?
IT'S SO LUSH AND BEAUTIFUL HERE.
THANKS.
I'M GLAD YOU LIKE IT.
OH?
BECAUSE THIS IS WHERE...
...WE'RE GOING TO LIVE.

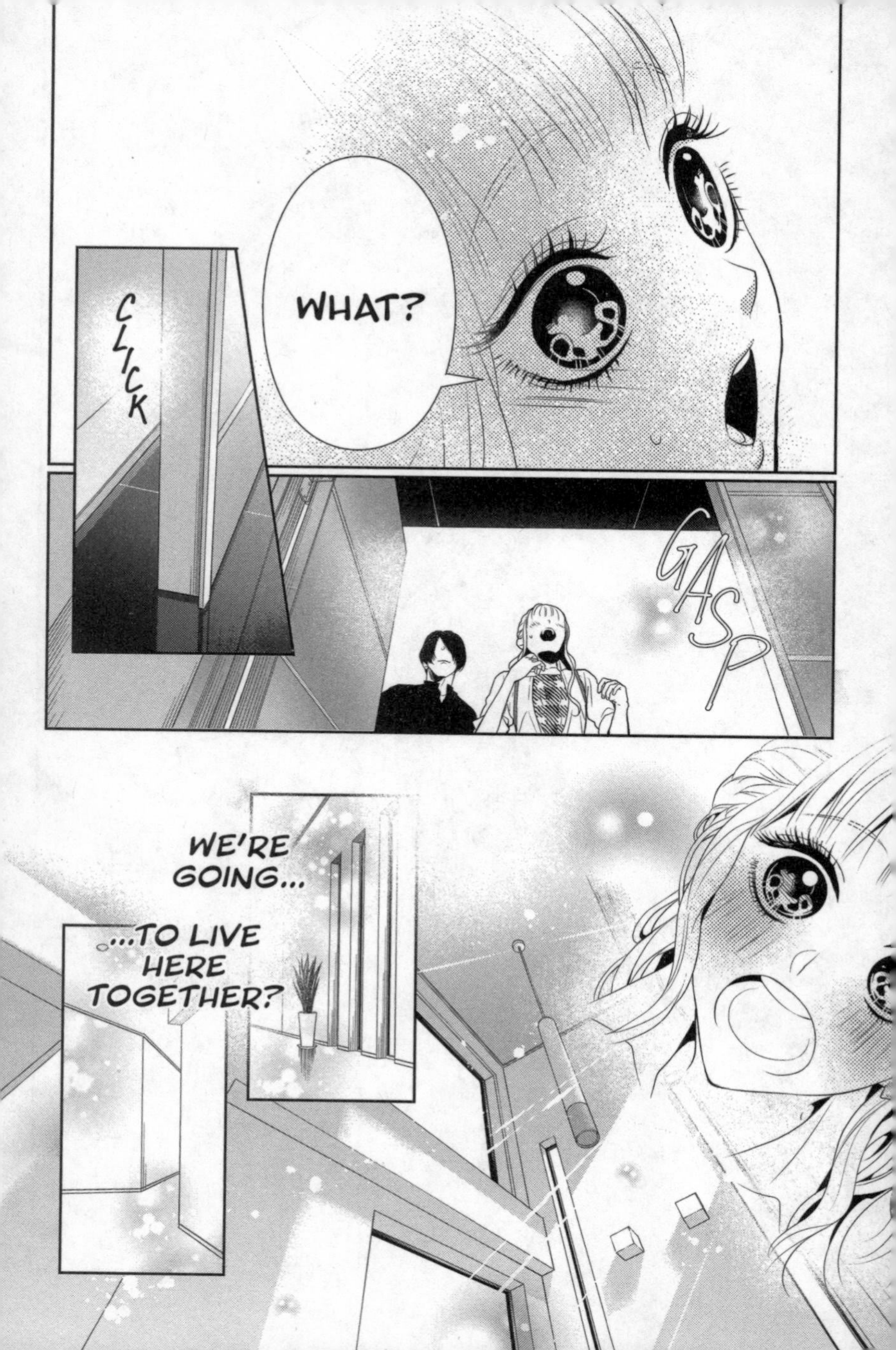
WHAT?
CLICK
GASP
WE'RE GOING...
...TO LIVE HERE TOGETHER?

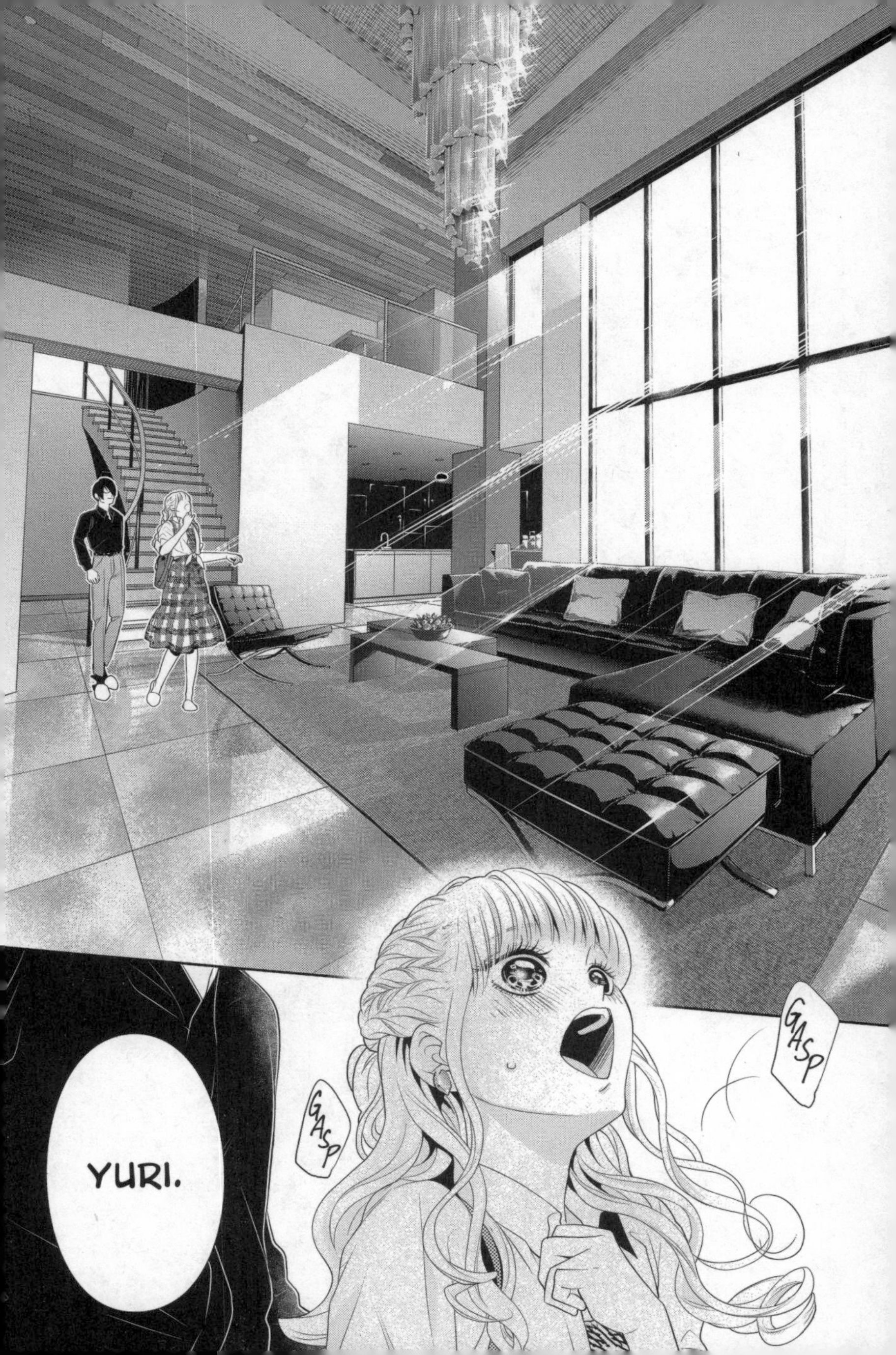
GASP
GASP
YURI.

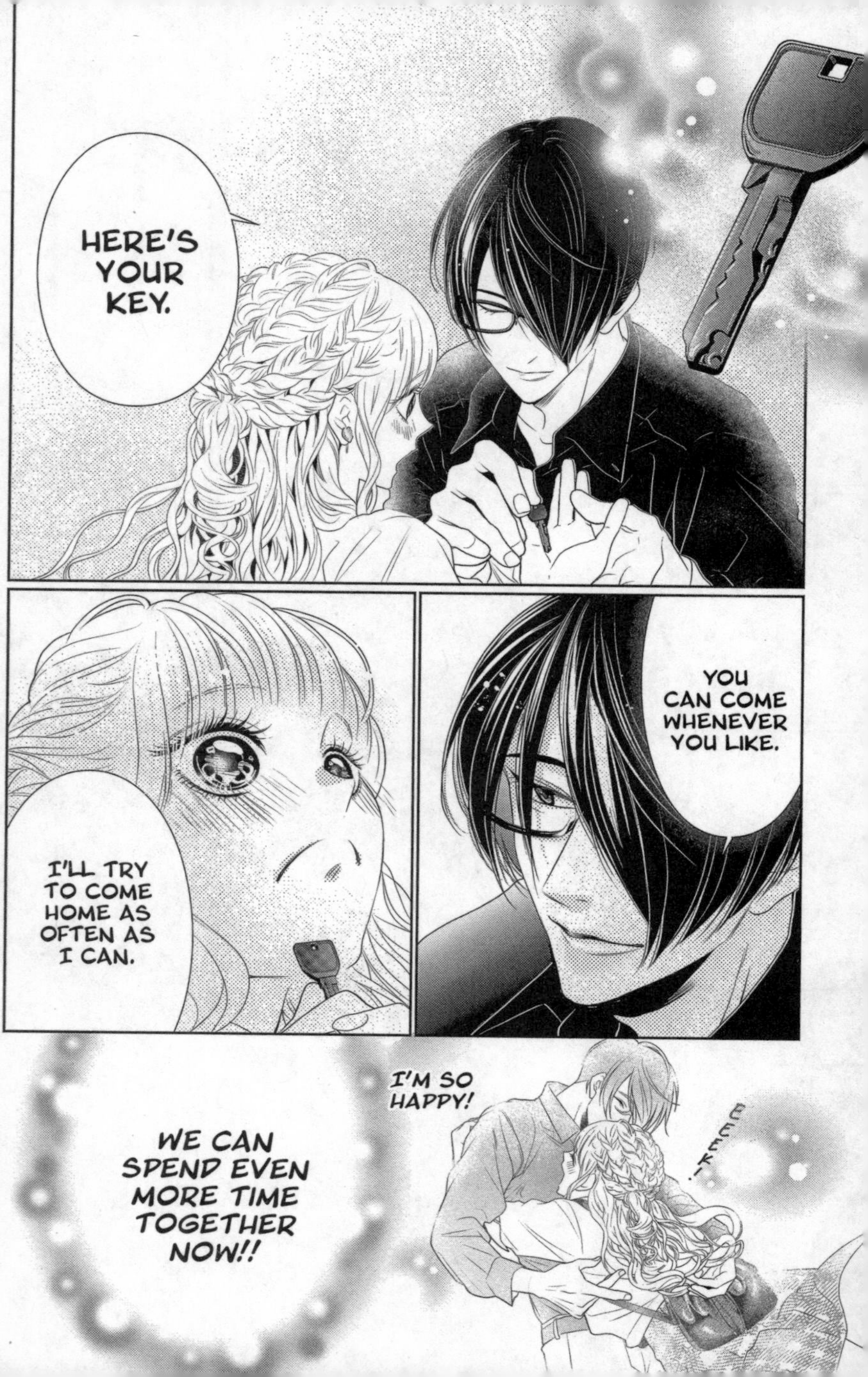
HERE'S YOUR KEY.
YOU CAN COME WHENEVER YOU LIKE.
I'LL TRY TO COME HOME AS OFTEN AS I CAN.
EEEEK!
I'M SO HAPPY!
WE CAN SPEND EVEN MORE TIME TOGETHER NOW!!

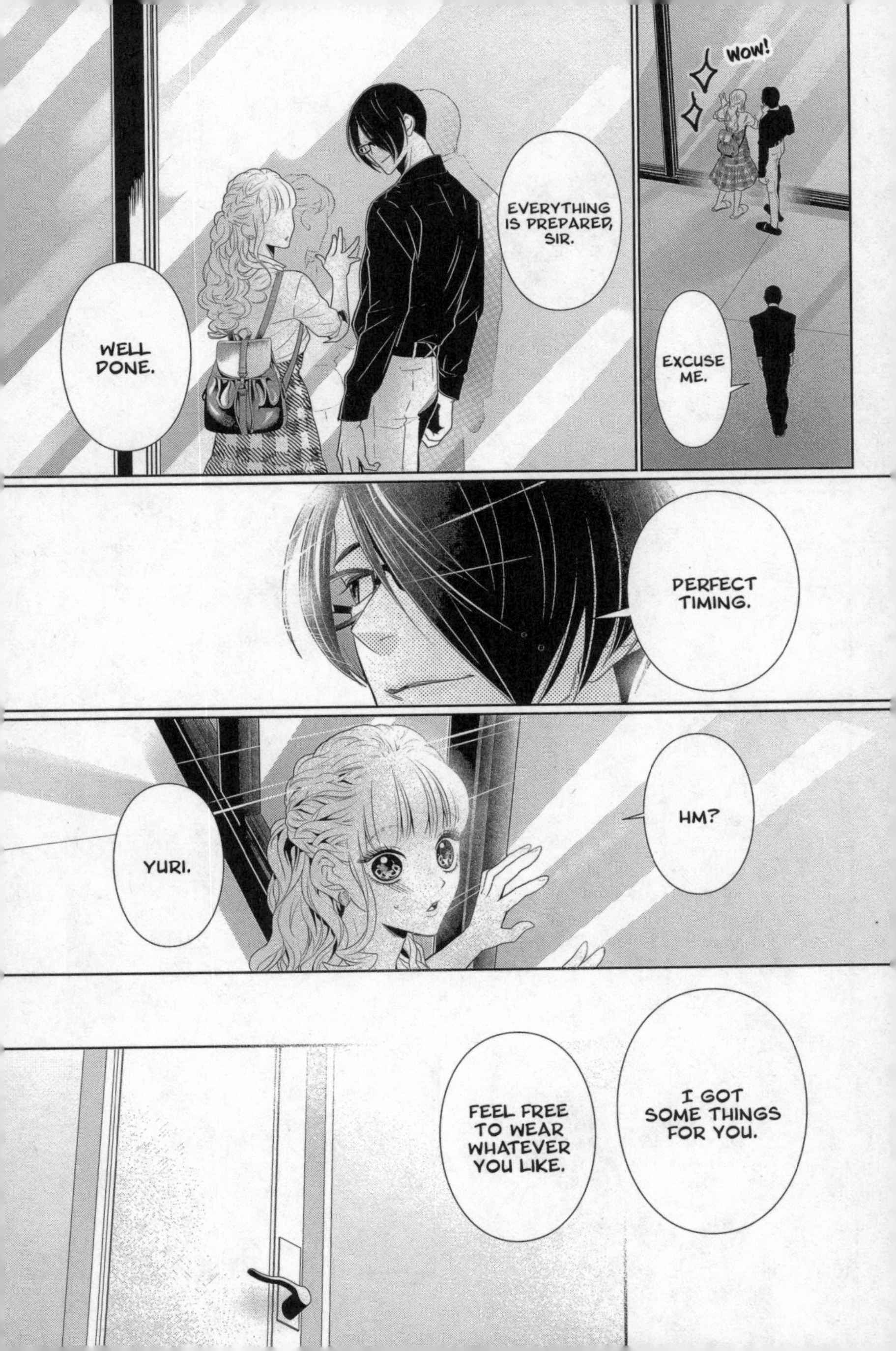
WOW!
EXCUSE ME.
EVERYTHING IS PREPARED, SIR.
WELL DONE.
PERFECT TIMING.
HM?
YURI.
I GOT SOME THINGS FOR YOU.
FEEL FREE TO WEAR WHATEVER YOU LIKE.

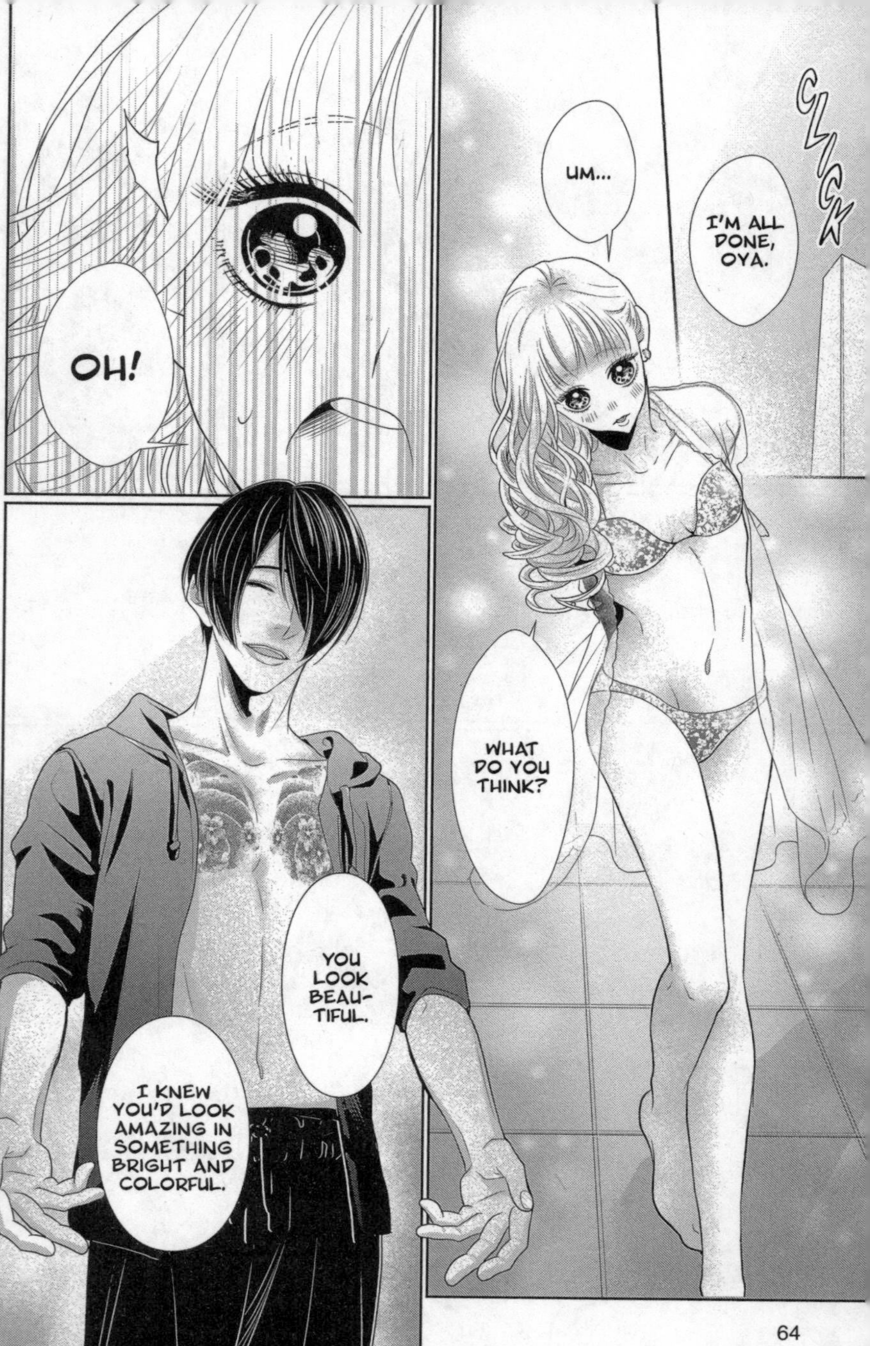
CLICK
I'M ALL DONE, OYA.
UM...
WHAT DO YOU THINK?
OH!
YOU LOOK BEAU-TIFUL.
I KNEW YOU'D LOOK AMAZING IN SOMETHING BRIGHT AND COLORFUL.

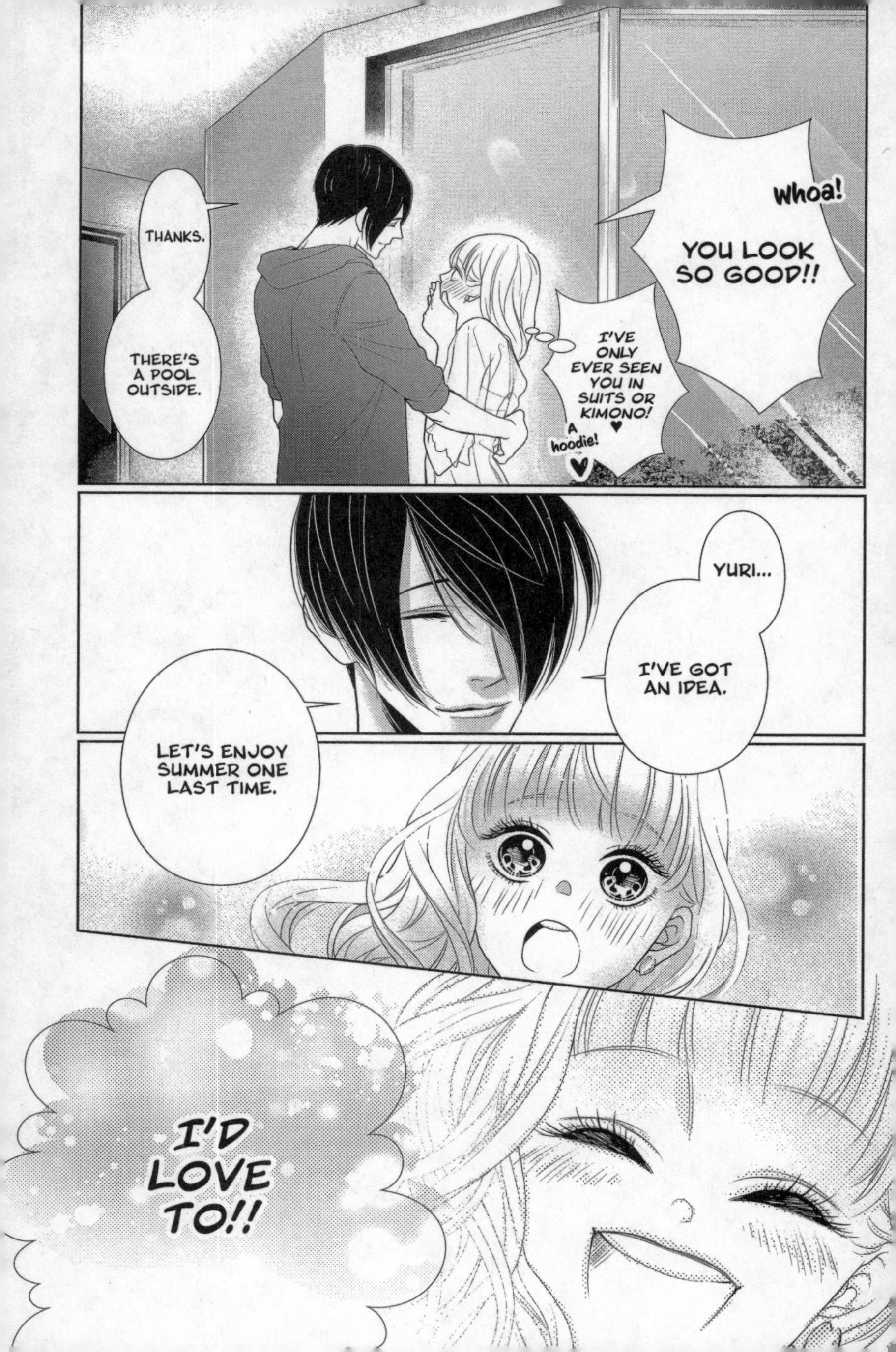
Whoa!
YOU LOOK SO GOOD!!
I'VE ONLY EVER SEEN YOU IN SUITS OR KIMONO! ♥
A hoodie! ♥
THANKS.
THERE'S A POOL OUTSIDE.
YURI...
I'VE GOT AN IDEA.
LET'S ENJOY SUMMER ONE LAST TIME.
I'D LOVE TO!!

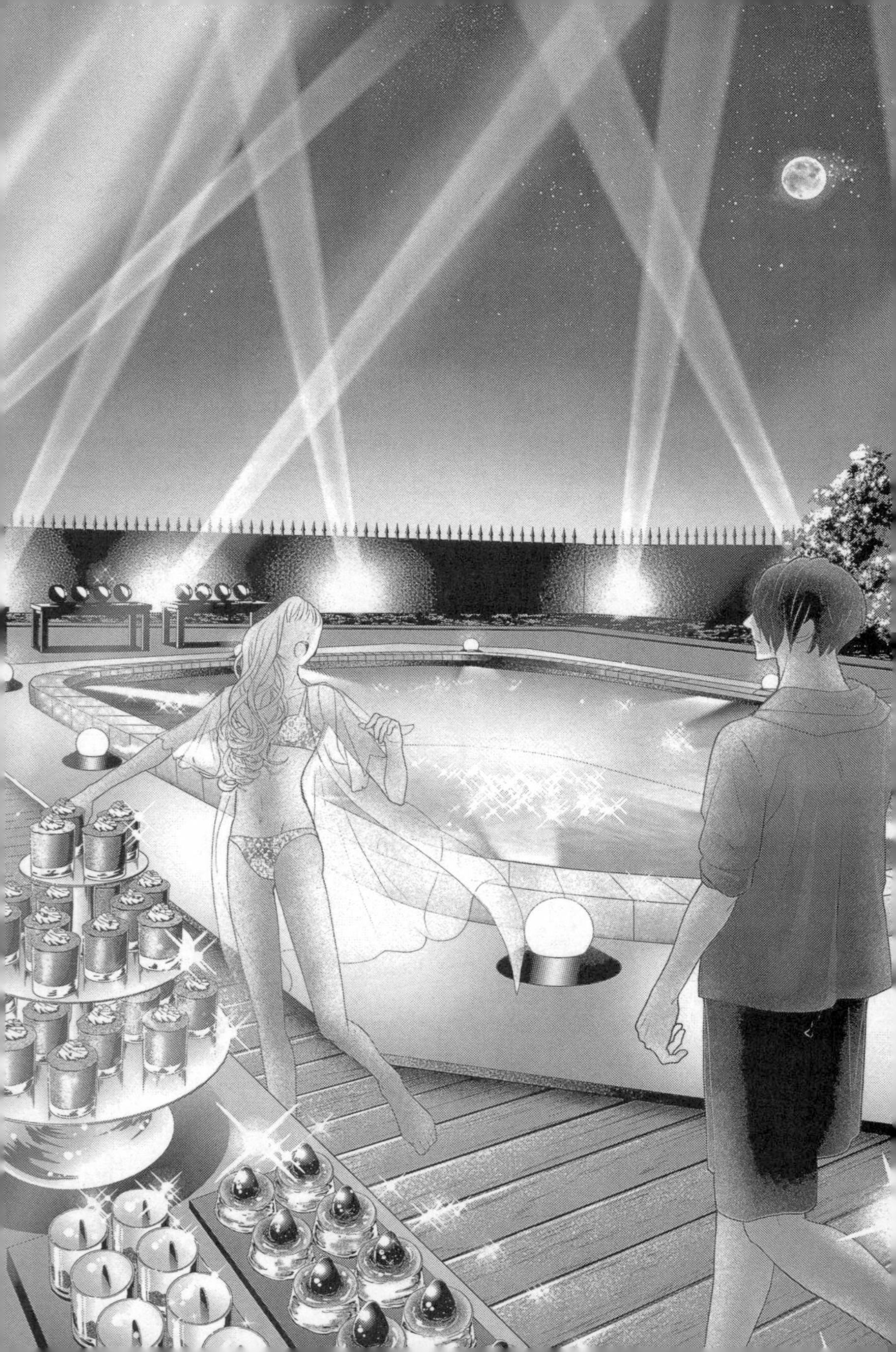

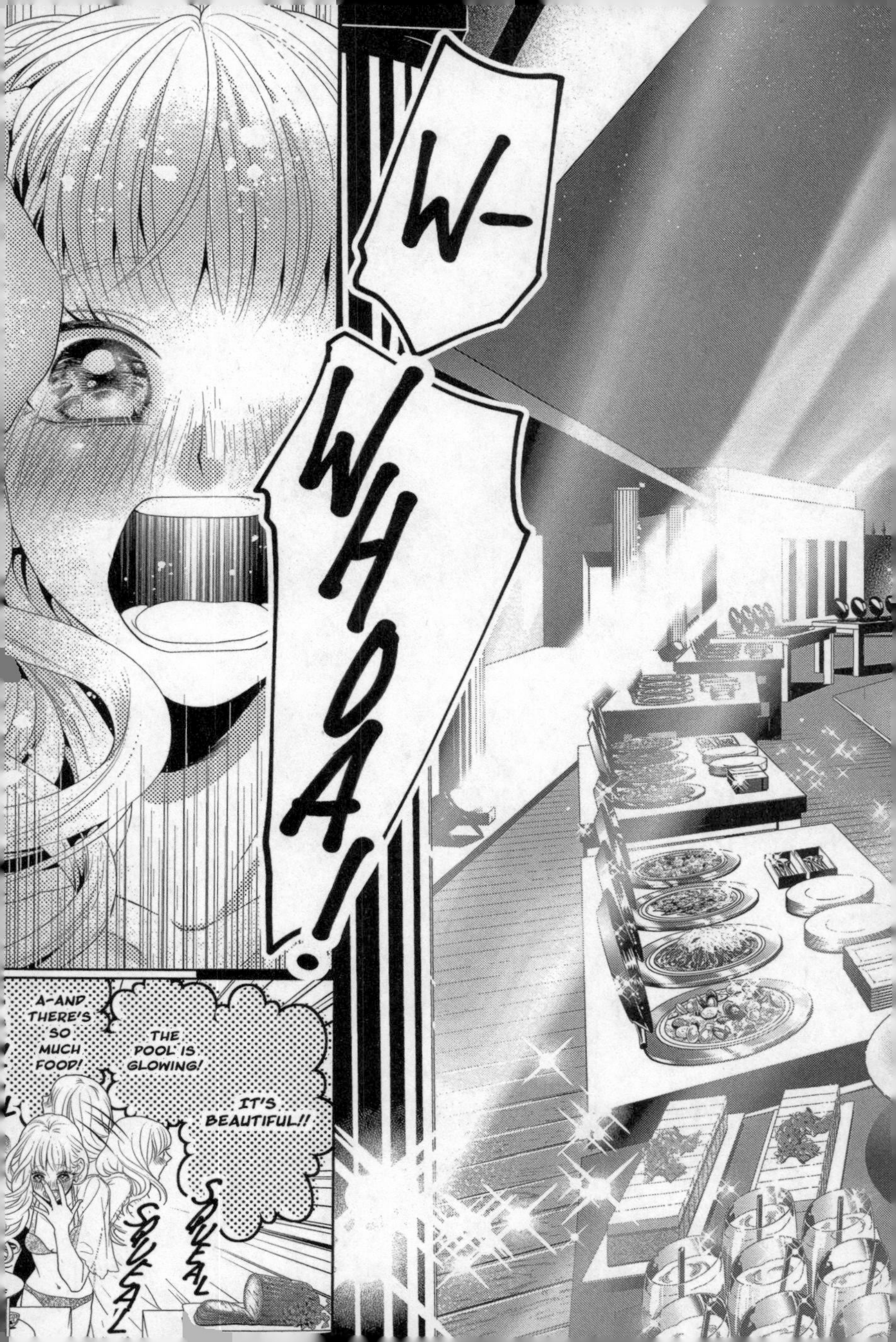
W-WHOA!
THE POOL IS GLOWING!
IT'S BEAUTIFUL!!
A-AND THERE'S SO MUCH FOOD!
SQUEAL
SQUEAL

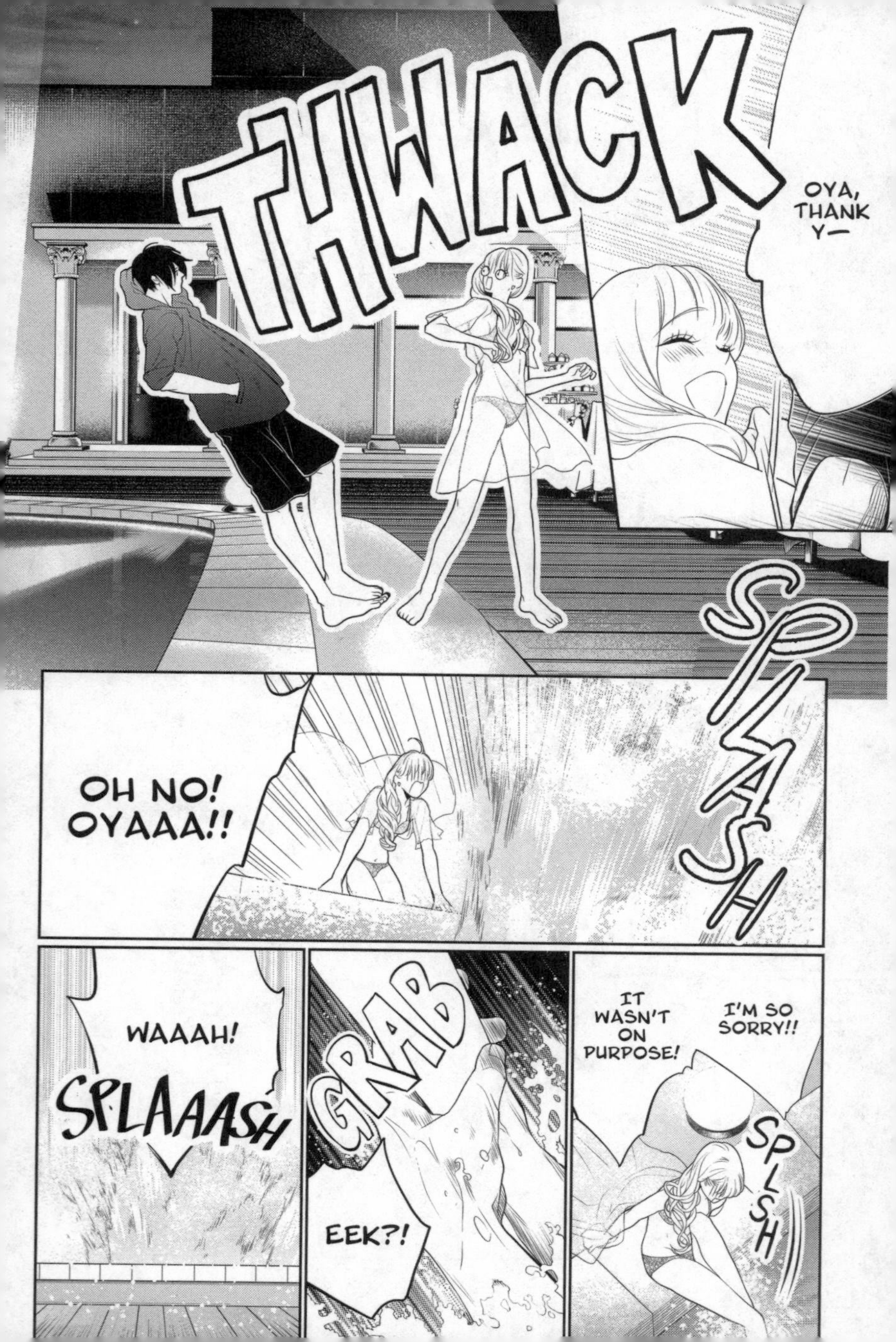
OYA, THANK Y—
THWACK
SPLASH
OH NO! OYAAA!!
IT WASN'T ON PURPOSE!
I'M SO SORRY!!
SPLSH
GRAB
EEK?!
WAAAH!
SPLAAASH

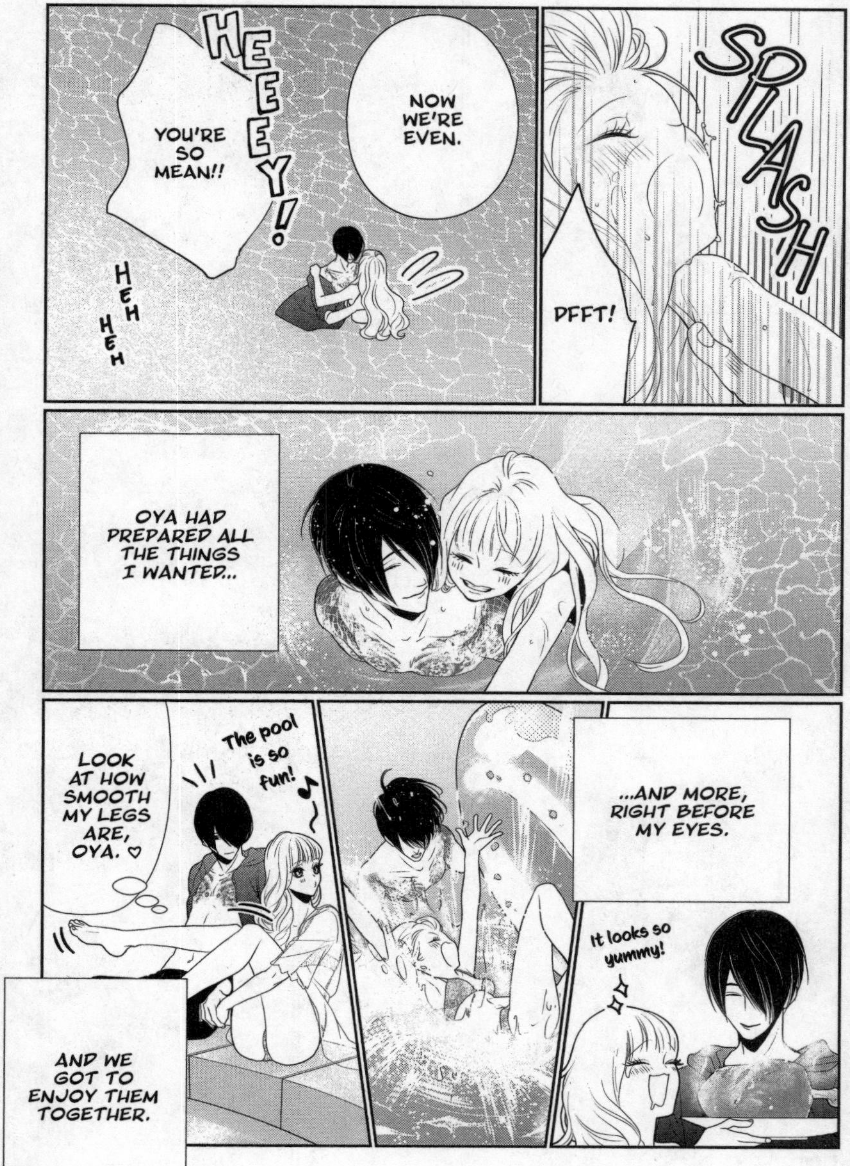
SPLASH
PFFT!
NOW WE'RE EVEN.
HEEEEY!
YOU'RE SO MEAN!!
HEH HEH HEH
OYA HAD PREPARED ALL THE THINGS I WANTED...
...AND MORE, RIGHT BEFORE MY EYES.
It looks so yummy!
The pool is so fun! ♪
LOOK AT HOW SMOOTH MY LEGS ARE, OYA. ♡
AND WE GOT TO ENJOY THEM TOGETHER.

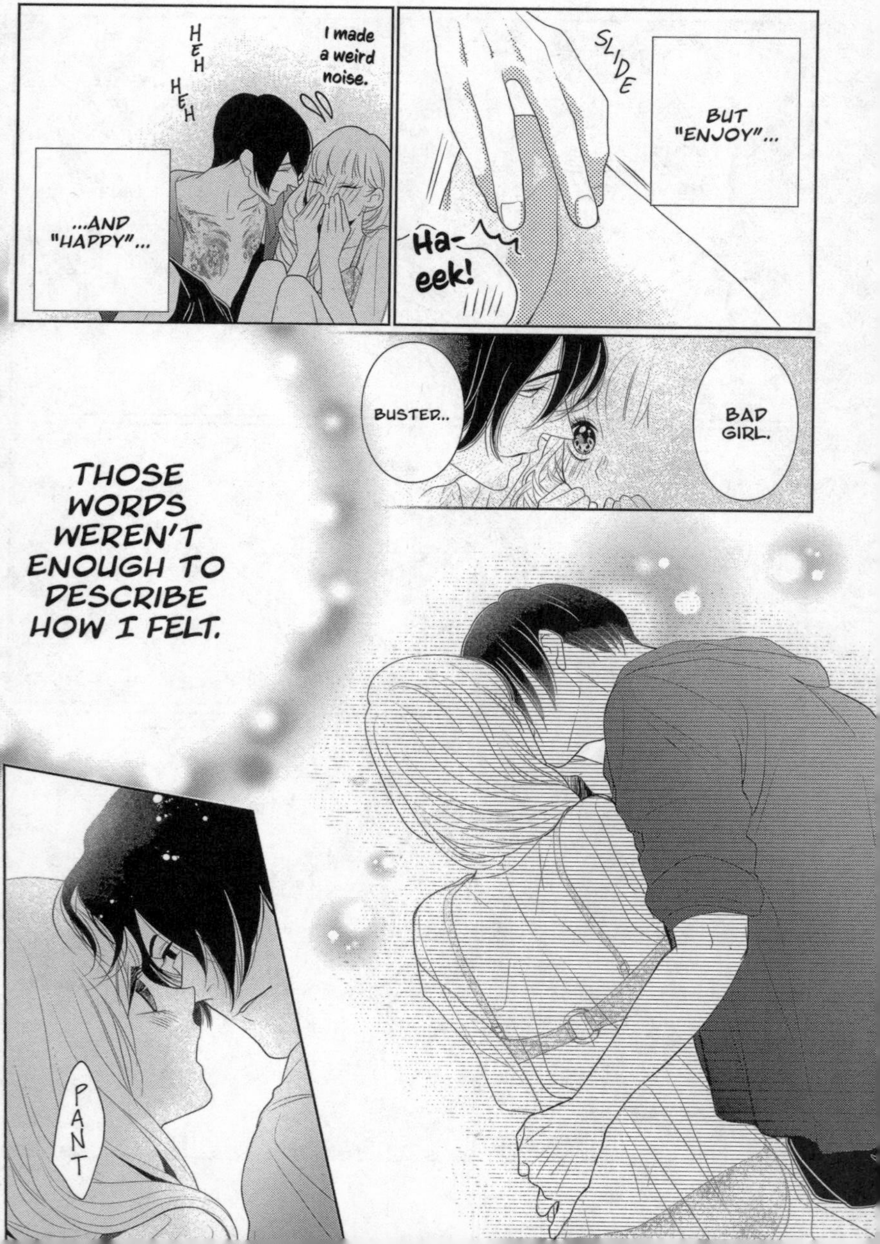
SLIDE
BUT "ENJOY"...
Ha-eek!
I made a weird noise.
HEH HEH
...AND "HAPPY"...
BAD GIRL.
BUSTED...
THOSE WORDS WEREN'T ENOUGH TO DESCRIBE HOW I FELT.
PANT

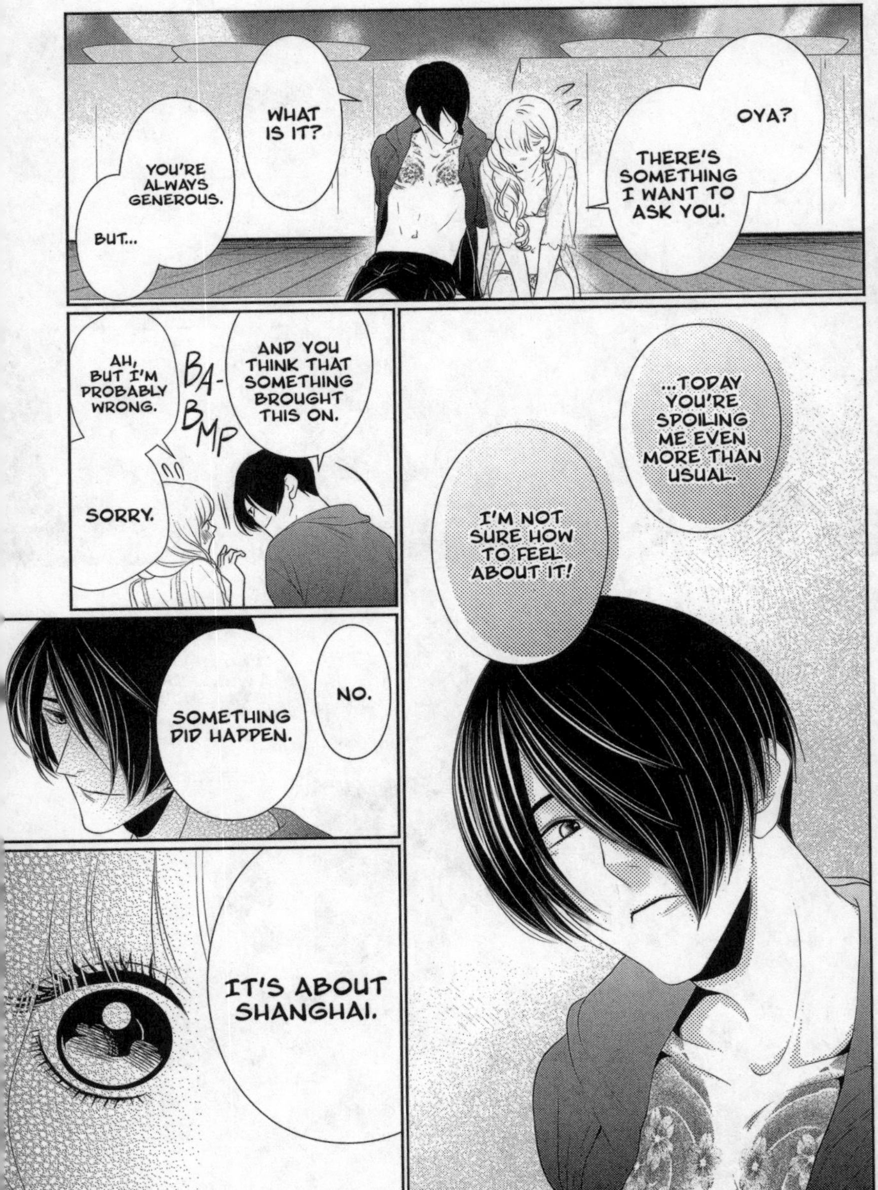

OYA?
THERE'S SOMETHING I WANT TO ASK YOU.
WHAT IS IT?
YOU'RE ALWAYS GENEROUS.
BUT...
...TODAY YOU'RE SPOILING ME EVEN MORE THAN USUAL.
I'M NOT SURE HOW TO FEEL ABOUT IT!
AND YOU THINK THAT SOMETHING BROUGHT THIS ON.
BA-BMP
AH, BUT I'M PROBABLY WRONG.
SORRY.
NO.
SOMETHING DID HAPPEN.
IT'S ABOUT SHANGHAI.

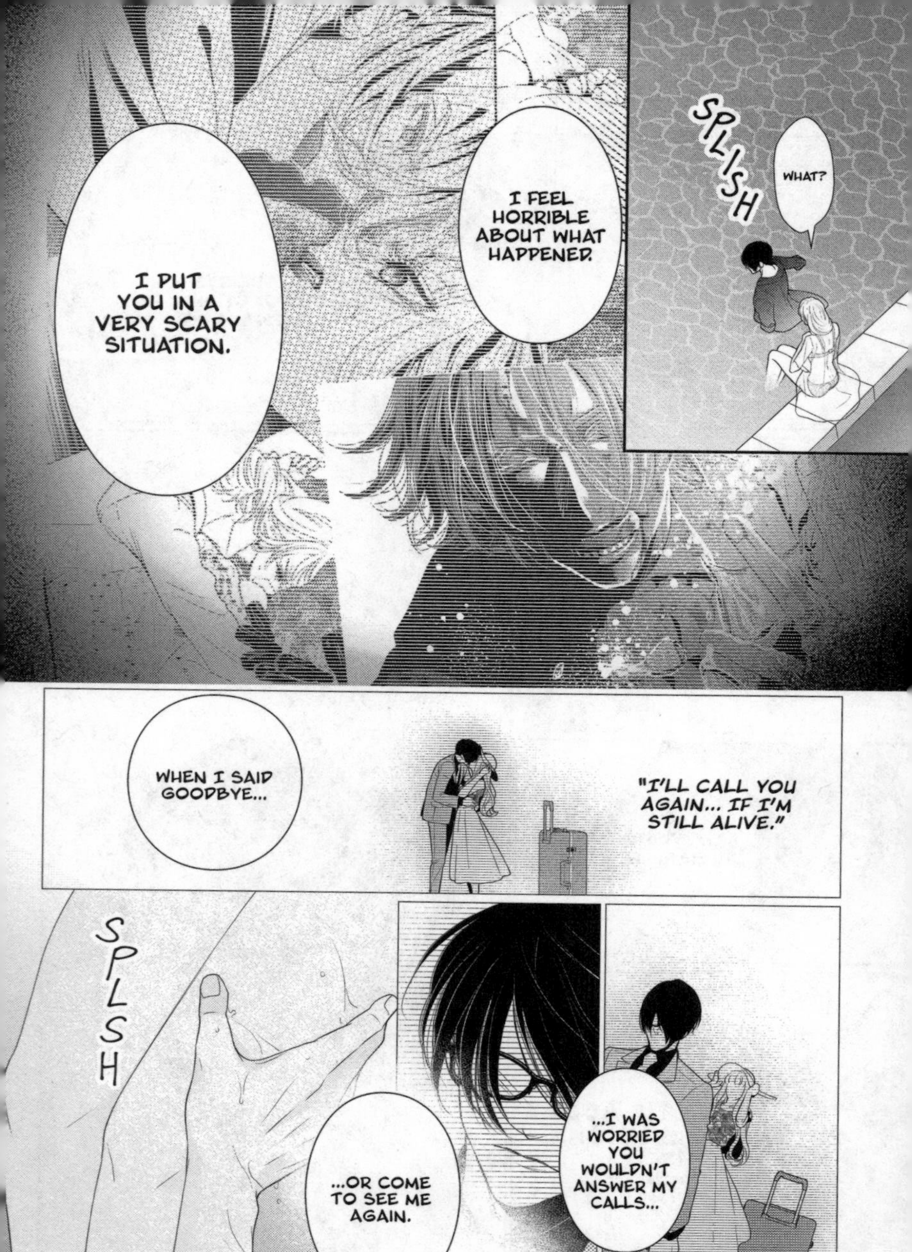
SPLISH
WHAT?
I FEEL HORRIBLE ABOUT WHAT HAPPENED.
I PUT YOU IN A VERY SCARY SITUATION.
"I'LL CALL YOU AGAIN... IF I'M STILL ALIVE."
WHEN I SAID GOODBYE...
...I WAS WORRIED YOU WOULDN'T ANSWER MY CALLS...
...OR COME TO SEE ME AGAIN.
SPLSH

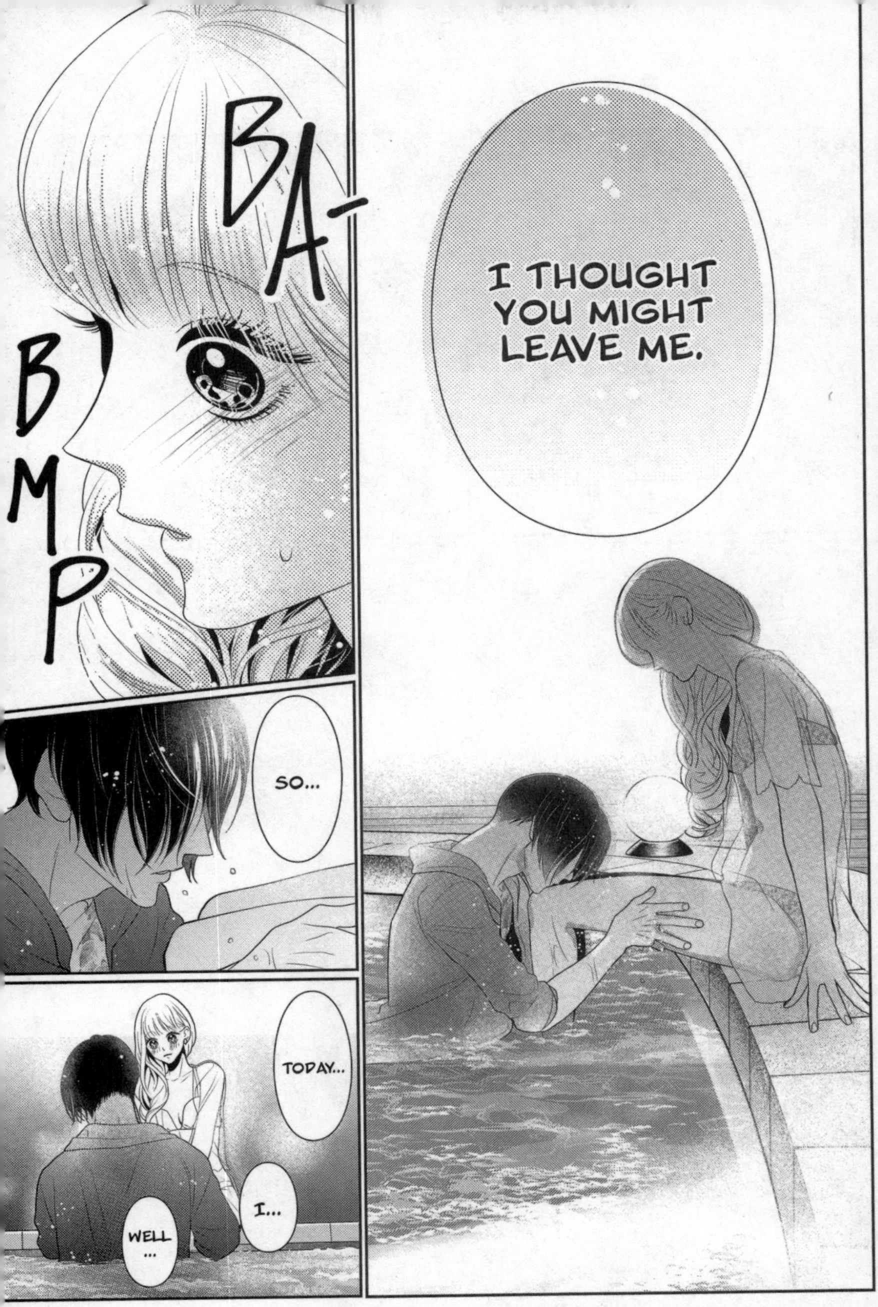
I THOUGHT YOU MIGHT LEAVE ME.
BA-BMP
SO...
TODAY...
I...
WELL...

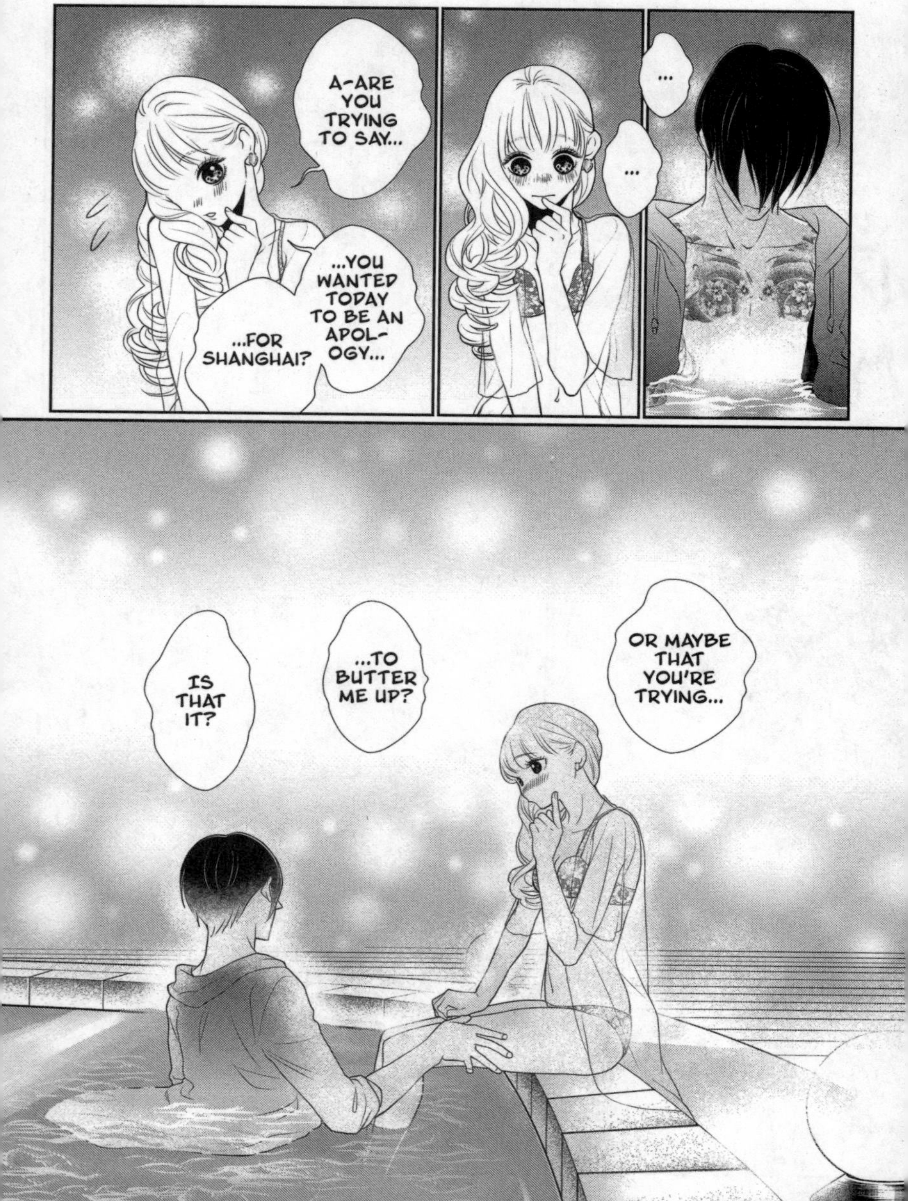
...
...
A-ARE YOU TRYING TO SAY...
...YOU WANTED TODAY TO BE AN APOLOGY...
...FOR SHANGHAI?
OR MAYBE THAT YOU'RE TRYING...
...TO BUTTER ME UP?
IS THAT IT?

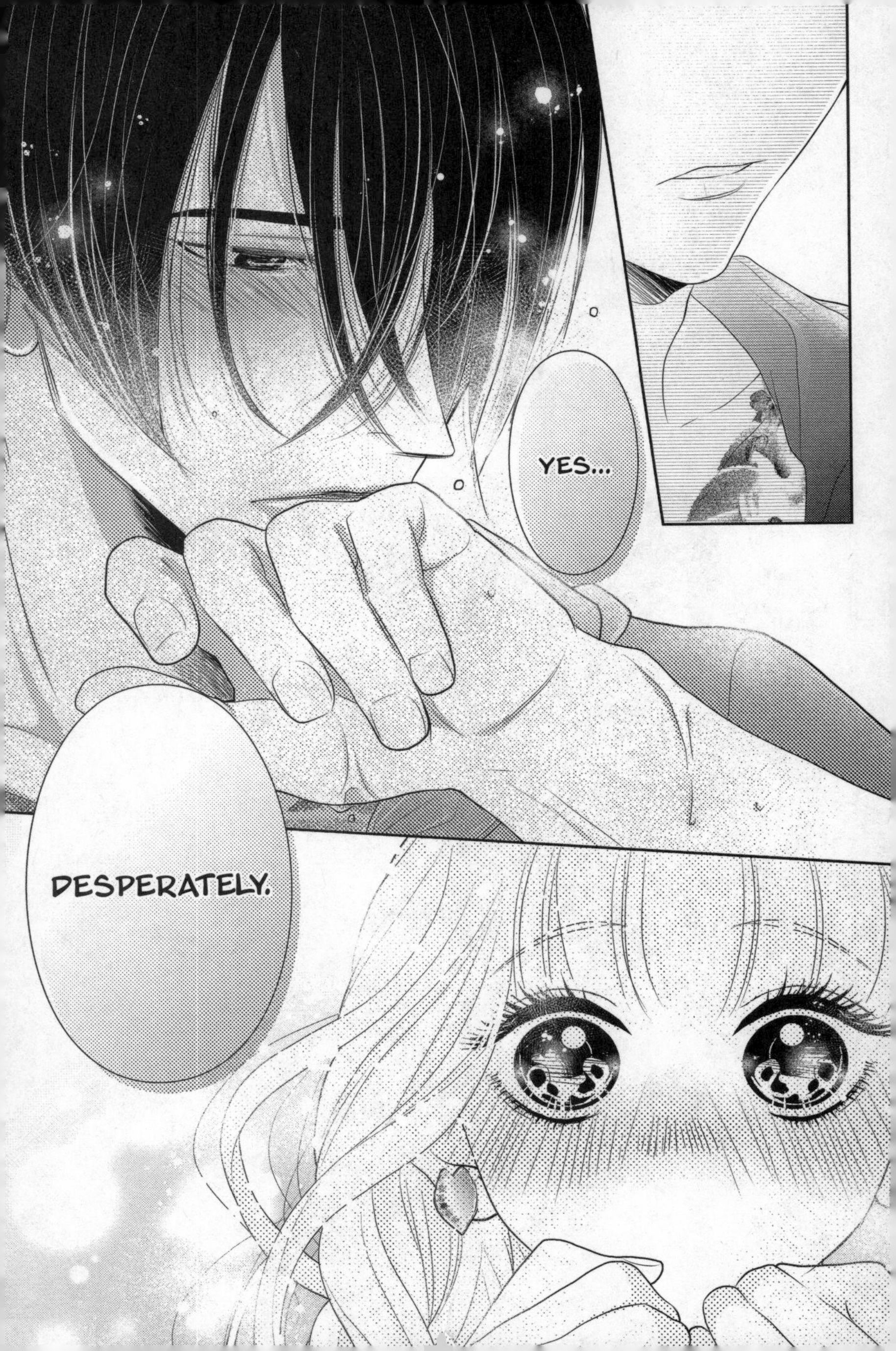
YES...
DESPERATELY.

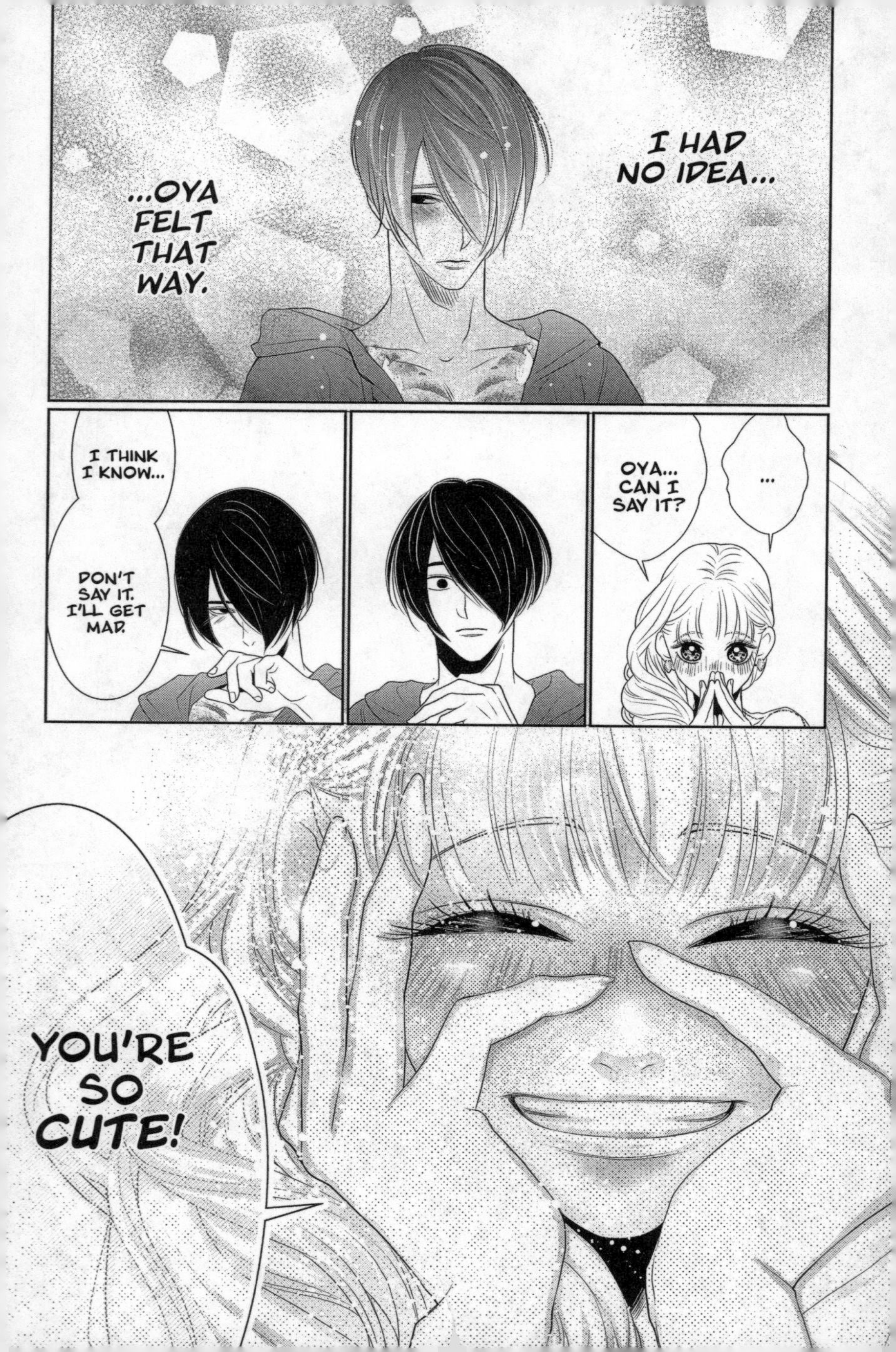
I HAD NO IDEA...
...OYA FELT THAT WAY.
...
OYA... CAN I SAY IT?
I THINK I KNOW...
DON'T SAY IT. I'LL GET MAD.
YOU'RE SO CUTE!

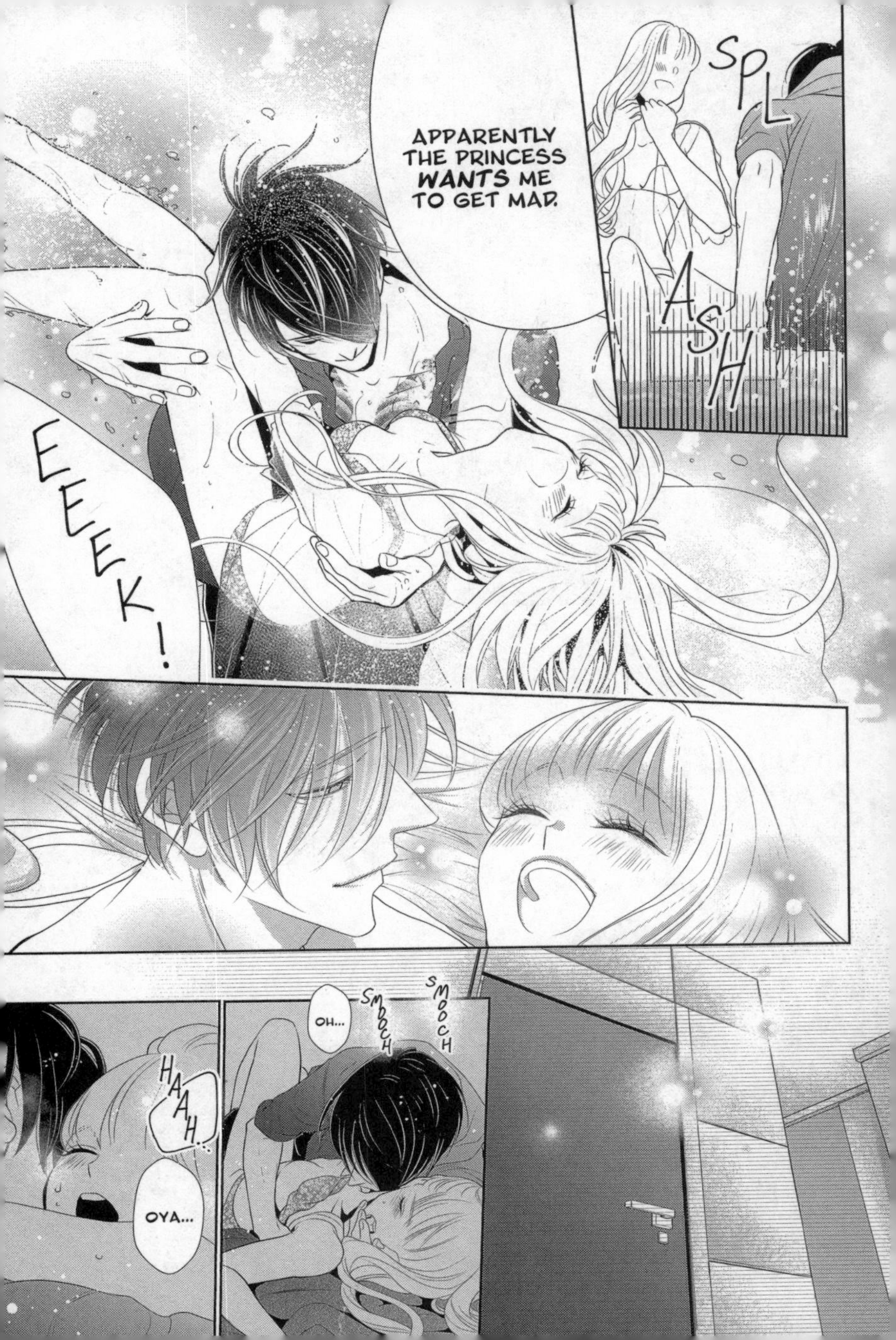
SPLASH
APPARENTLY THE PRINCESS WANTS ME TO GET MAD.
EEEEK!
SMOOCH
SMOOCH
OH...
HAAAH...
OYA...

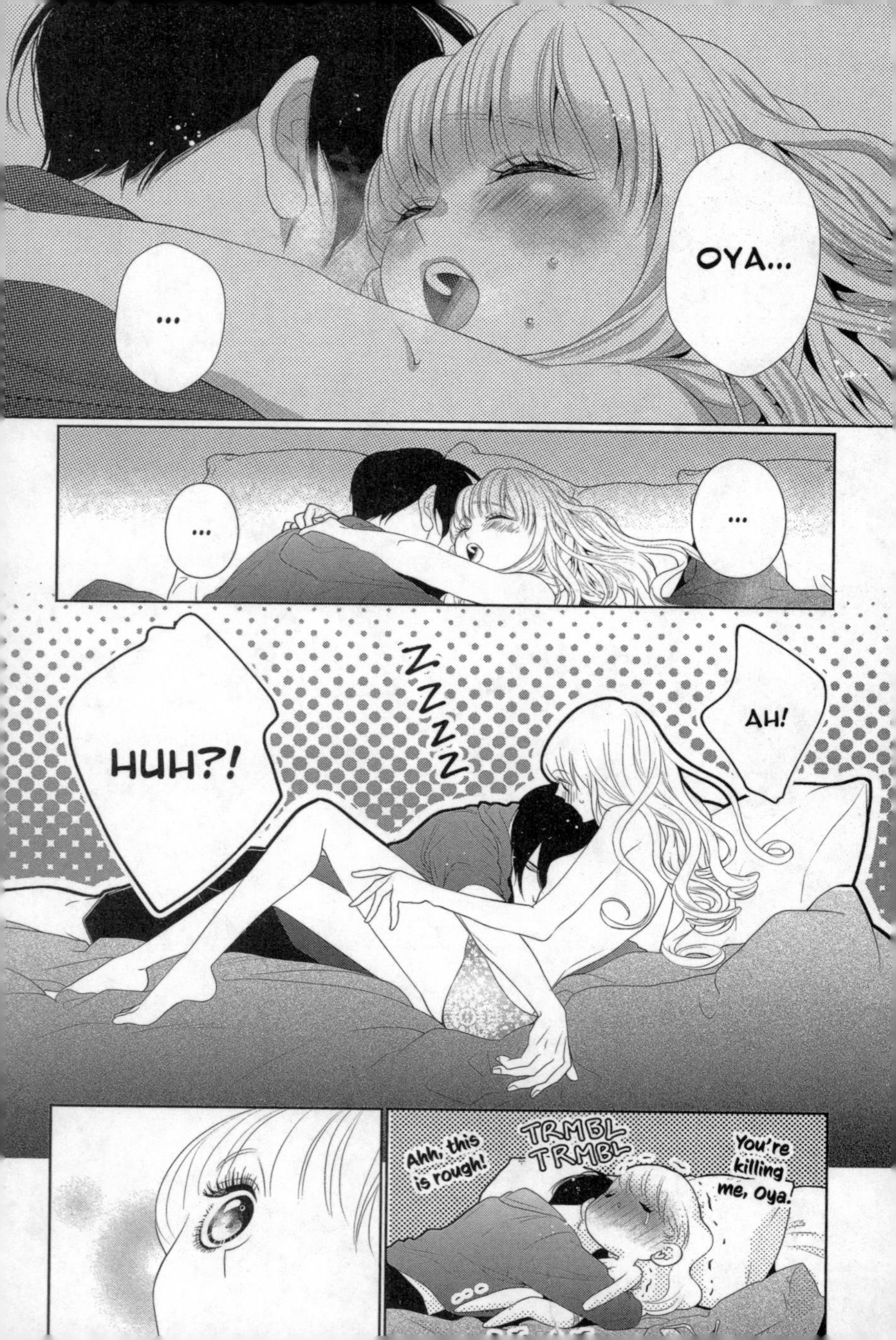
OYA...
...
...
...
AH!
ZZZZ
HUH?!
You're killing me, Oya.
TRMBL TRMBL
Ahh, this is rough!

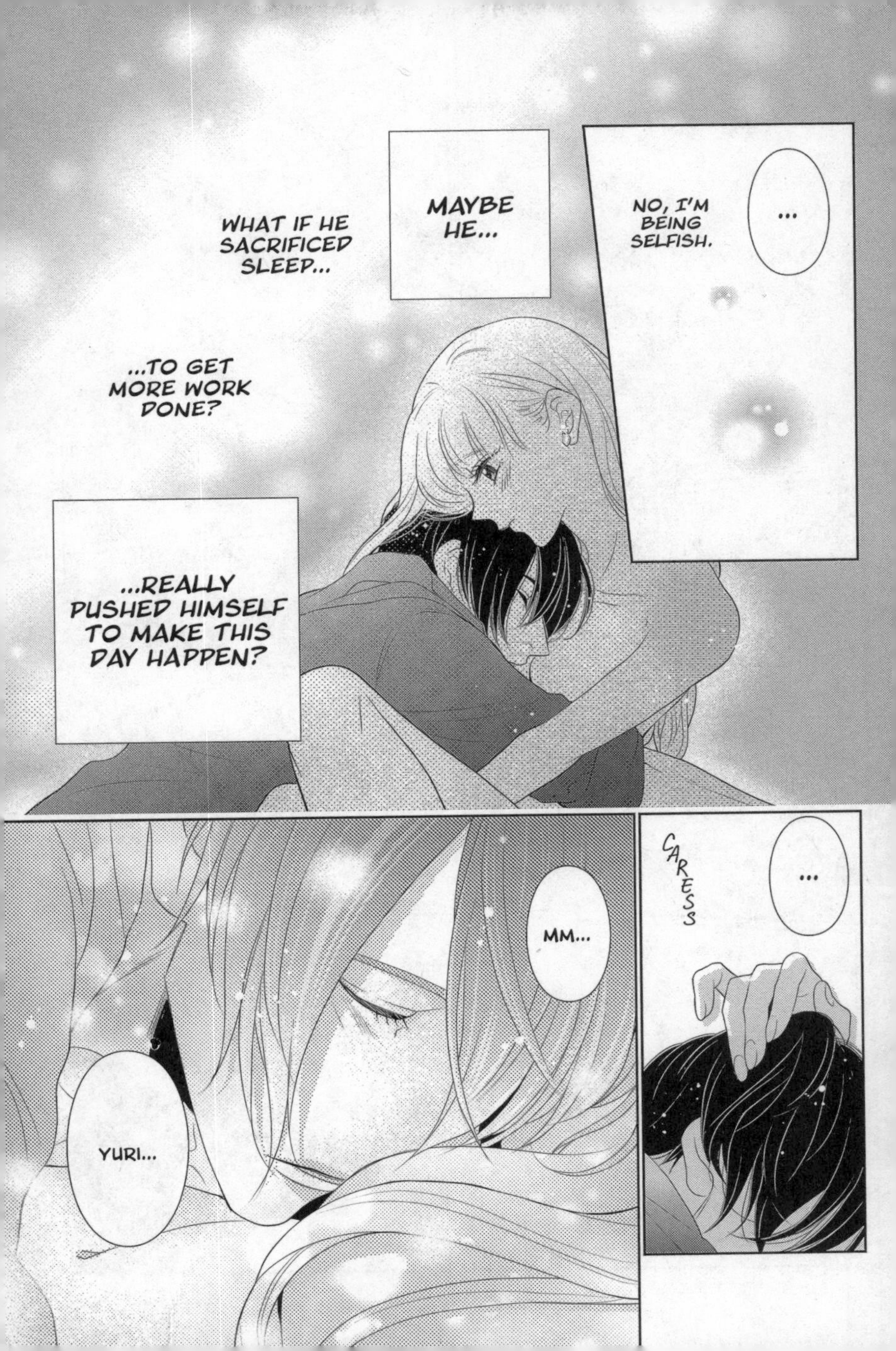
MAYBE HE...
WHAT IF HE SACRIFICED SLEEP...
...TO GET MORE WORK DONE?
...REALLY PUSHED HIMSELF TO MAKE THIS DAY HAPPEN?
...
NO, I'M BEING SELFISH.
...
CARESS
MM...
YURI...

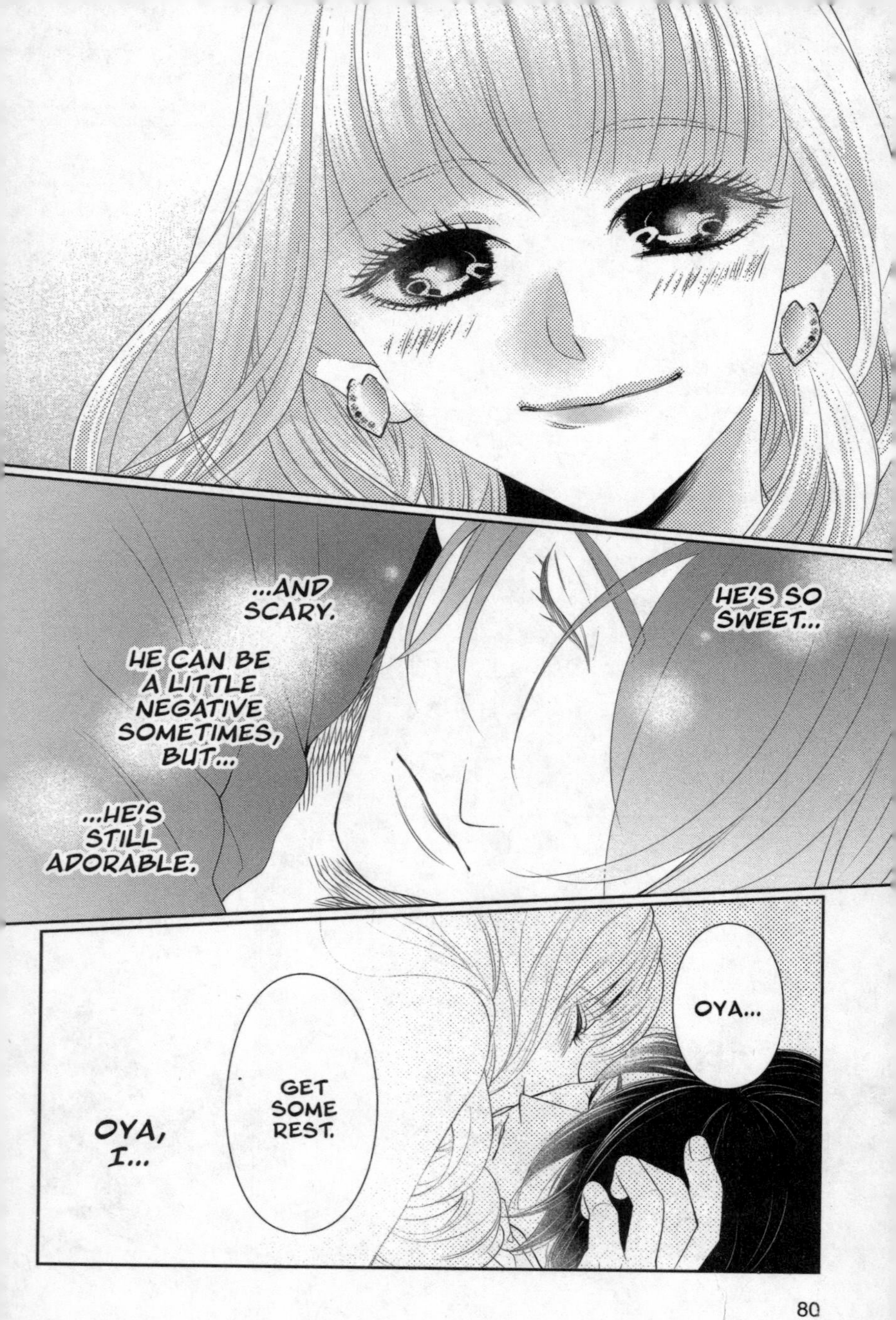
HE'S SO SWEET...
...AND SCARY.
HE CAN BE A LITTLE NEGATIVE SOMETIMES, BUT...
...HE'S STILL ADORABLE.
OYA...
GET SOME REST.
OYA, I...

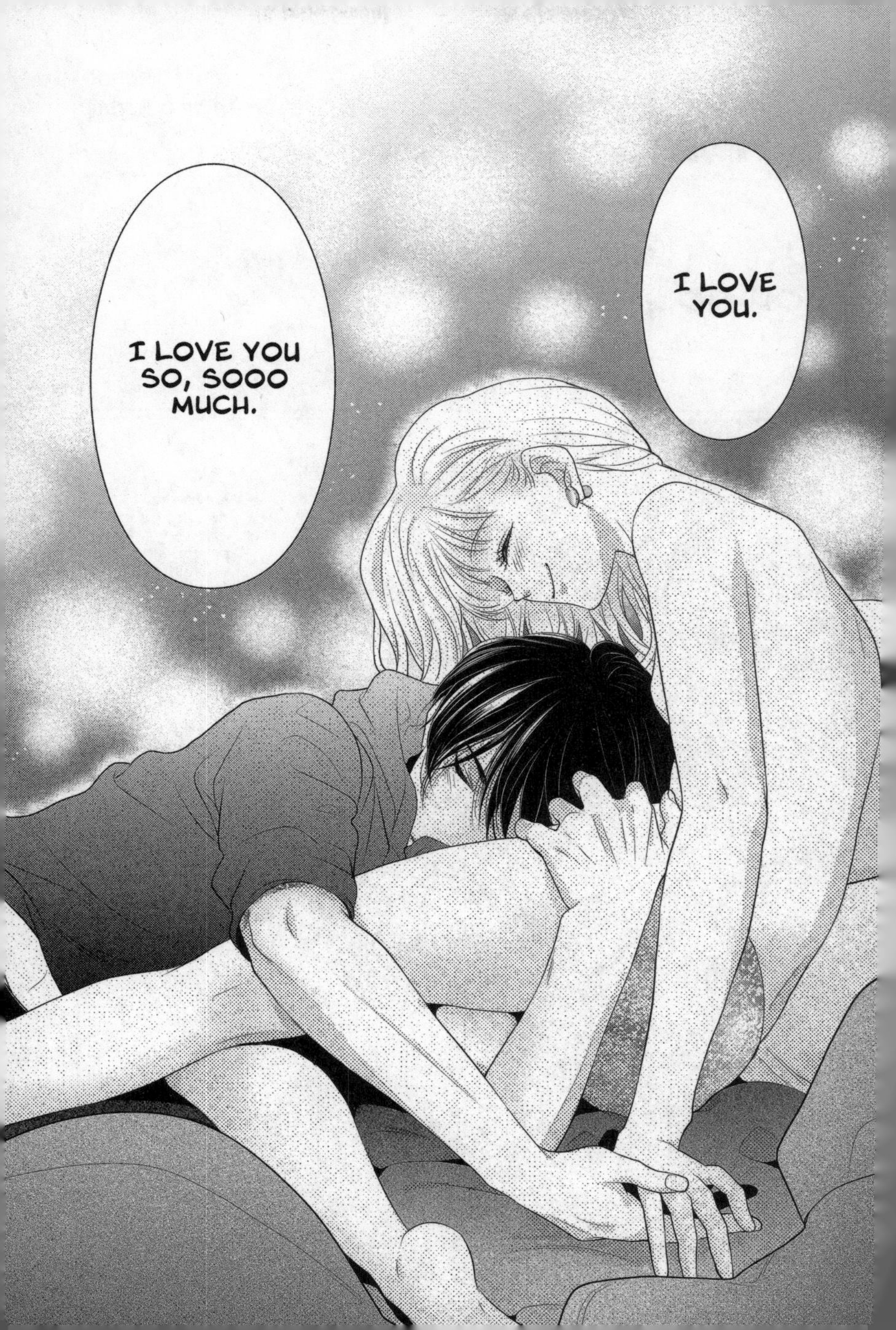
I LOVE YOU.
I LOVE YOU SO, SOOO MUCH.

bonus
bullet 09 secret scene

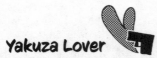

Yakuza Lover Oya's Mistake

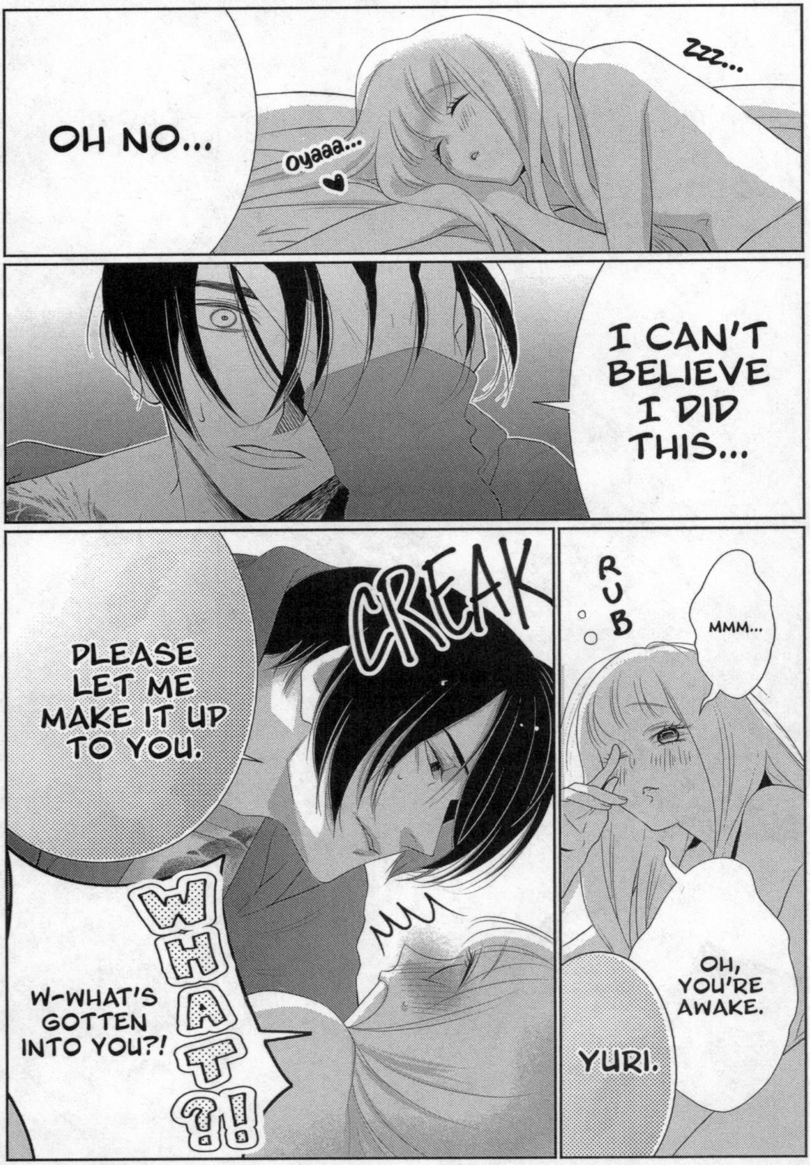
Zzz...
Oyaaa... ♥
OH NO...
I CAN'T BELIEVE I DID THIS...
RUB
MMM...
OH, YOU'RE AWAKE.
YURI.
CREAK
PLEASE LET ME MAKE IT UP TO YOU.
WHAT?!
W-WHAT'S GOTTEN INTO YOU?!

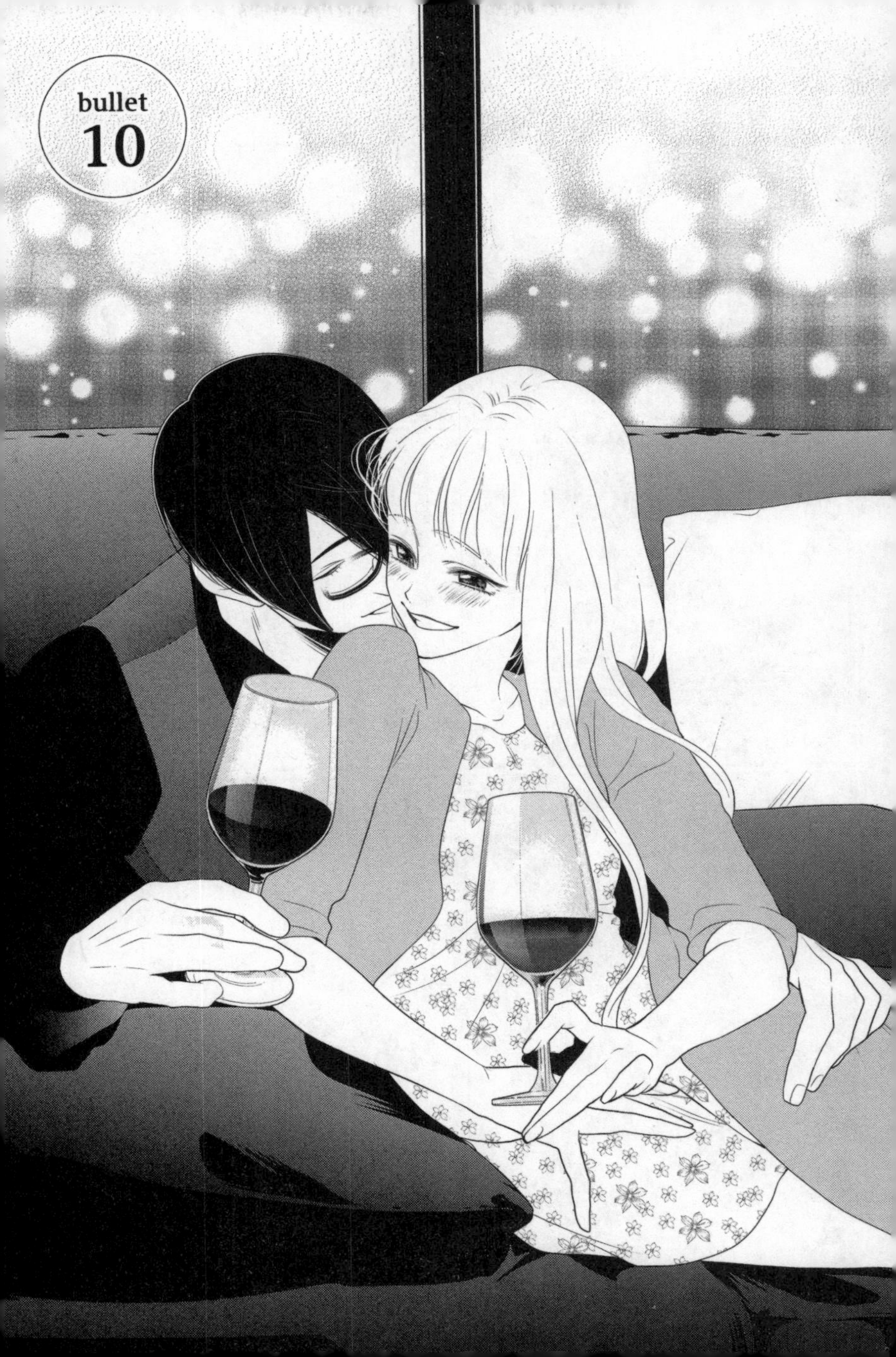
bullet
10

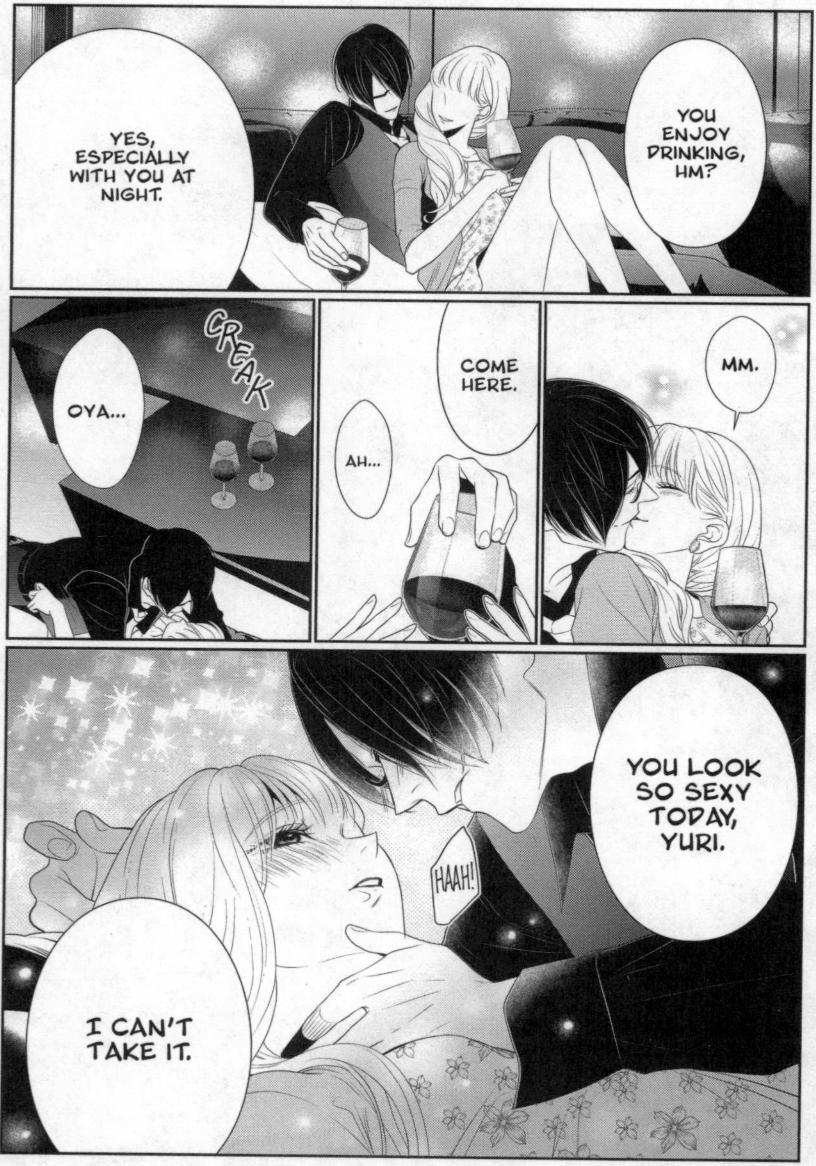
YOU ENJOY DRINKING, HM?
YES, ESPECIALLY WITH YOU AT NIGHT.
MM.
COME HERE.
AH...
CREAK
OYA...
YOU LOOK SO SEXY TODAY, YURI.
HAAH!
I CAN'T TAKE IT.

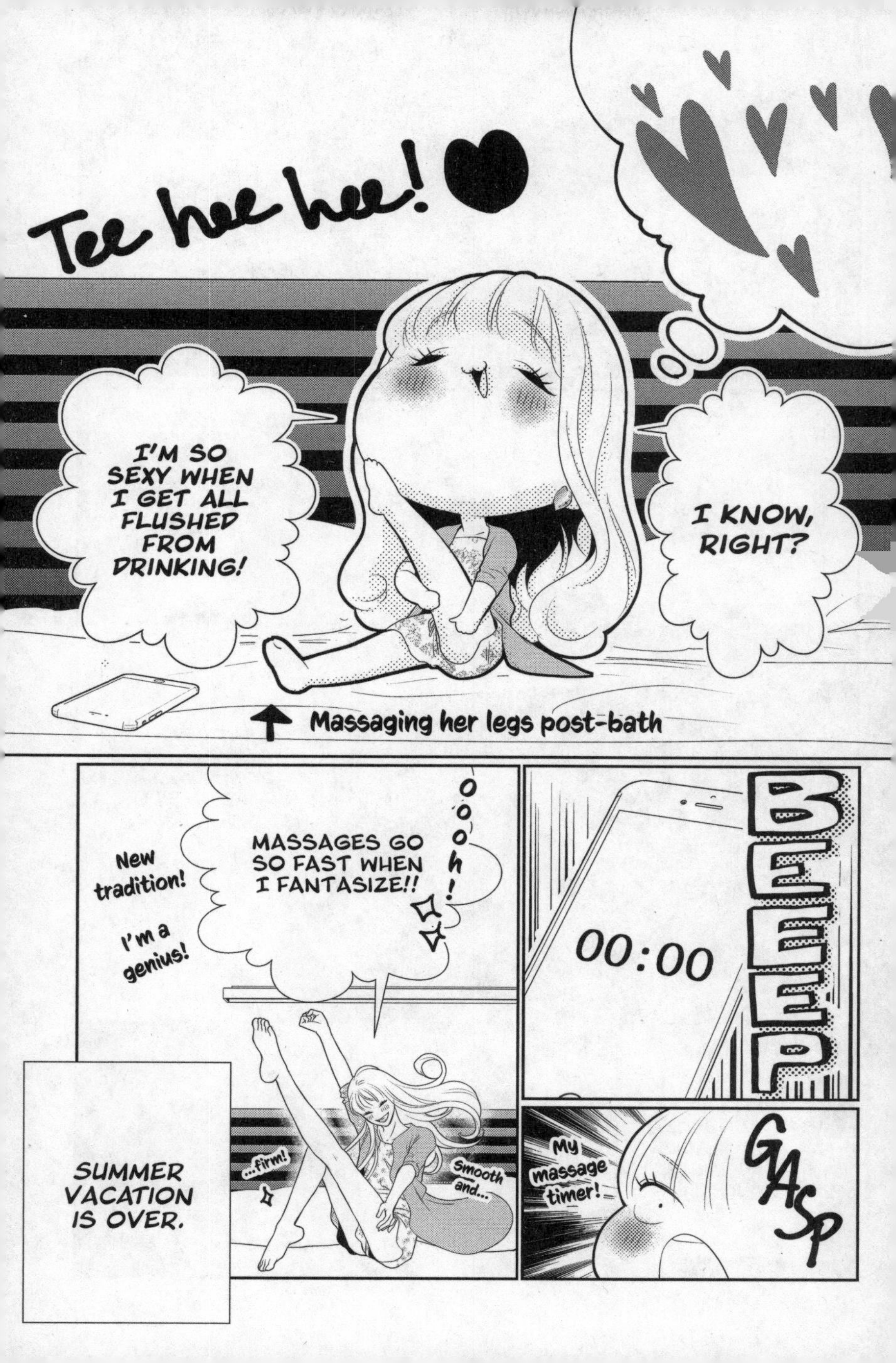

Tee hee hee!
I KNOW, RIGHT?
I'M SO SEXY WHEN I GET ALL FLUSHED FROM DRINKING!
Massaging her legs post-bath
00:00
BEEP
GASP
My massage timer!
Ooooh!
MASSAGES GO SO FAST WHEN I FANTASIZE!!
New tradition!
I'm a genius!
Smooth and...
...firm!
SUMMER VACATION IS OVER.

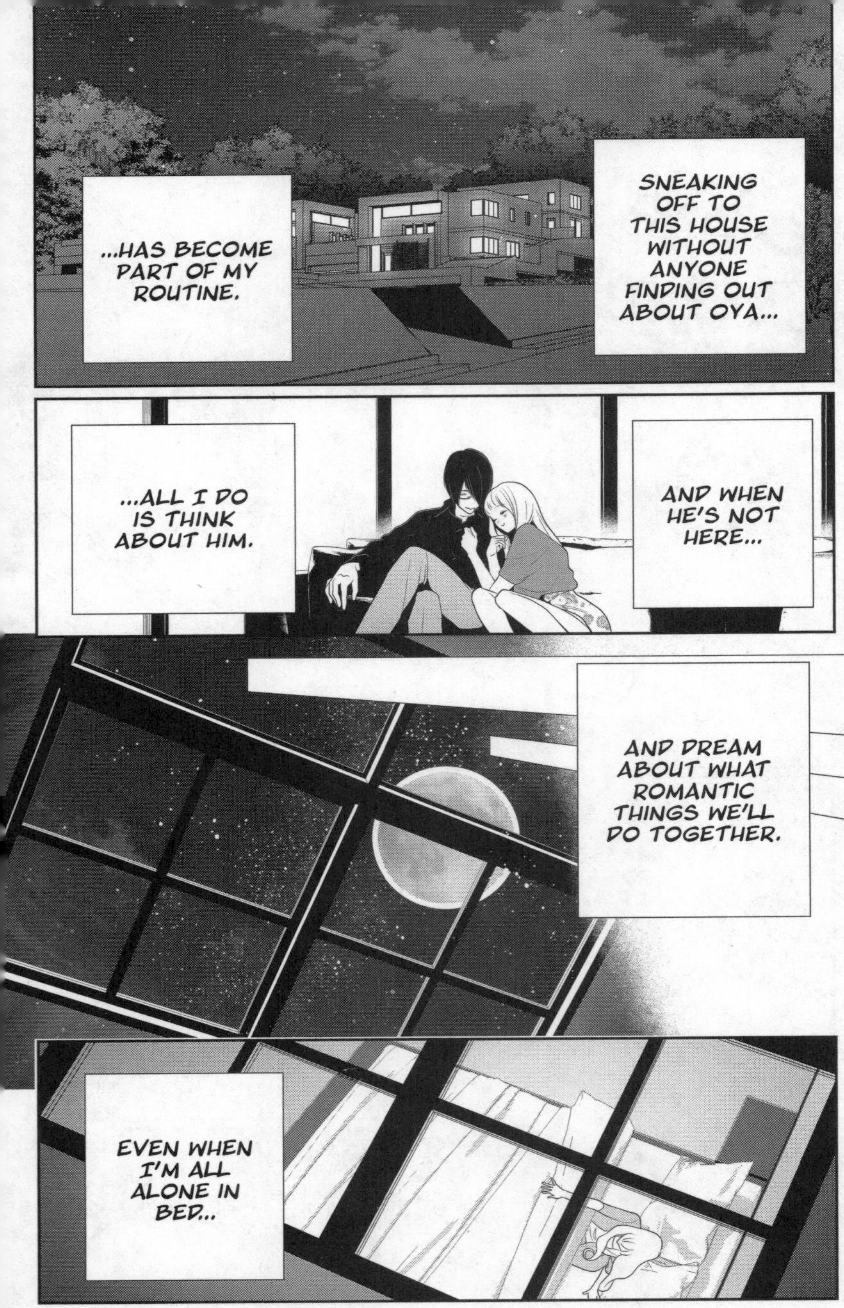
SNEAKING OFF TO THIS HOUSE WITHOUT ANYONE FINDING OUT ABOUT OYA...
...HAS BECOME PART OF MY ROUTINE.
AND WHEN HE'S NOT HERE...
...ALL I DO IS THINK ABOUT HIM.
AND DREAM ABOUT WHAT ROMANTIC THINGS WE'LL DO TOGETHER.
EVEN WHEN I'M ALL ALONE IN BED...

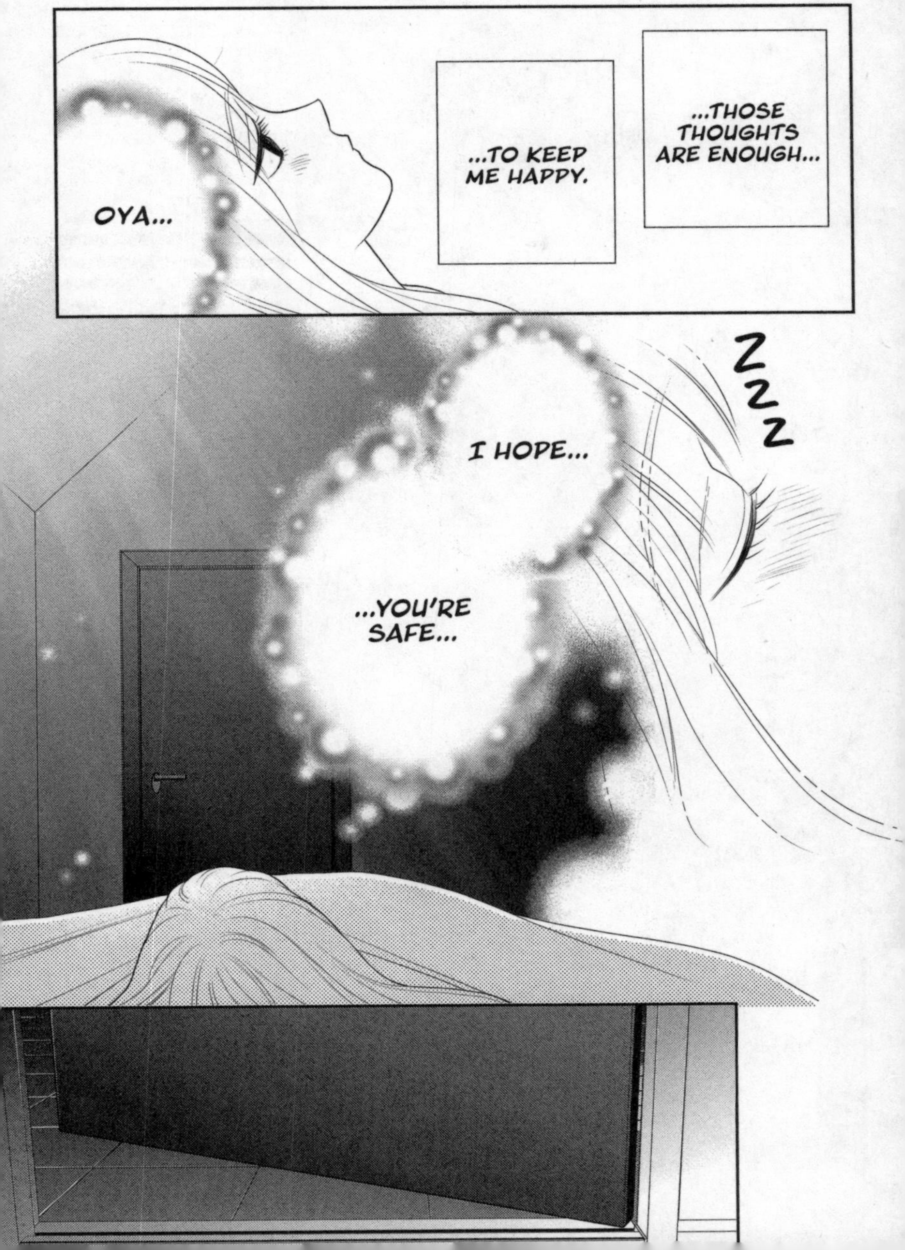
...THOSE THOUGHTS ARE ENOUGH...
...TO KEEP ME HAPPY.
OYA...
ZZZ
I HOPE...
...YOU'RE SAFE...

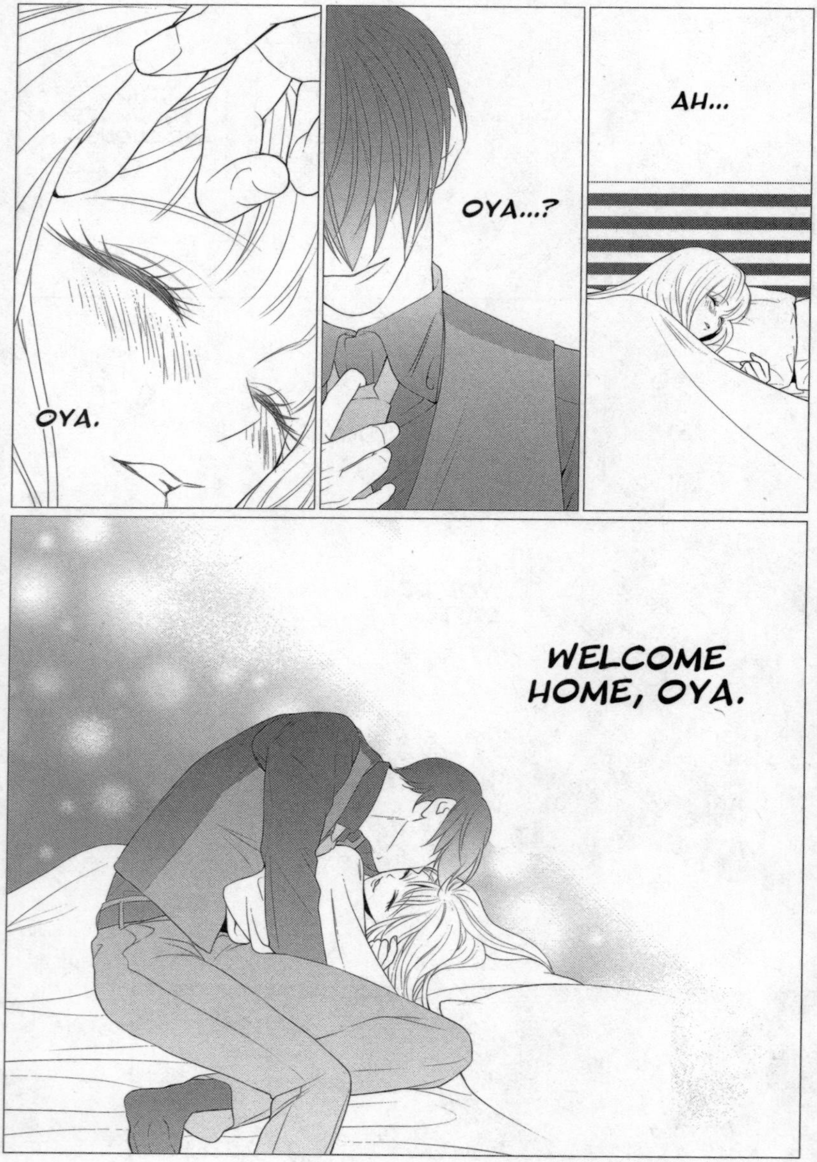
AH...
OYA...?
OYA.
WELCOME HOME, OYA.

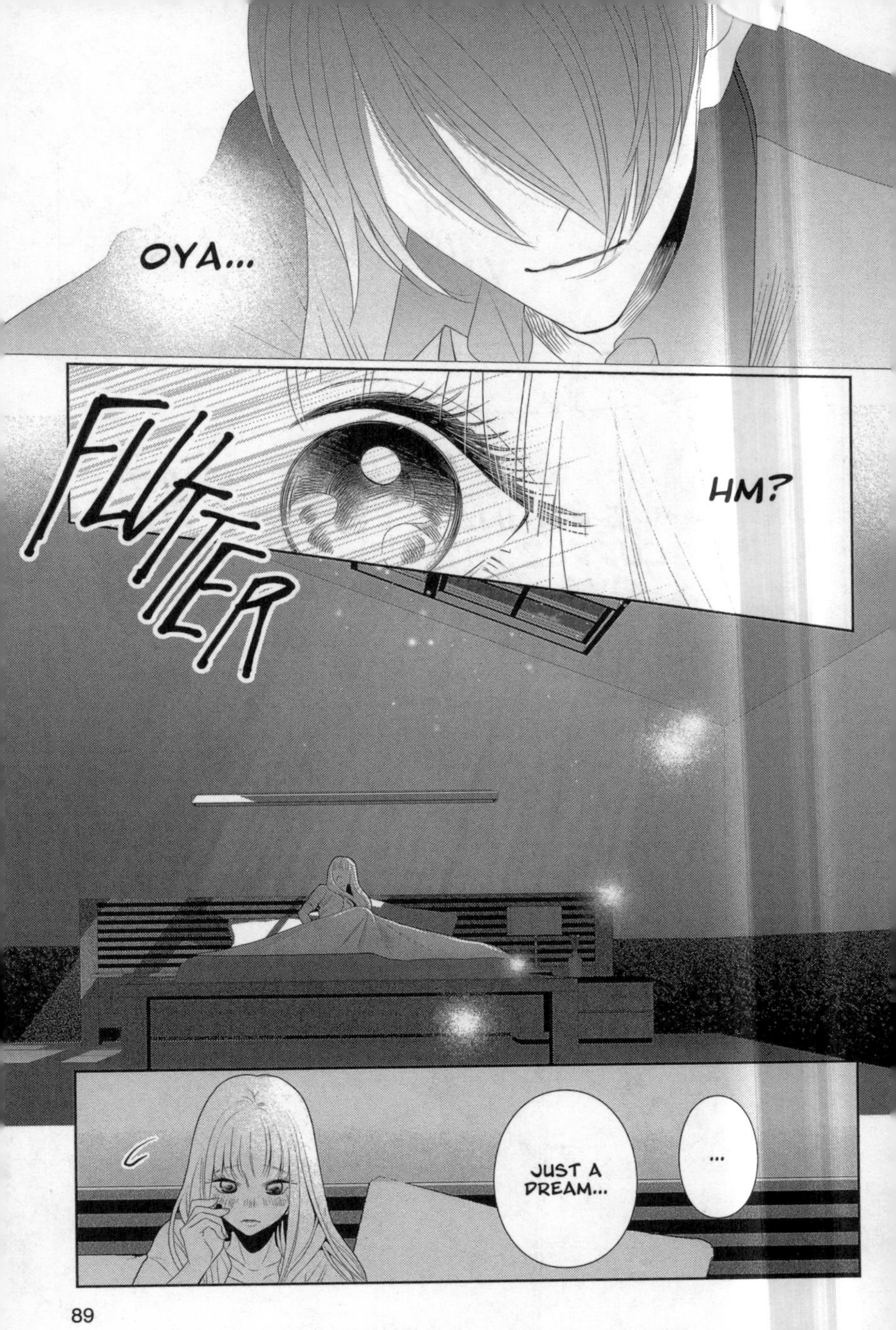
OYA...
HM?
FLUTTER
...
JUST A DREAM...

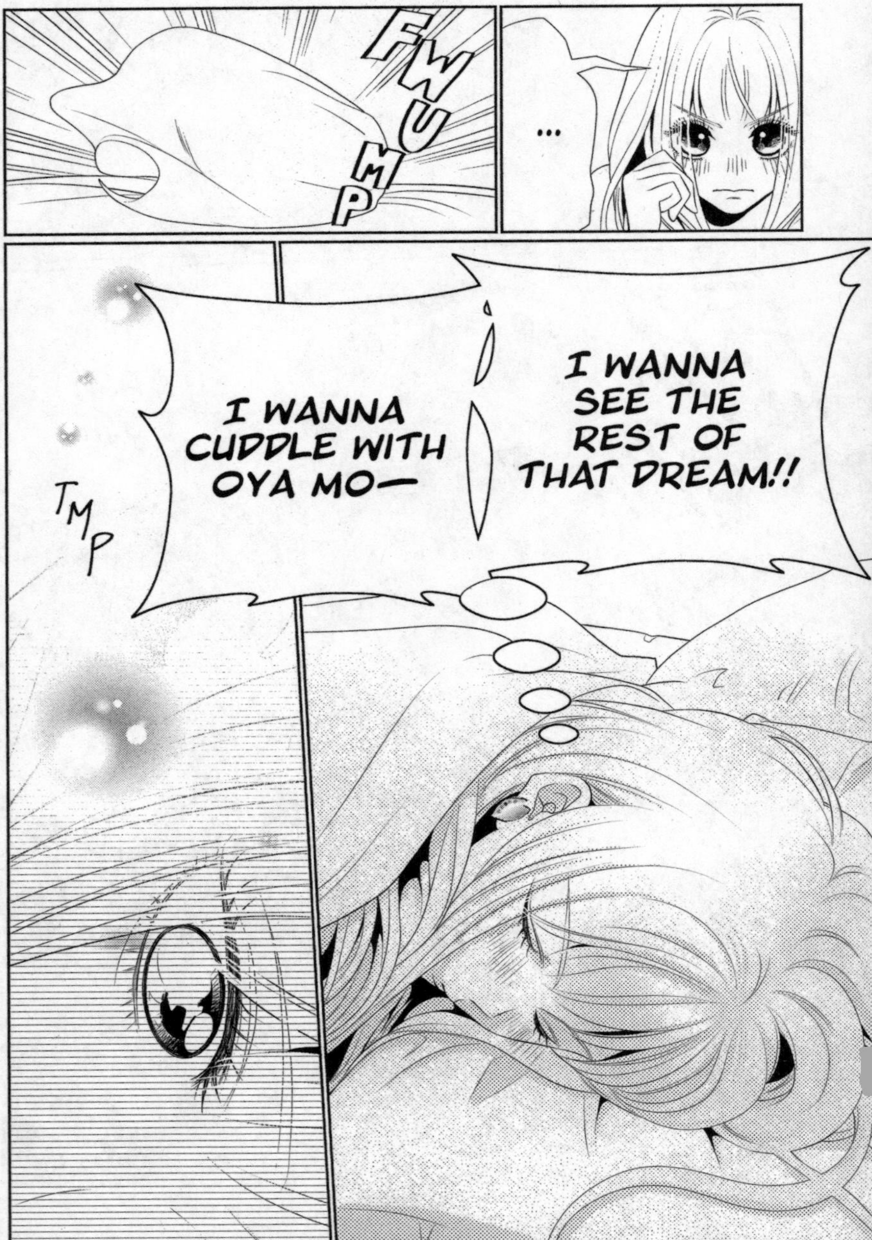
...
FWUMP
I WANNA SEE THE REST OF THAT DREAM!!
I WANNA CUDDLE WITH OYA MO—
TMP

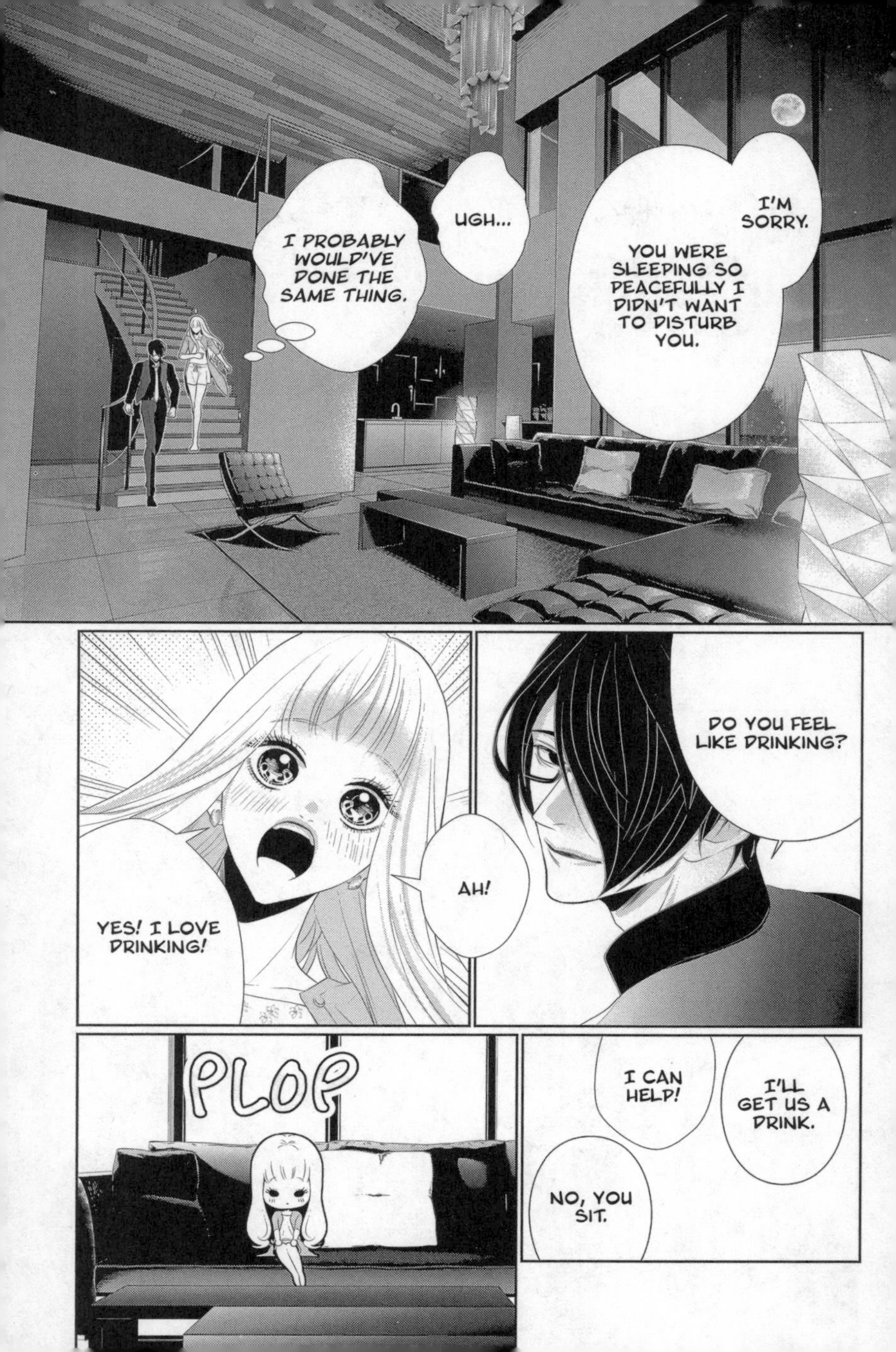
I'M SORRY.
YOU WERE SLEEPING SO PEACEFULLY I DIDN'T WANT TO DISTURB YOU.
UGH...
I PROBABLY WOULD'VE DONE THE SAME THING.
DO YOU FEEL LIKE DRINKING?
AH!
YES! I LOVE DRINKING!
I'LL GET US A DRINK.
I CAN HELP!
NO, YOU SIT.
PLOP

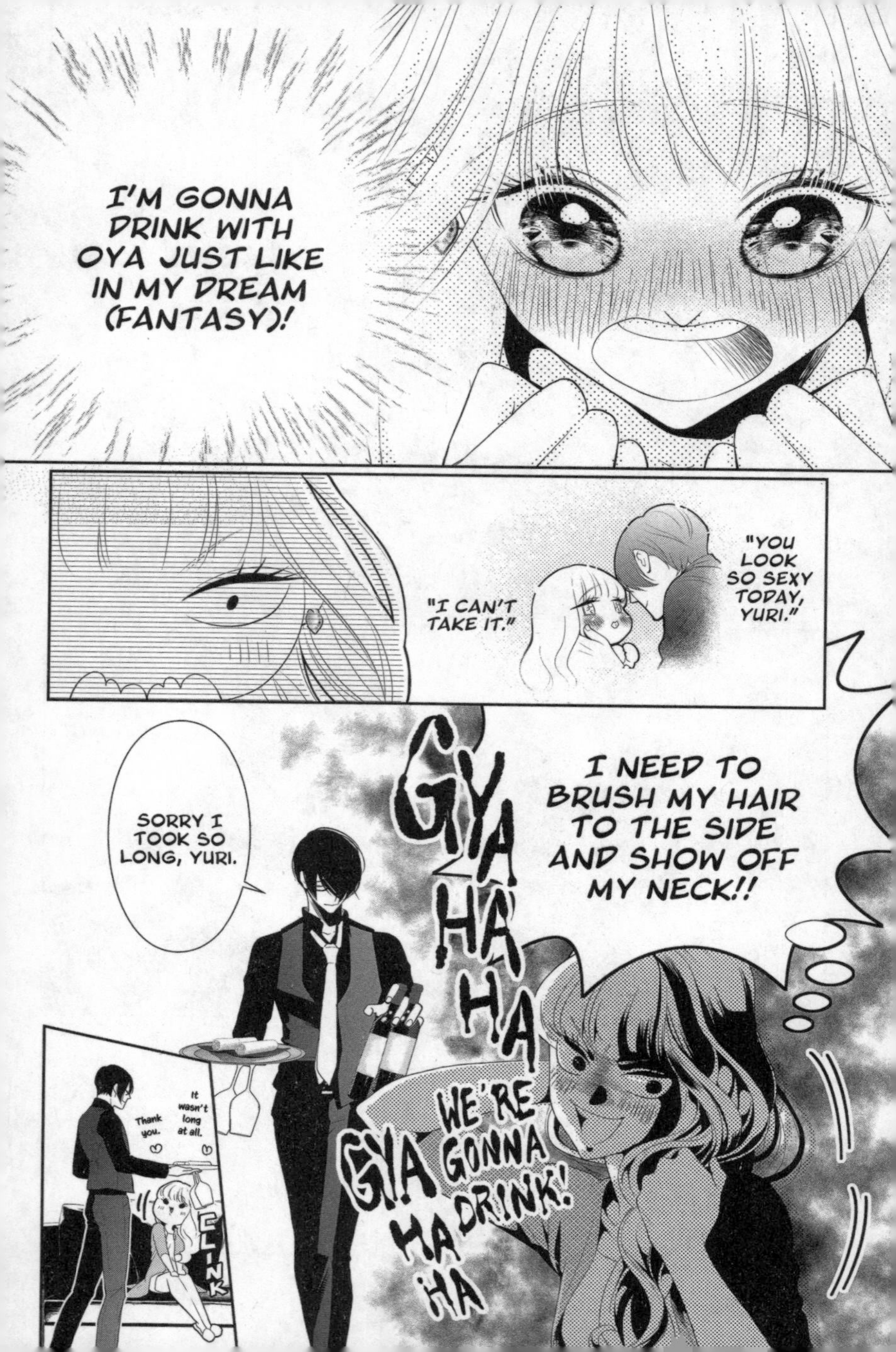
I'M GONNA DRINK WITH OYA JUST LIKE IN MY DREAM (FANTASY)!
"YOU LOOK SO SEXY TODAY, YURI."
"I CAN'T TAKE IT."
I NEED TO BRUSH MY HAIR TO THE SIDE AND SHOW OFF MY NECK!!
GYA HA HA HA
WE'RE GONNA DRINK!
GYA HA HA HA
SORRY I TOOK SO LONG, YURI.
It wasn't long at all.
Thank you.
CLINK

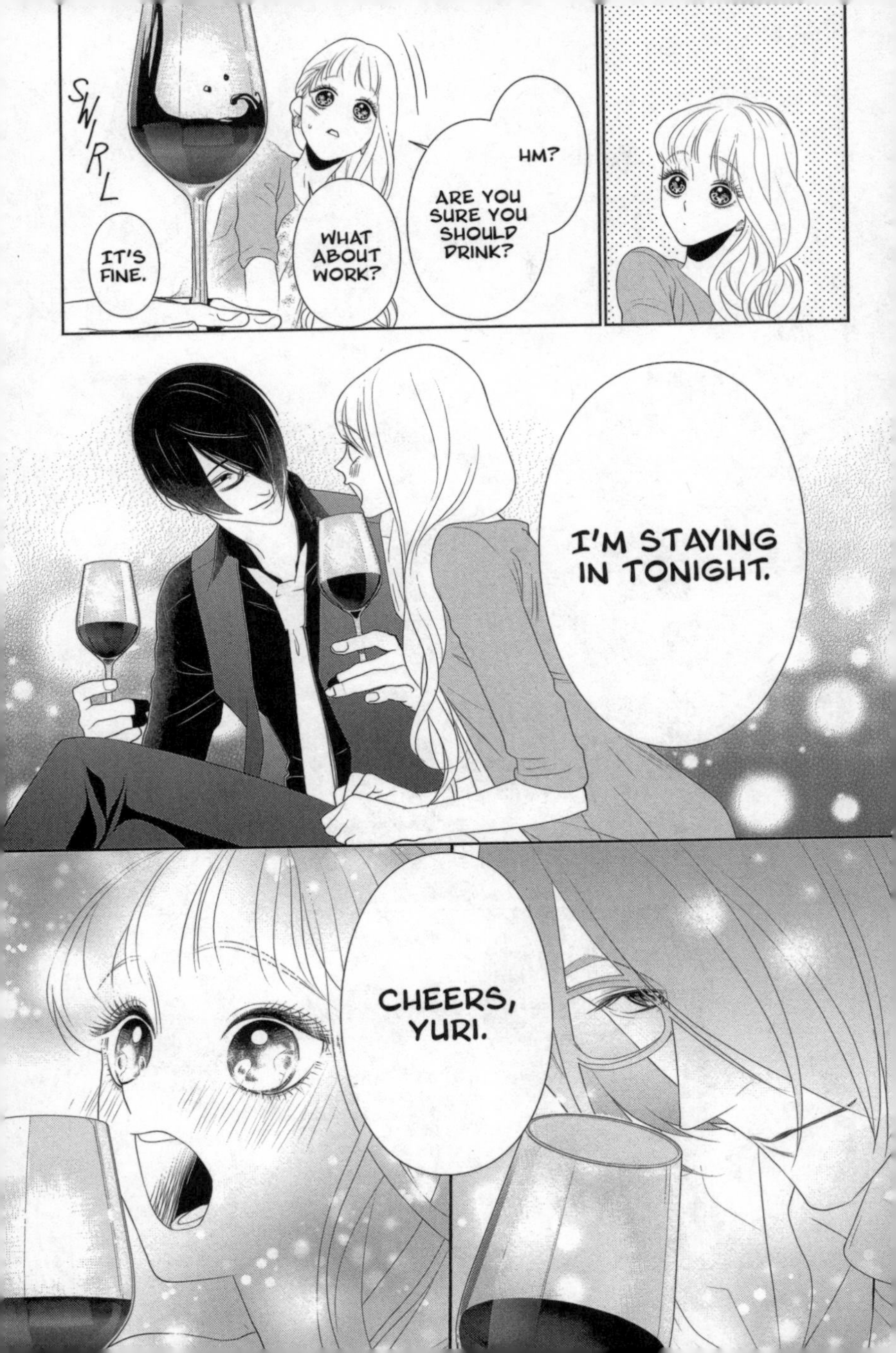
HM? ARE YOU SURE YOU SHOULD DRINK?
WHAT ABOUT WORK?
SWIRL
IT'S FINE.
I'M STAYING IN TONIGHT.
CHEERS, YURI.

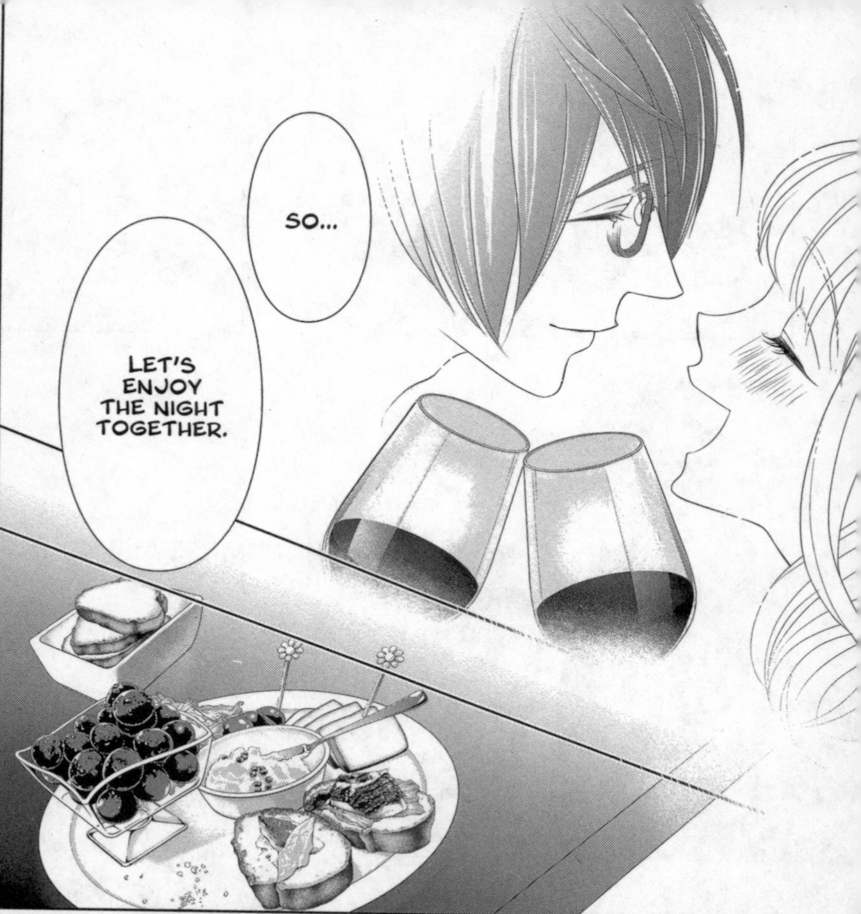
SO...
LET'S ENJOY THE NIGHT TOGETHER.

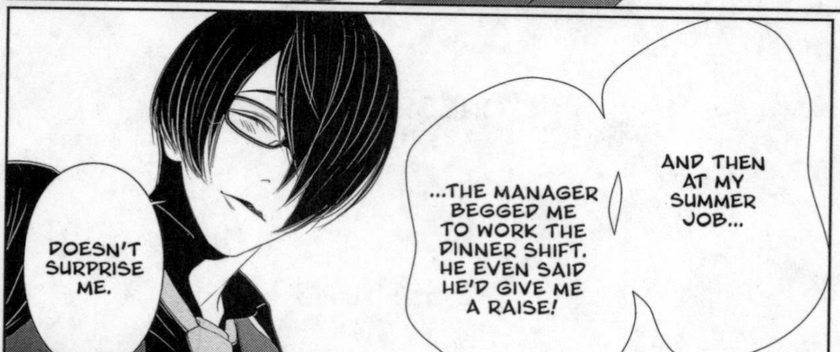
AND THEN AT MY SUMMER JOB...
...THE MANAGER BEGGED ME TO WORK THE DINNER SHIFT. HE EVEN SAID HE'D GIVE ME A RAISE!
DOESN'T SURPRISE ME.

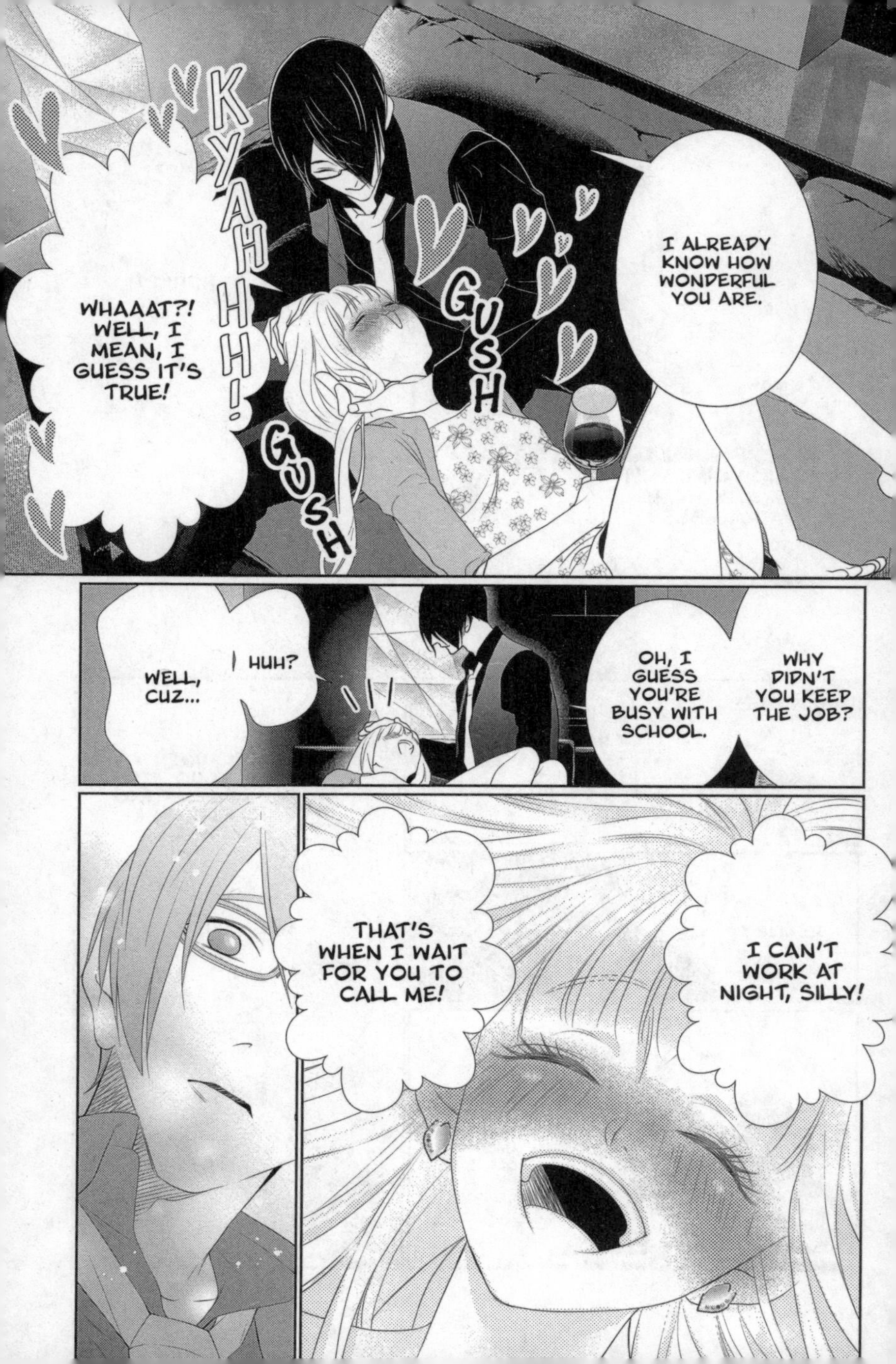
I ALREADY KNOW HOW WONDERFUL YOU ARE.
GUSH
KYAHHHH!
WHAAAT?! WELL, I MEAN, I GUESS IT'S TRUE!
GUSH
WHY DIDN'T YOU KEEP THE JOB?
OH, I GUESS YOU'RE BUSY WITH SCHOOL.
HUH?
WELL, CUZ...
I CAN'T WORK AT NIGHT, SILLY!
THAT'S WHEN I WAIT FOR YOU TO CALL ME!

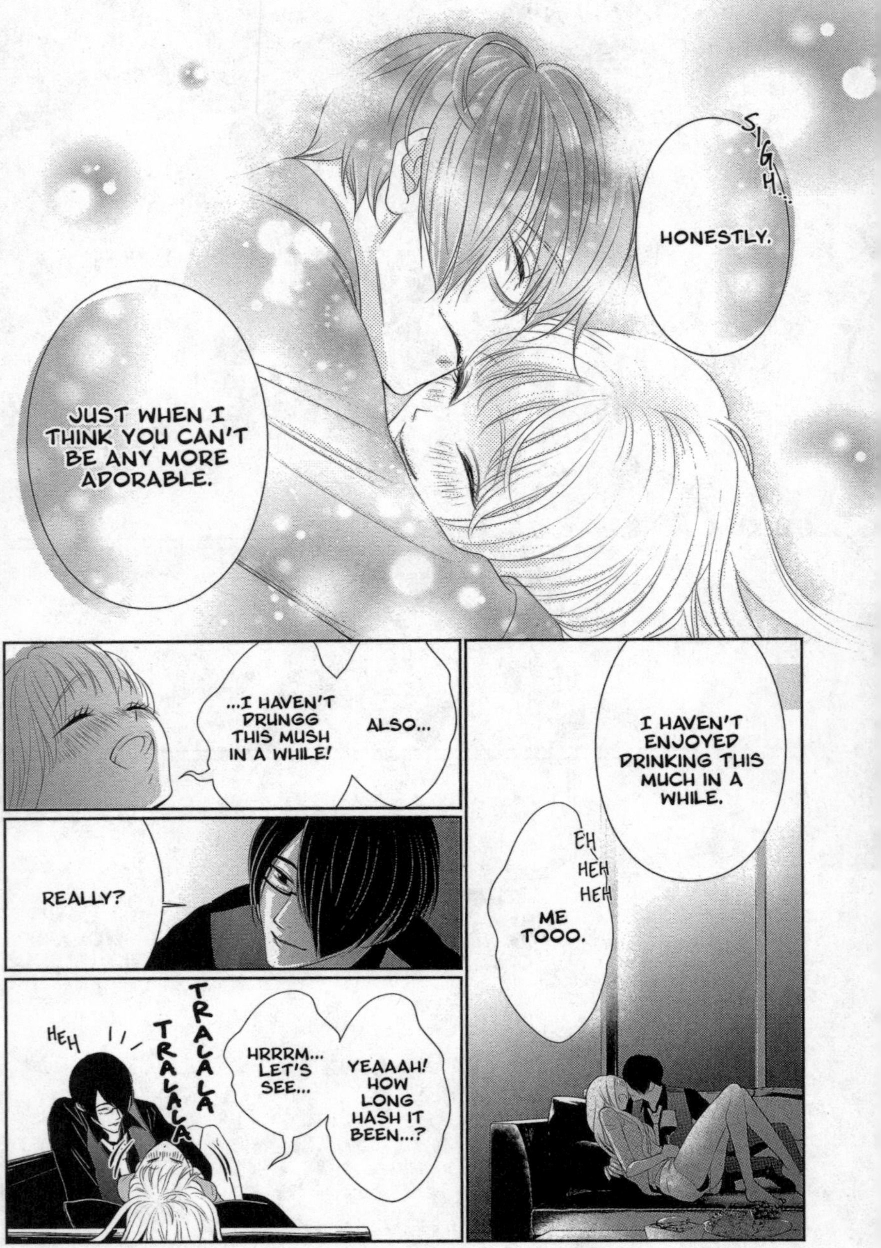
SIGH...
HONESTLY.
JUST WHEN I THINK YOU CAN'T BE ANY MORE ADORABLE.
I HAVEN'T ENJOYED DRINKING THIS MUCH IN A WHILE.
EH HEH HEH
ME TOOO.
ALSO...
...I HAVEN'T DRUNGG THIS MUSH IN A WHILE!
REALLY?
TRALALA
TRALALA
YEAAAH! HOW LONG HASH IT BEEN...?
HRRRM... LET'S SEE...
HEH

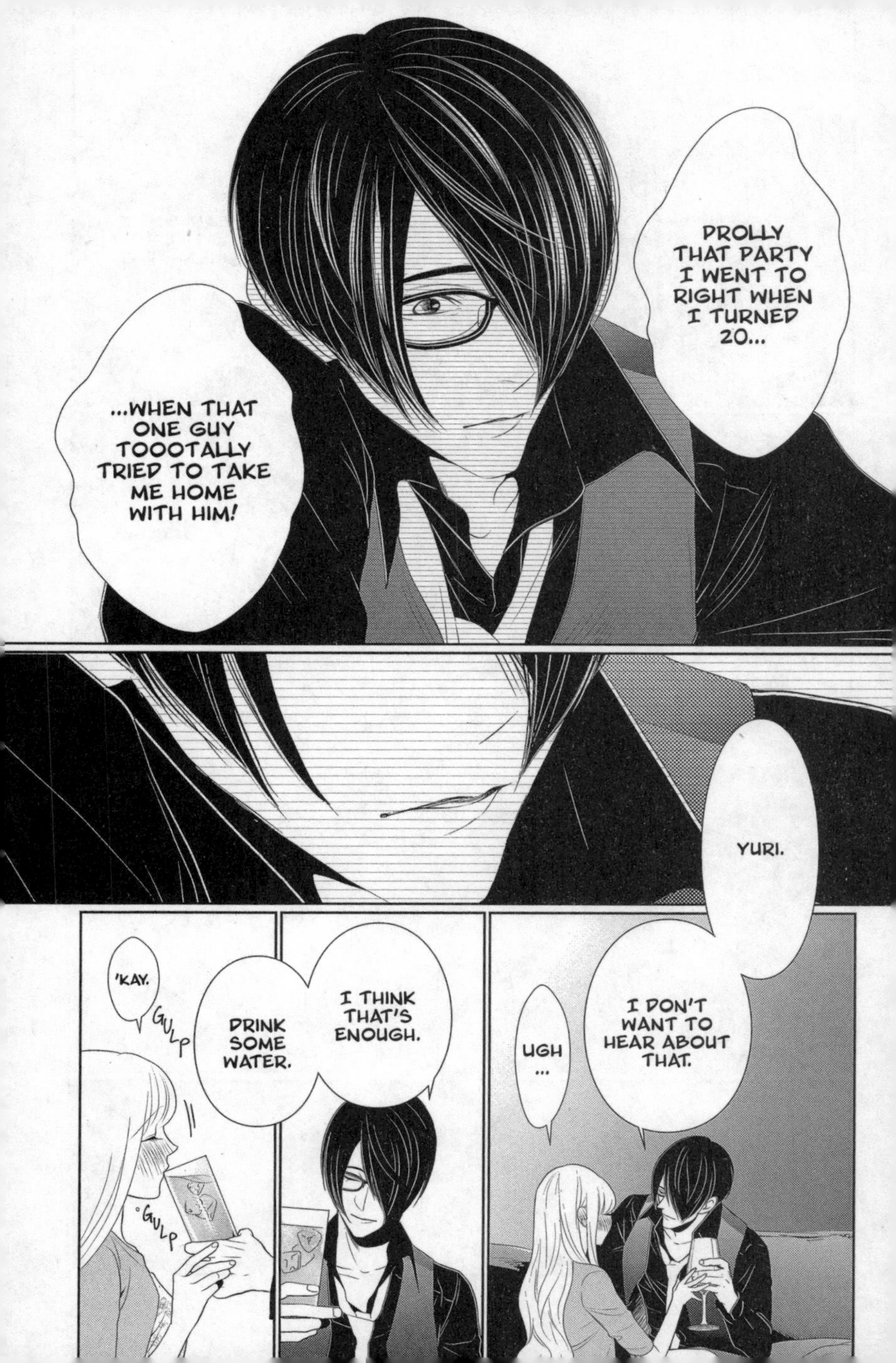
PROLLY THAT PARTY I WENT TO RIGHT WHEN I TURNED 20...
...WHEN THAT ONE GUY TOOOTALLY TRIED TO TAKE ME HOME WITH HIM!
YURI.
I DON'T WANT TO HEAR ABOUT THAT.
UGH ...
I THINK THAT'S ENOUGH.
DRINK SOME WATER.
'KAY.
GULP
GULP

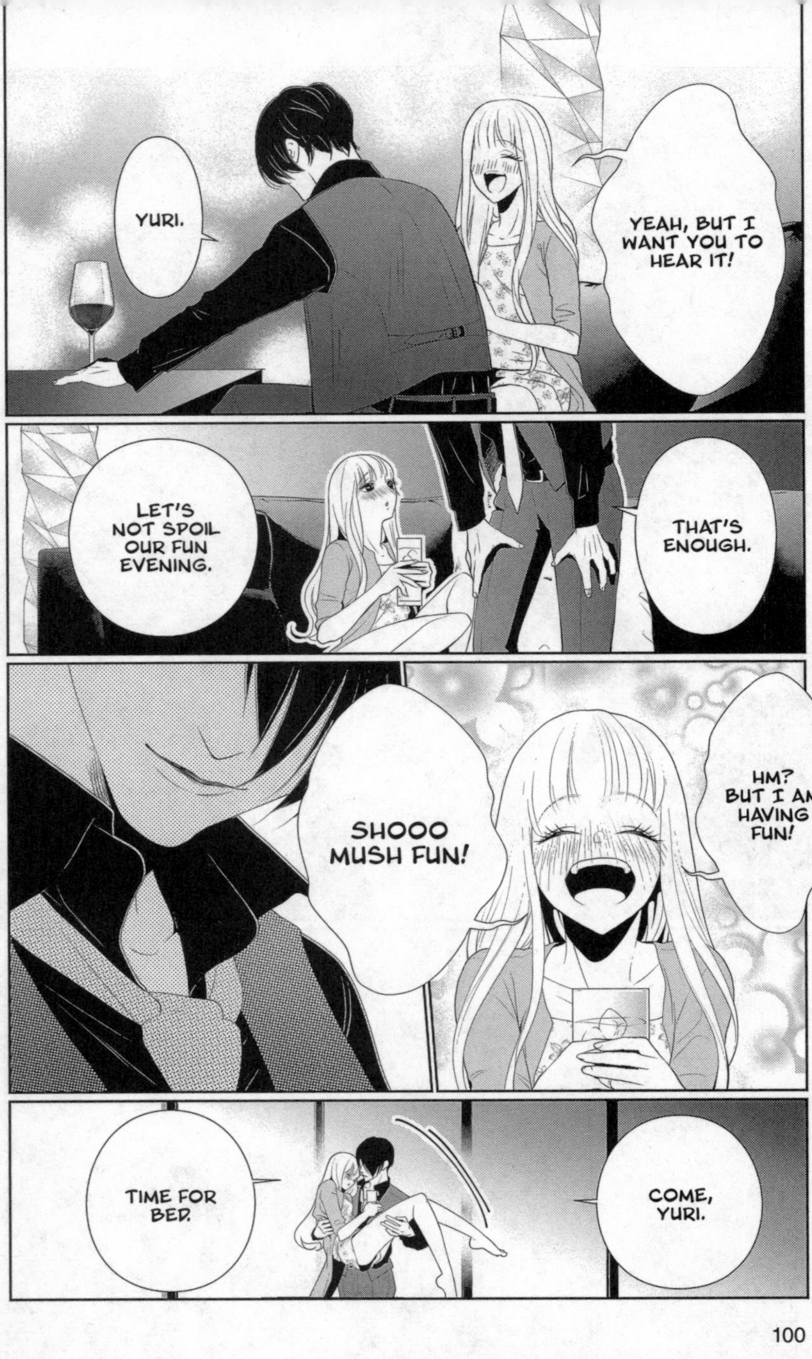
YEAH, BUT I WANT YOU TO HEAR IT!
YURI.
THAT'S ENOUGH.
LET'S NOT SPOIL OUR FUN EVENING.
HM? BUT I AM HAVING FUN!
SHOOO MUSH FUN!
COME, YURI.
TIME FOR BED.

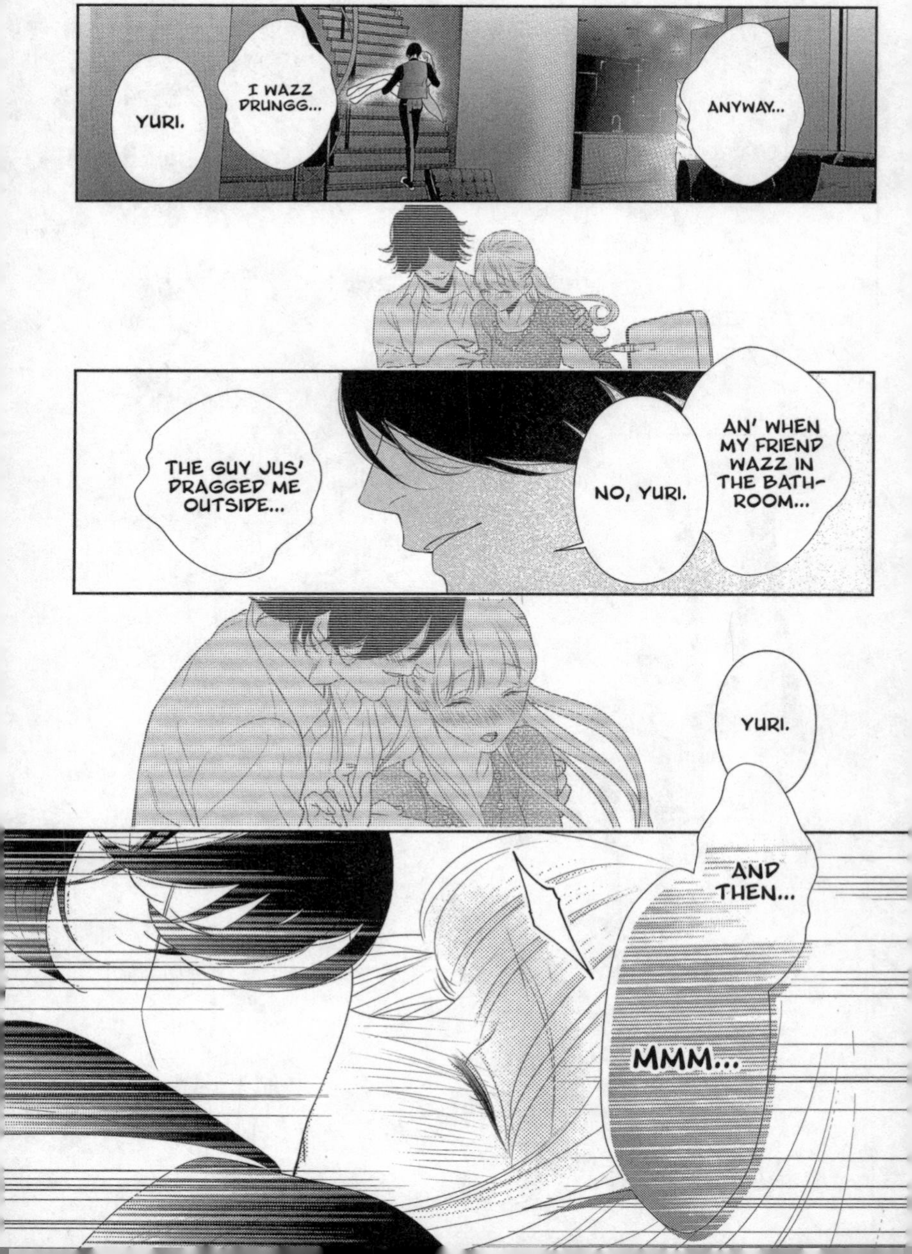
ANYWAY...
I WAZZ DRUNGG...
YURI.
AN' WHEN MY FRIEND WAZZ IN THE BATH-ROOM...
NO, YURI.
THE GUY JUS' DRAGGED ME OUTSIDE...
YURI.
AND THEN...
MMM...

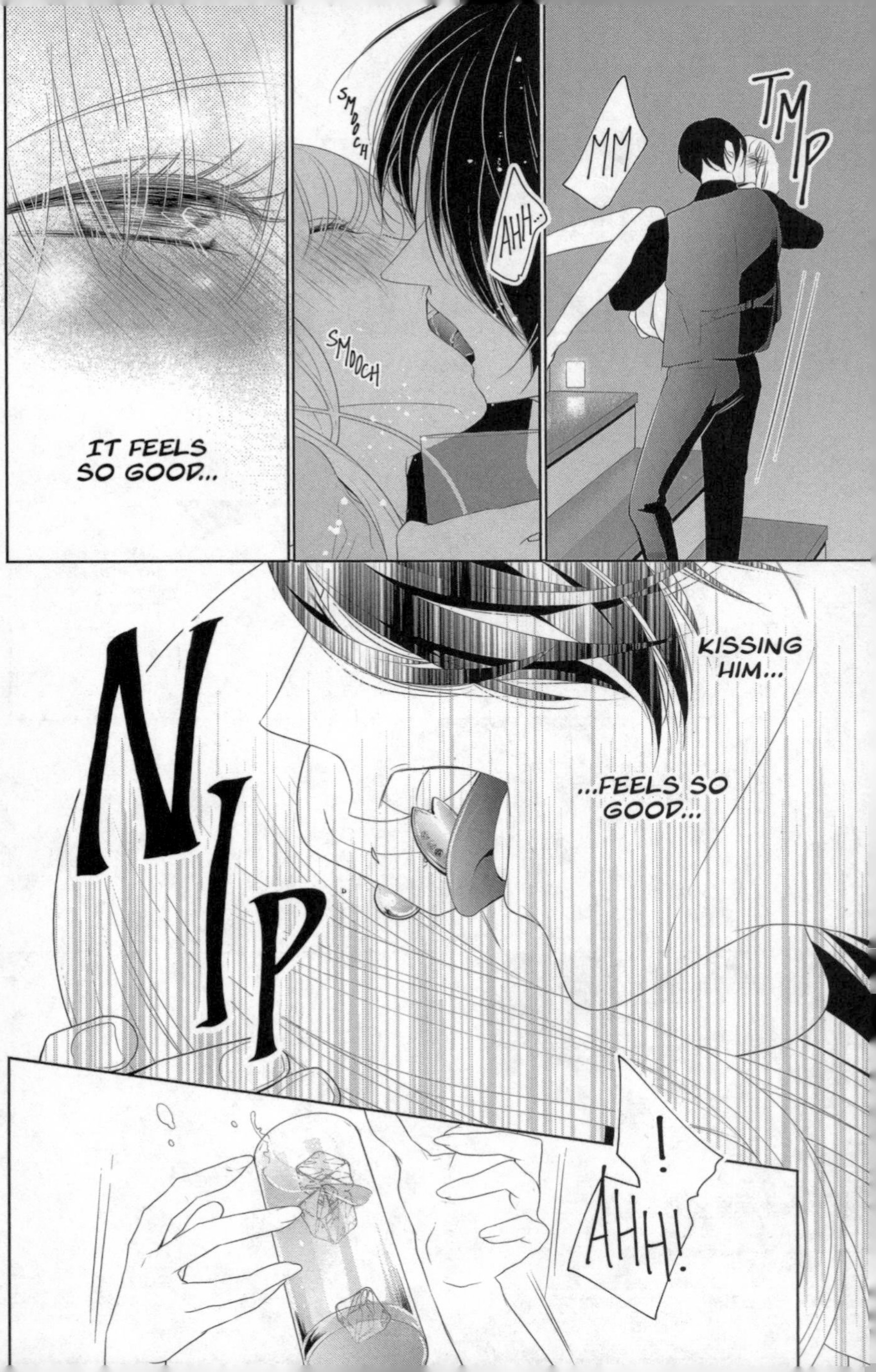
TMP
MM
AHH...
SMOOCH
SMOOCH
IT FEELS SO GOOD...
KISSING HIM...
...FEELS SO GOOD...
NIP
!
AHH!

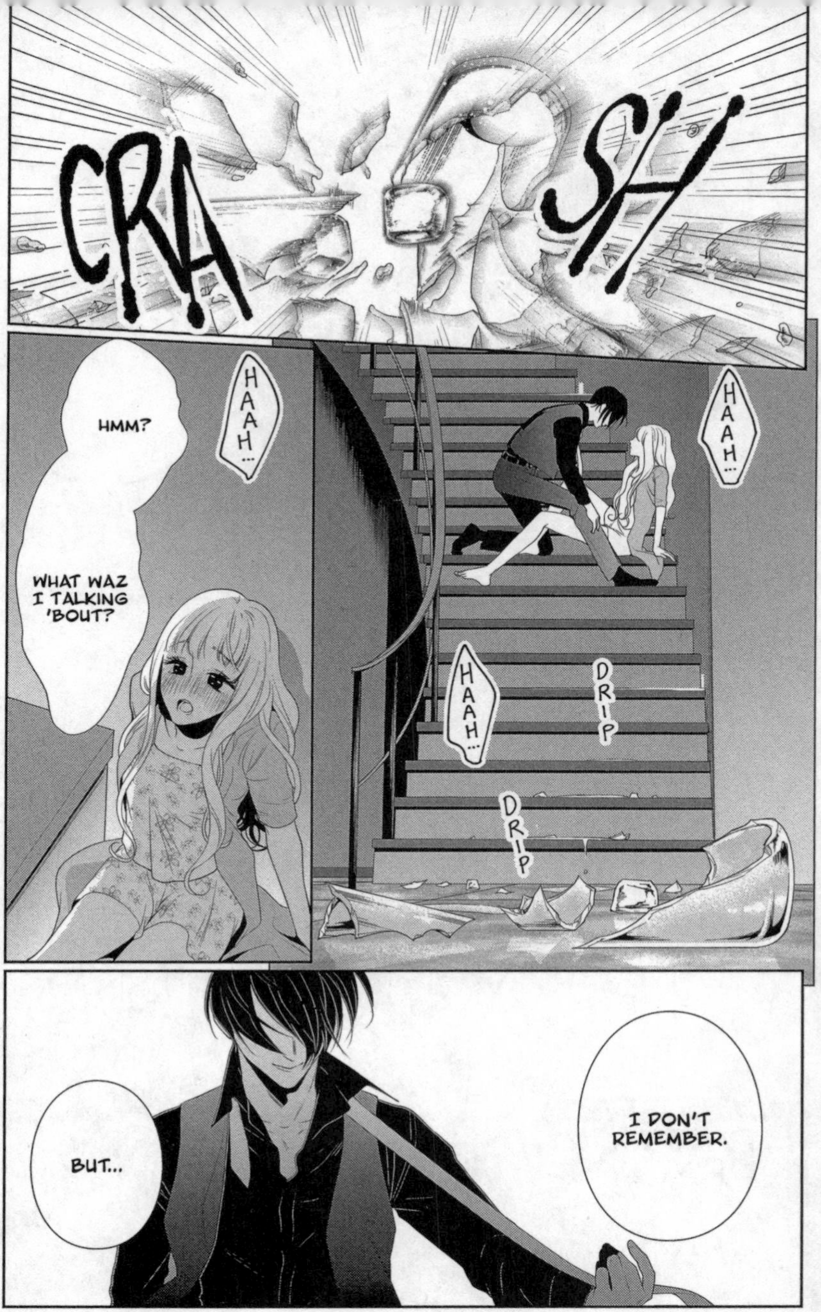
CRASH
HAAAH...
HAAAH...
DRIP
DRIP
HAAAH...
HMM?
WHAT WAZ I TALKING 'BOUT?
I DON'T REMEMBER.
BUT...

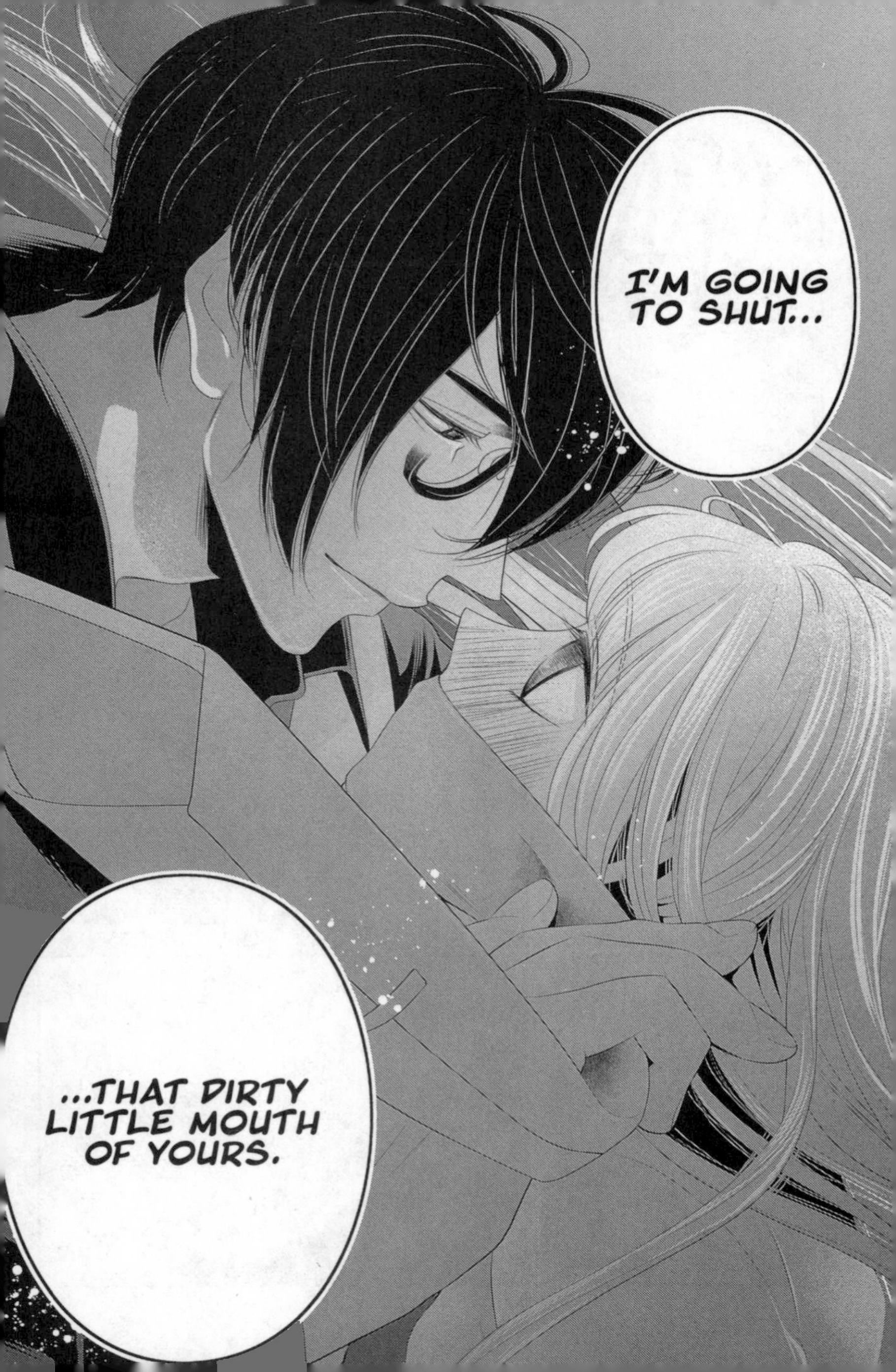
I'M GOING TO SHUT...
...THAT DIRTY LITTLE MOUTH OF YOURS.

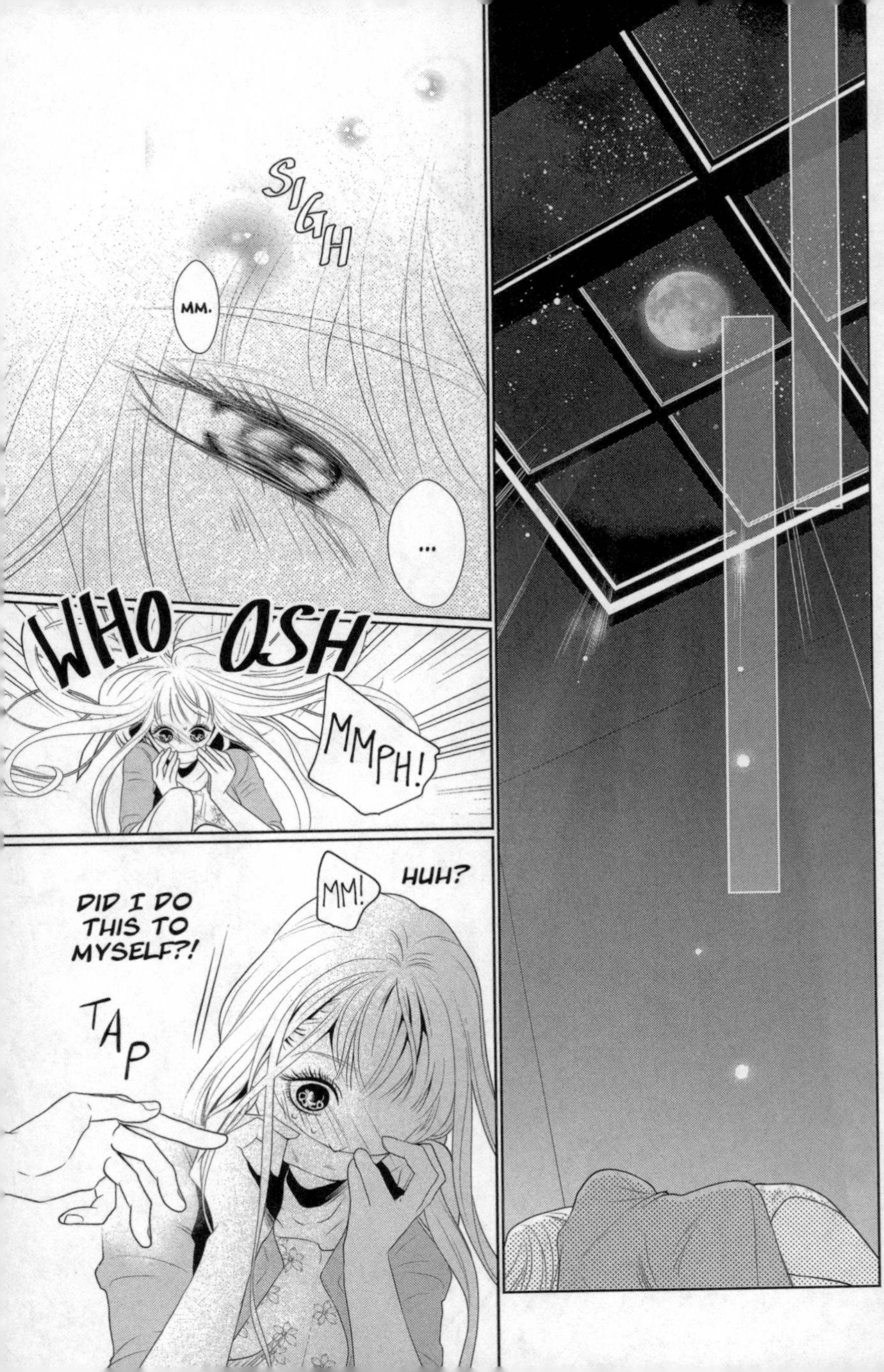
SIGH
MM.
...
WHOOSH
MMPH!
HUH?
MM!
DID I DO THIS TO MYSELF?!
TAP

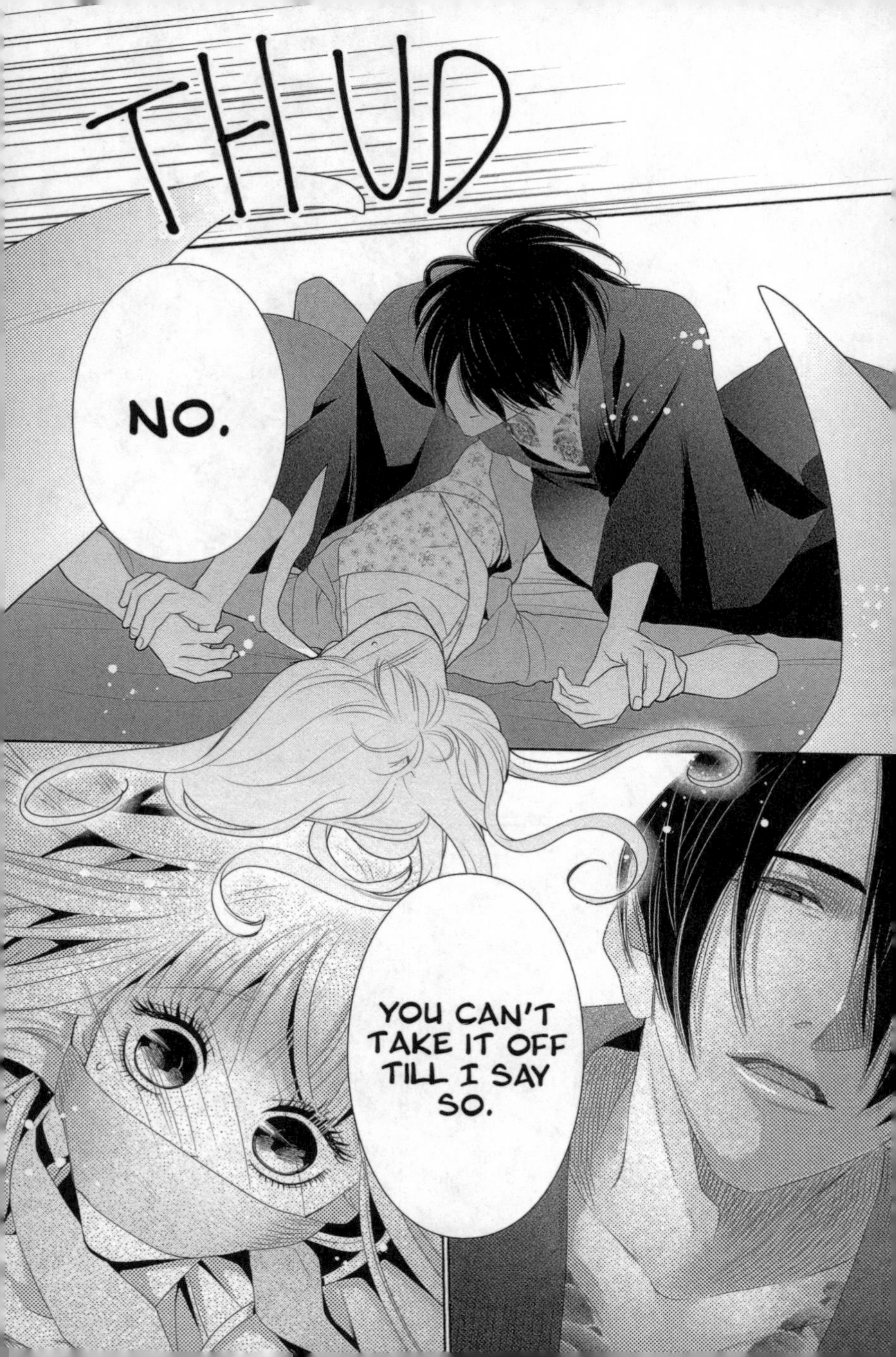
THUD
NO.
YOU CAN'T TAKE IT OFF TILL I SAY SO.

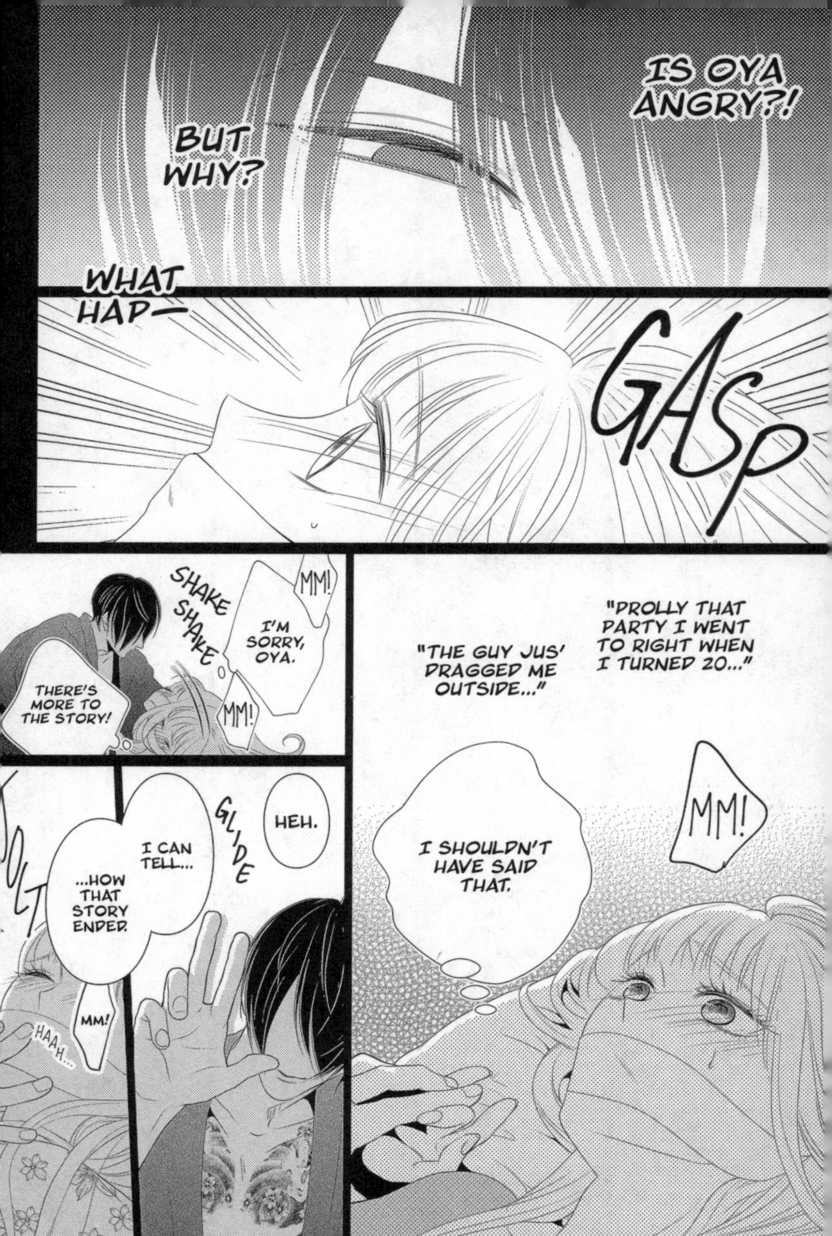
IS OYA ANGRY?!
BUT WHY?
WHAT HAP—
GASP
"PROLLY THAT PARTY I WENT TO RIGHT WHEN I TURNED 20..."
"THE GUY JUS' DRAGGED ME OUTSIDE..."
MM!
I SHOULDN'T HAVE SAID THAT.
MM!
I'M SORRY, OYA.
SHAKE SHAKE
THERE'S MORE TO THE STORY!
MM!
HEH.
GLIDE
I CAN TELL...
...HOW THAT STORY ENDED.
MM!
HAAH...

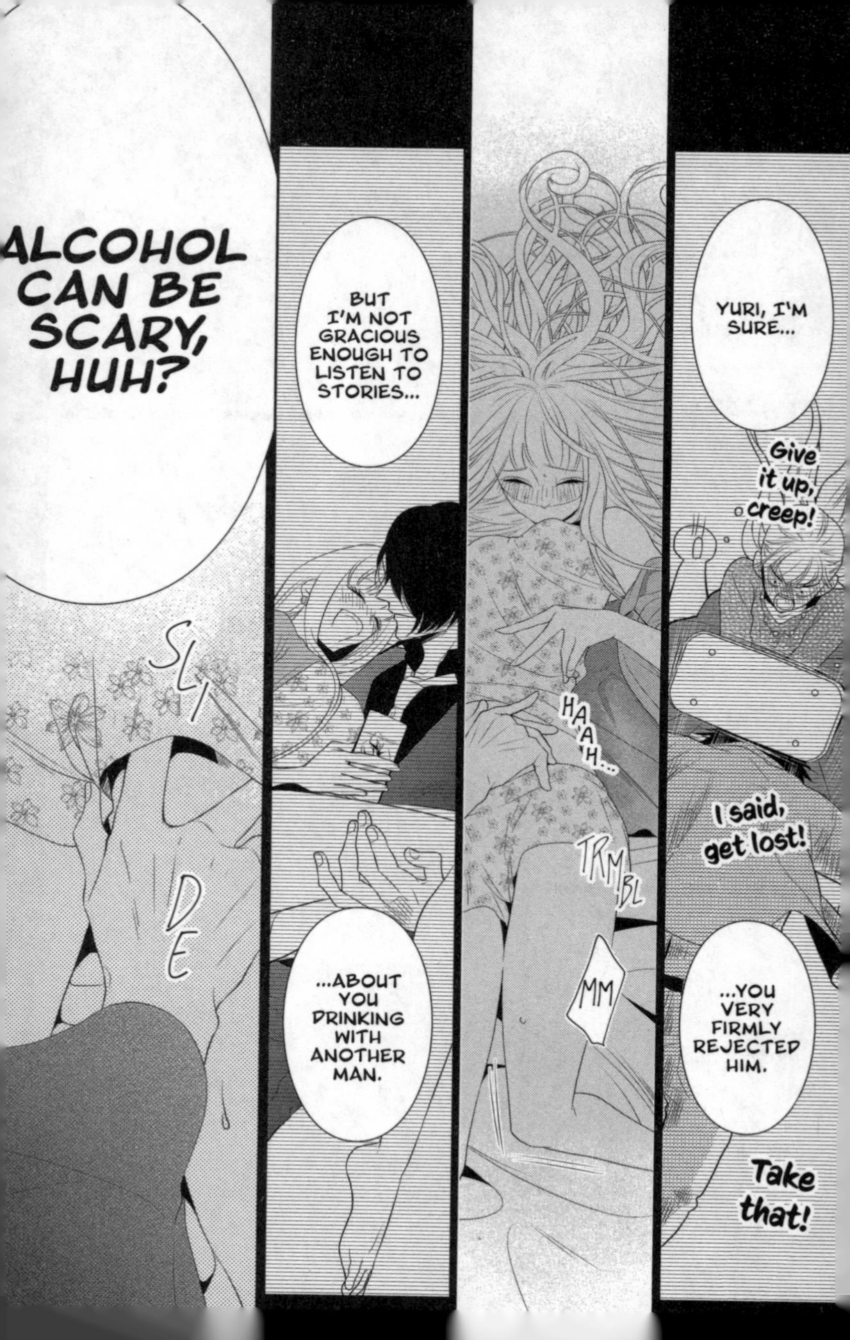
YURI, I'M SURE...
Give it up, creep!
I said, get lost!
...YOU VERY FIRMLY REJECTED HIM.
Take that!
HAAAH...
TRMBL
MM
BUT I'M NOT GRACIOUS ENOUGH TO LISTEN TO STORIES...
...ABOUT YOU DRINKING WITH ANOTHER MAN.
ALCOHOL CAN BE SCARY, HUH?
SLI
DE

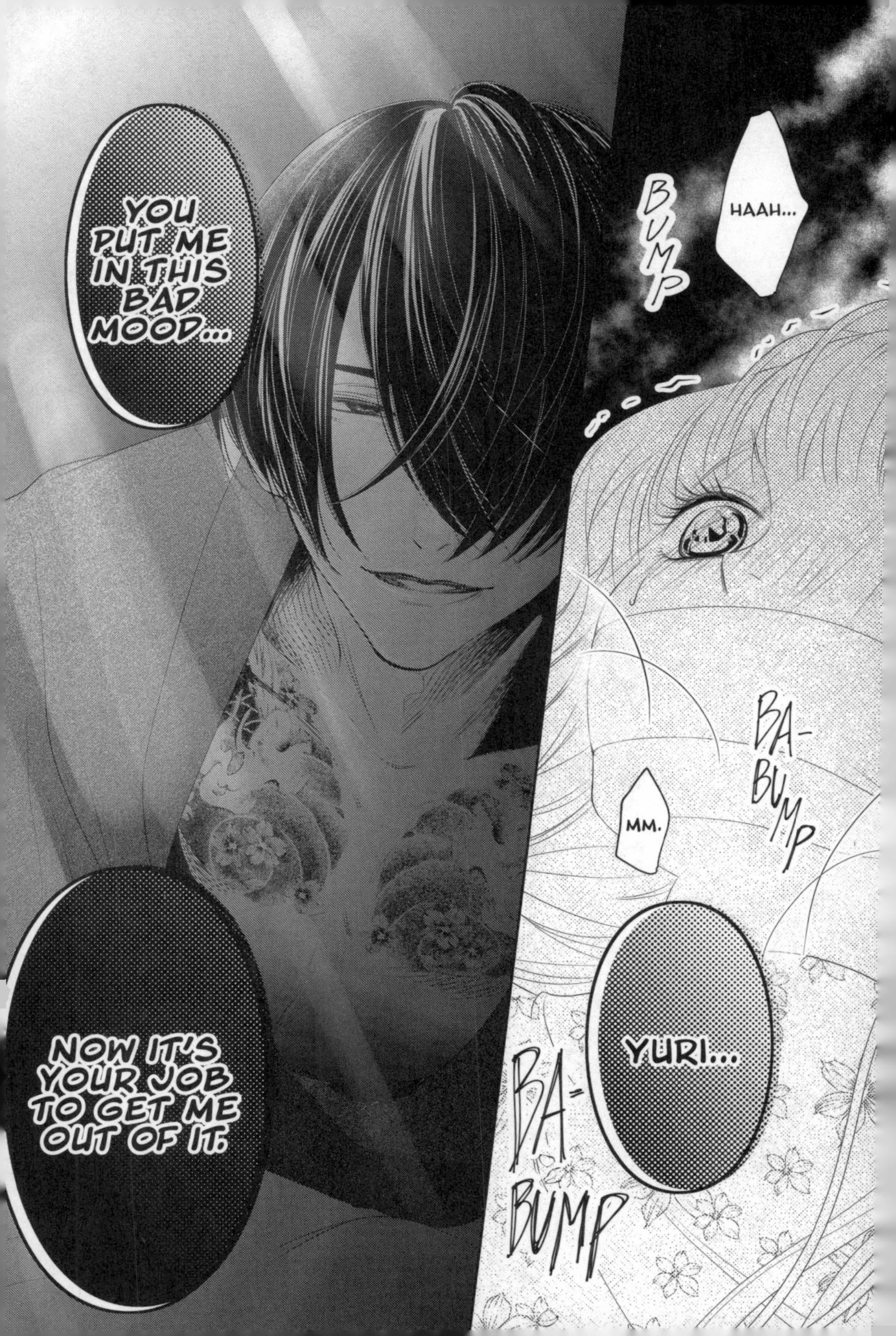
HAAH...
BUMP
BA-BUMP
MM.
YURI...
BA-BUMP
YOU PUT ME IN THIS BAD MOOD...
NOW IT'S YOUR JOB TO GET ME OUT OF IT.

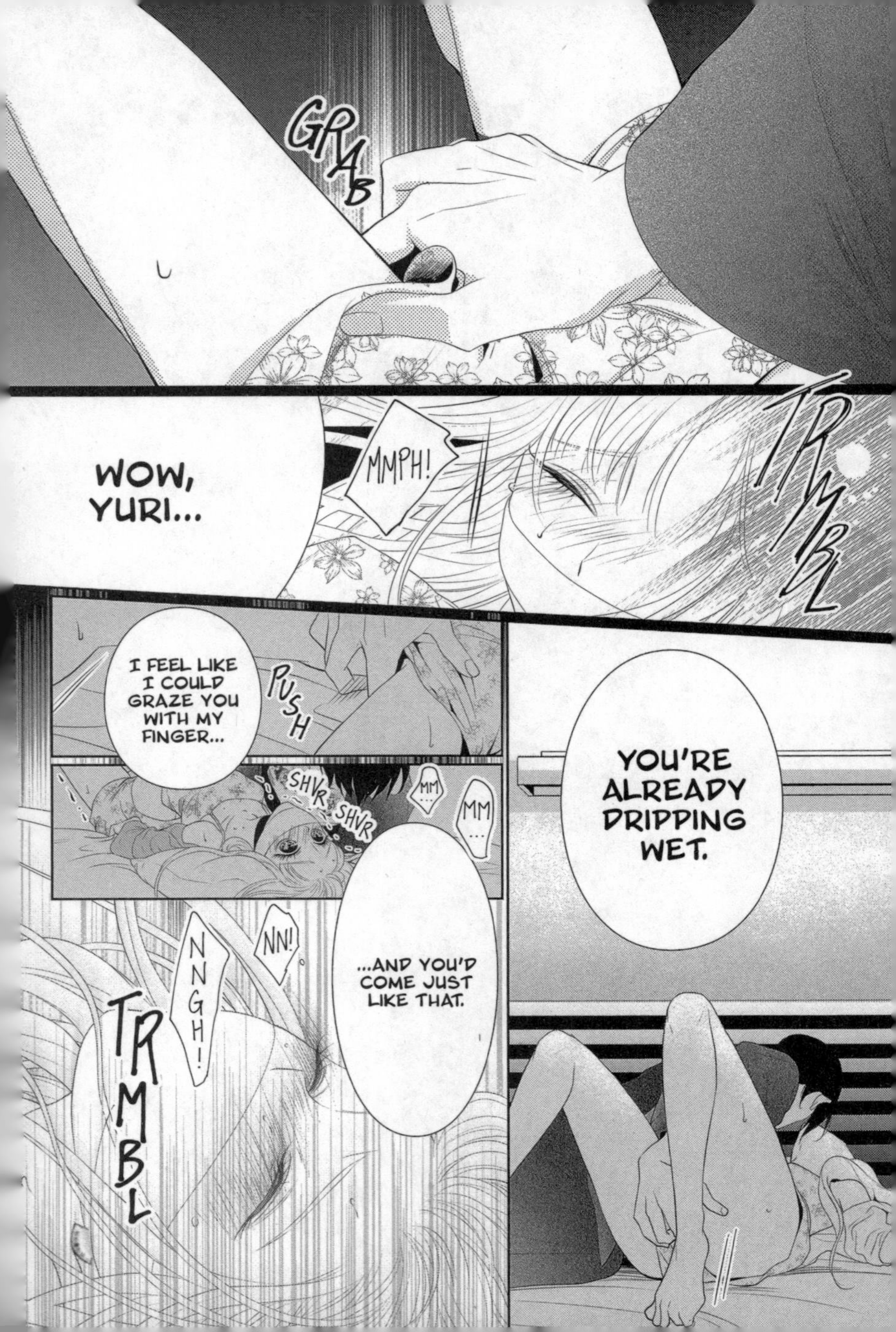
GRAB
TRMBL
MMPH!
WOW, YURI...
YOU'RE ALREADY DRIPPING WET.
I FEEL LIKE I COULD GRAZE YOU WITH MY FINGER...
PUSH
MM...
MM...
SHVR SHVR
...AND YOU'D COME JUST LIKE THAT.
NN!
NNGH!
TRMBL

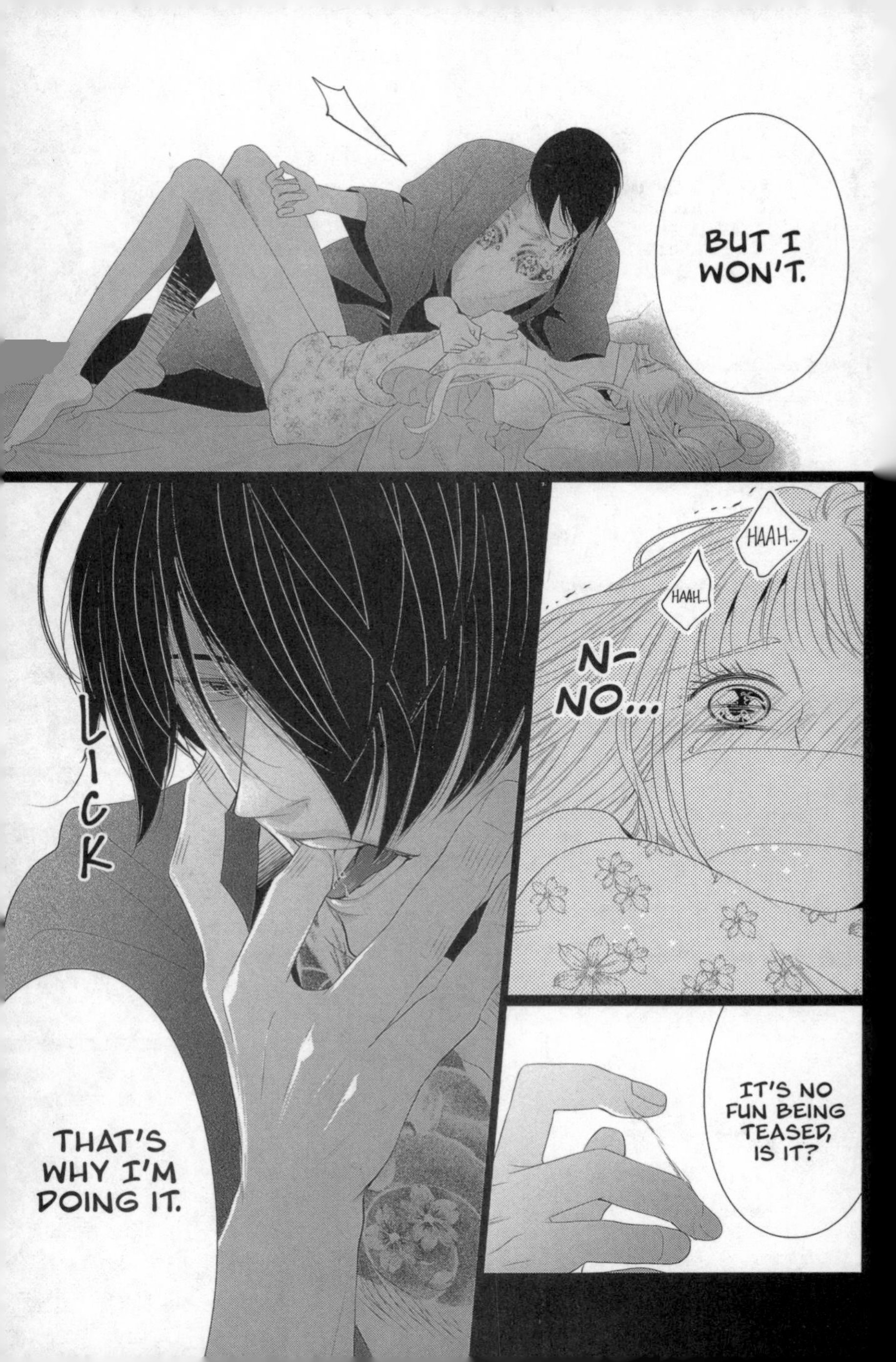
BUT I WON'T.
HAAH...
HAAH...
N-NO...
IT'S NO FUN BEING TEASED, IS IT?
LICK
THAT'S WHY I'M DOING IT.

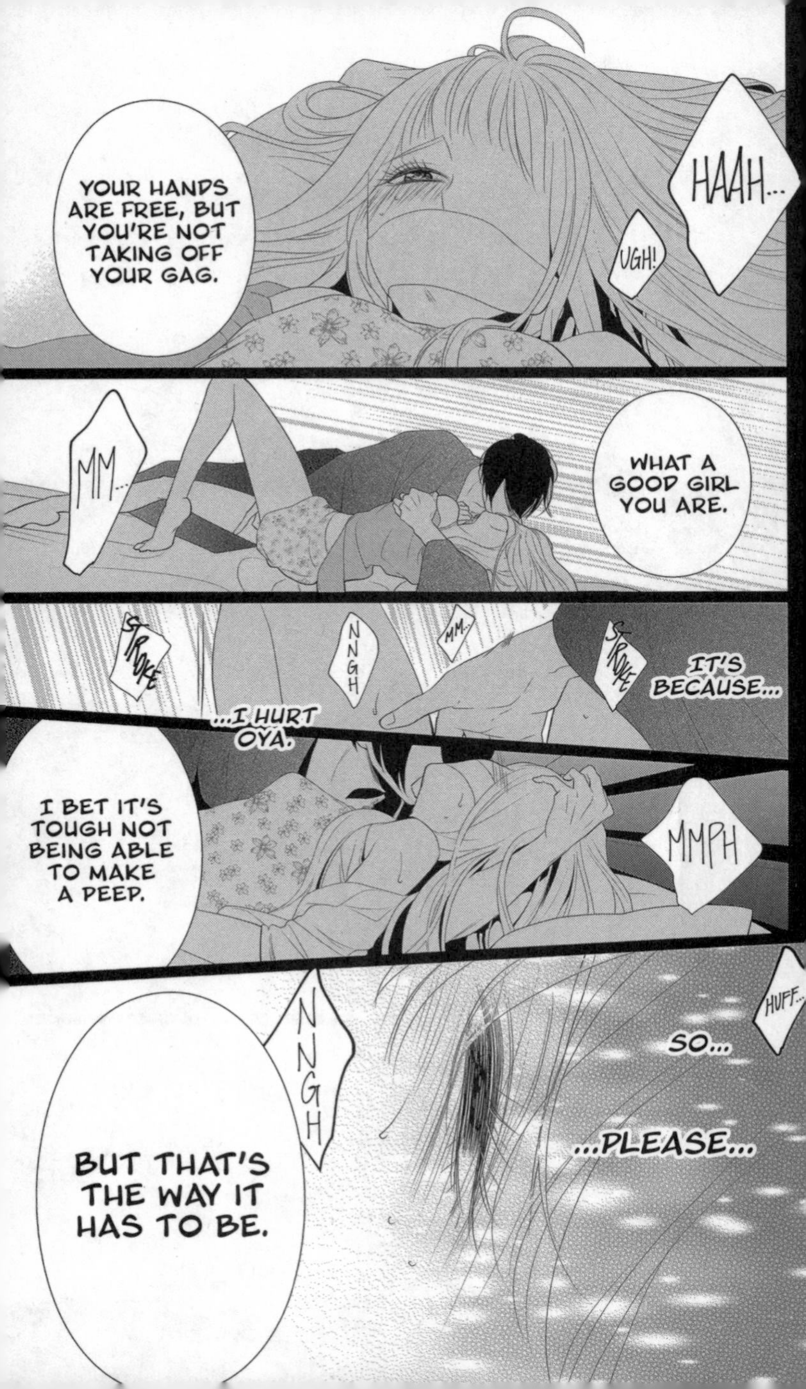
HAAH...
UGH!
YOUR HANDS ARE FREE, BUT YOU'RE NOT TAKING OFF YOUR GAG.
WHAT A GOOD GIRL YOU ARE.
MM...
STROKE
IT'S BECAUSE...
MM...
NNGH
STROKE
...I HURT OYA.
MMPH
I BET IT'S TOUGH NOT BEING ABLE TO MAKE A PEEP.
HUFF...
SO...
...PLEASE...
NNGH
BUT THAT'S THE WAY IT HAS TO BE.

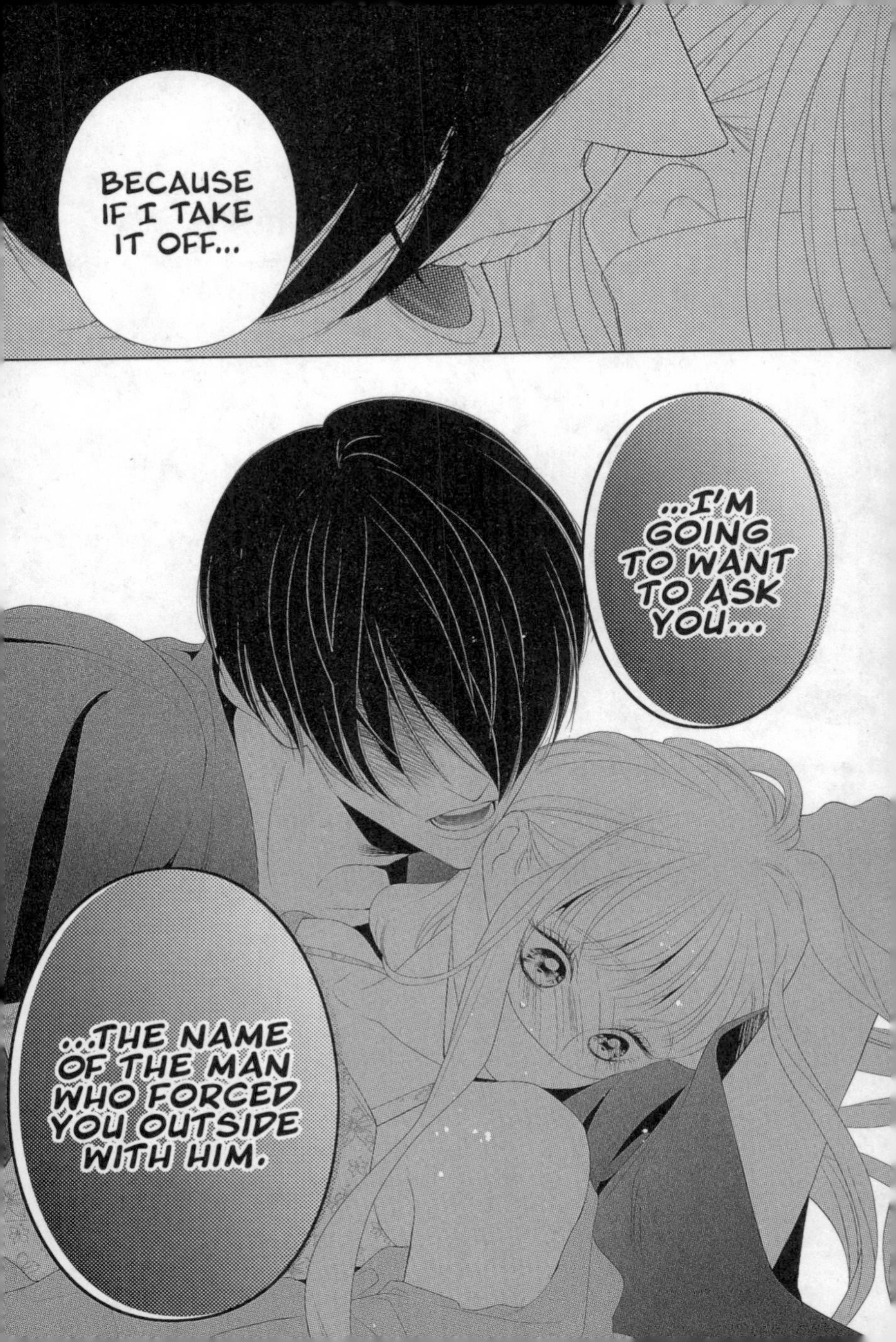
BECAUSE IF I TAKE IT OFF...
...I'M GOING TO WANT TO ASK YOU...
...THE NAME OF THE MAN WHO FORCED YOU OUTSIDE WITH HIM.

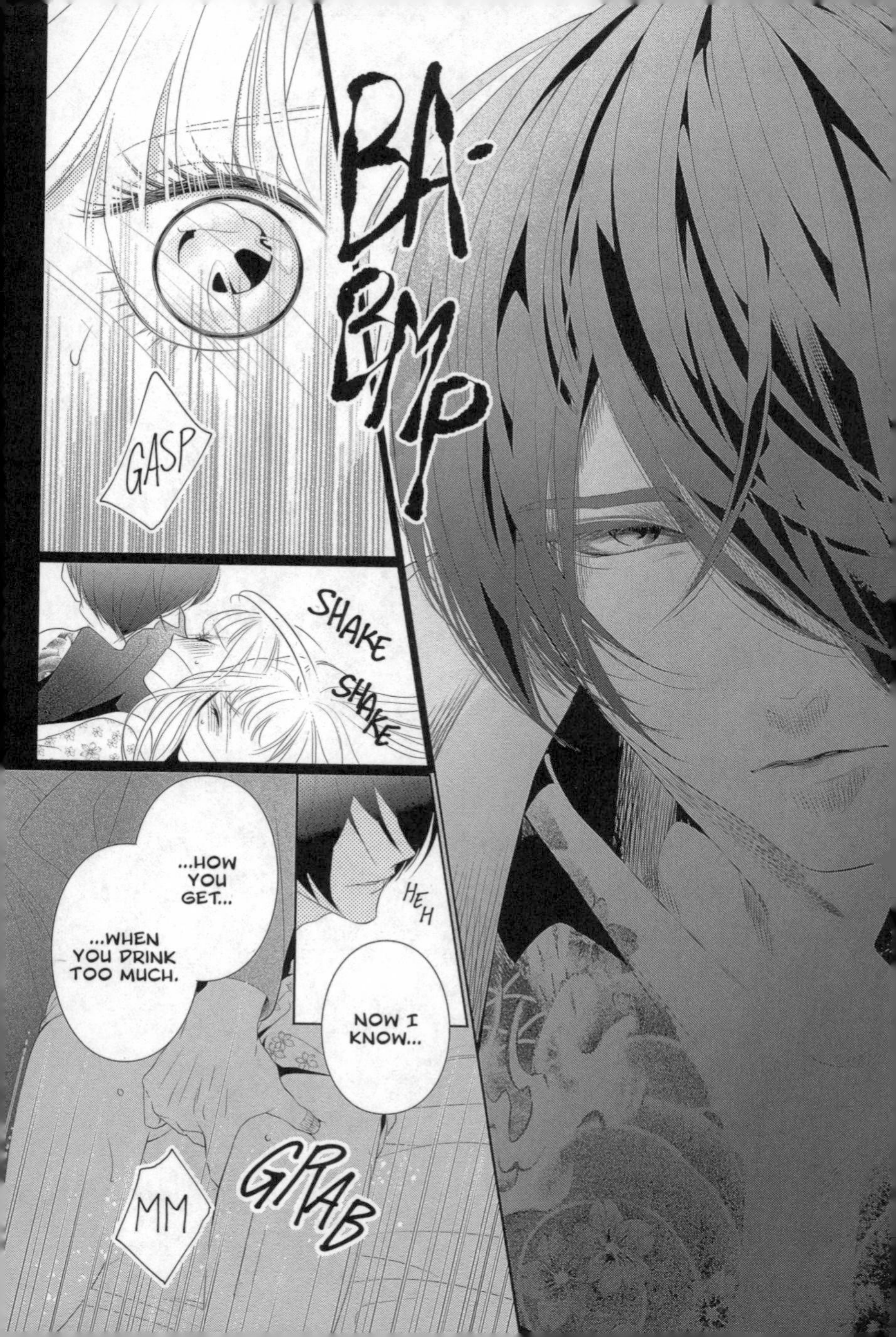
BA-BUMP
GASP
SHAKE
SHAKE
HEH
NOW I KNOW...
...HOW YOU GET...
...WHEN YOU DRINK TOO MUCH.
GRAB
MM

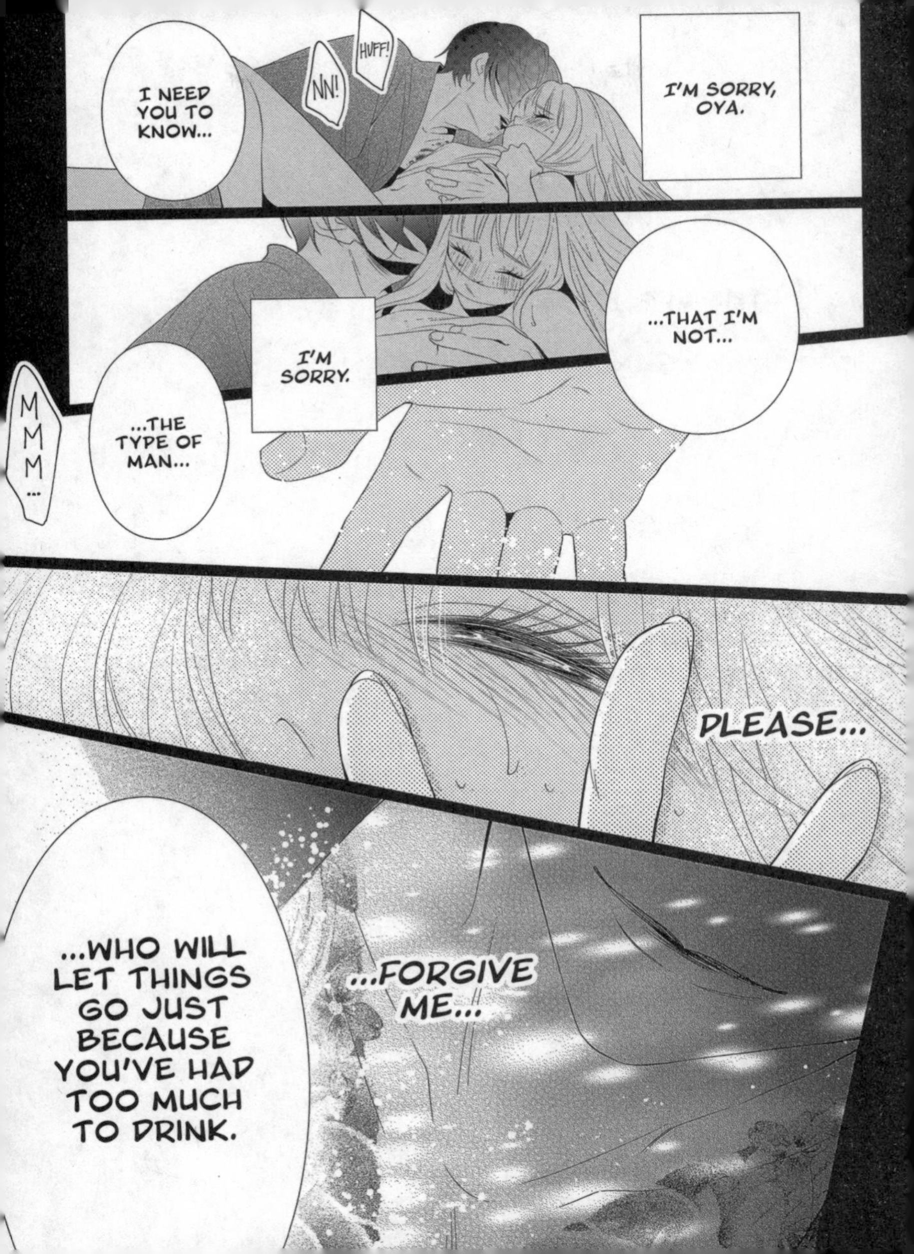
I'M SORRY, OYA.
HUFF!
NN!
I NEED YOU TO KNOW...
...THAT I'M NOT...
I'M SORRY.
...THE TYPE OF MAN...
MMM...
PLEASE...
...FORGIVE ME...
...WHO WILL LET THINGS GO JUST BECAUSE YOU'VE HAD TOO MUCH TO DRINK.

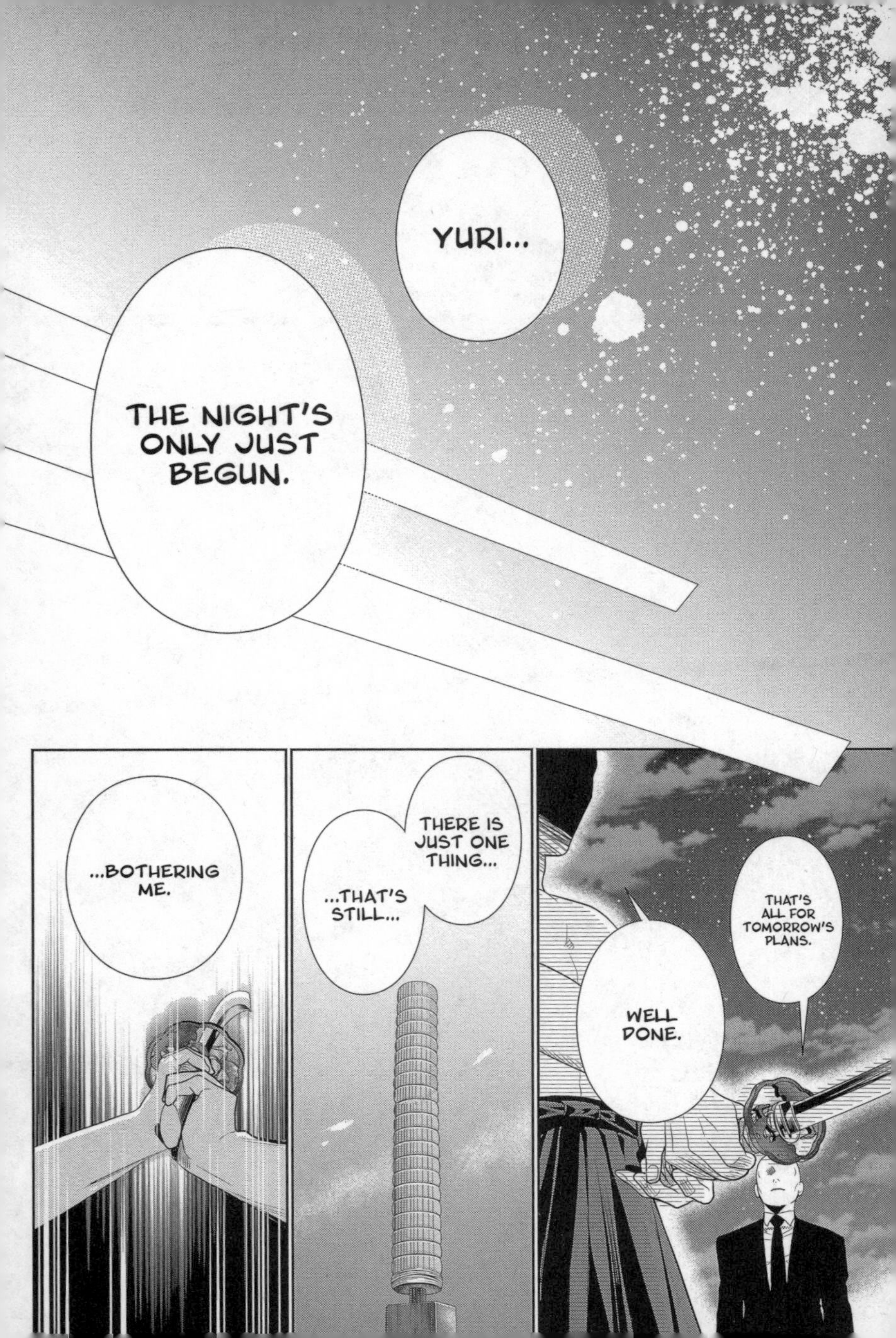
YURI...
THE NIGHT'S ONLY JUST BEGUN.
THAT'S ALL FOR TOMORROW'S PLANS.
WELL DONE.
THERE IS JUST ONE THING...
...THAT'S STILL...
...BOTHERING ME.

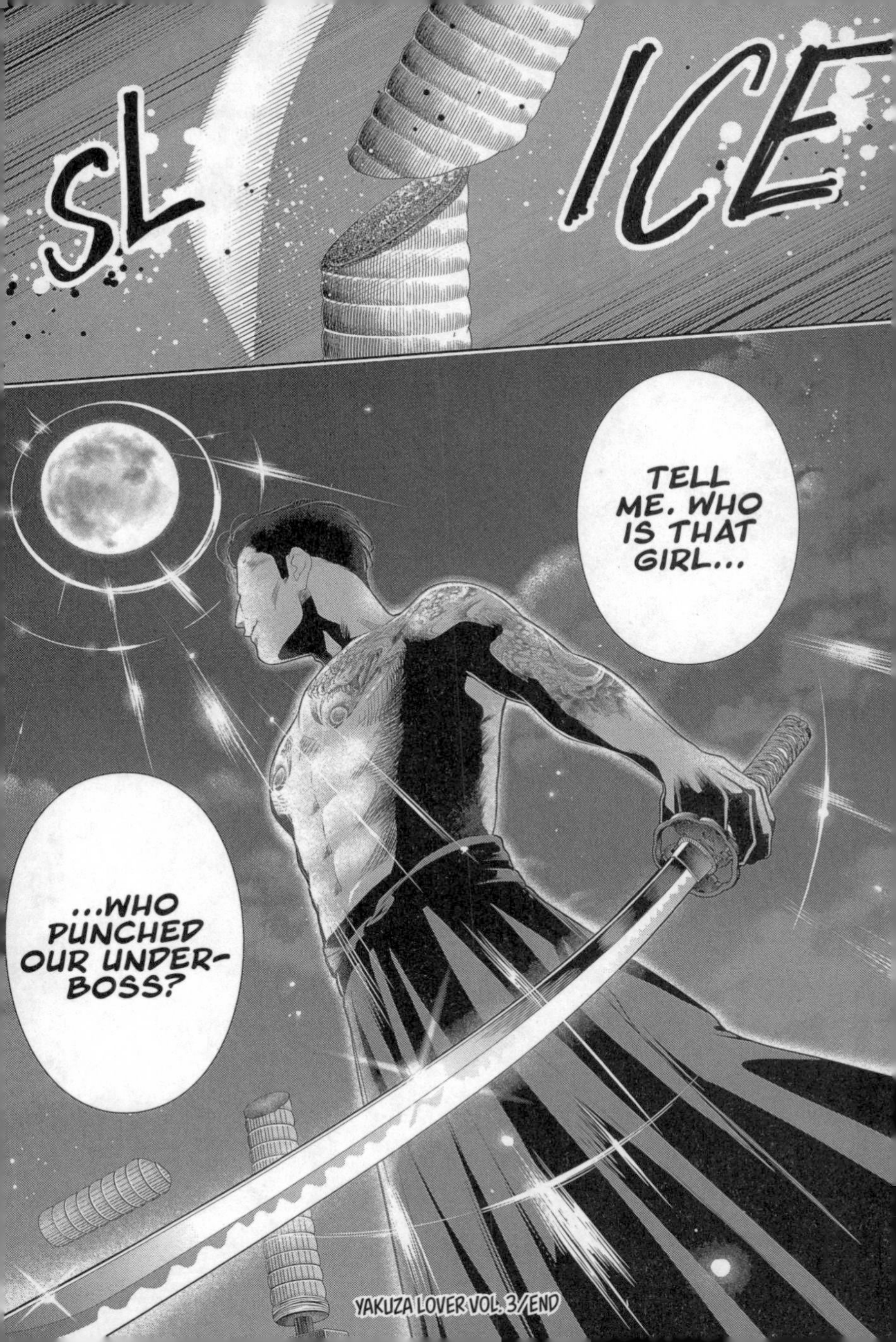
SLICE
TELL ME. WHO IS THAT GIRL...
...WHO PUNCHED OUR UNDER-BOSS?
YAKUZA LOVER VOL. 3/END

Yakuza Lover Rough Sketches

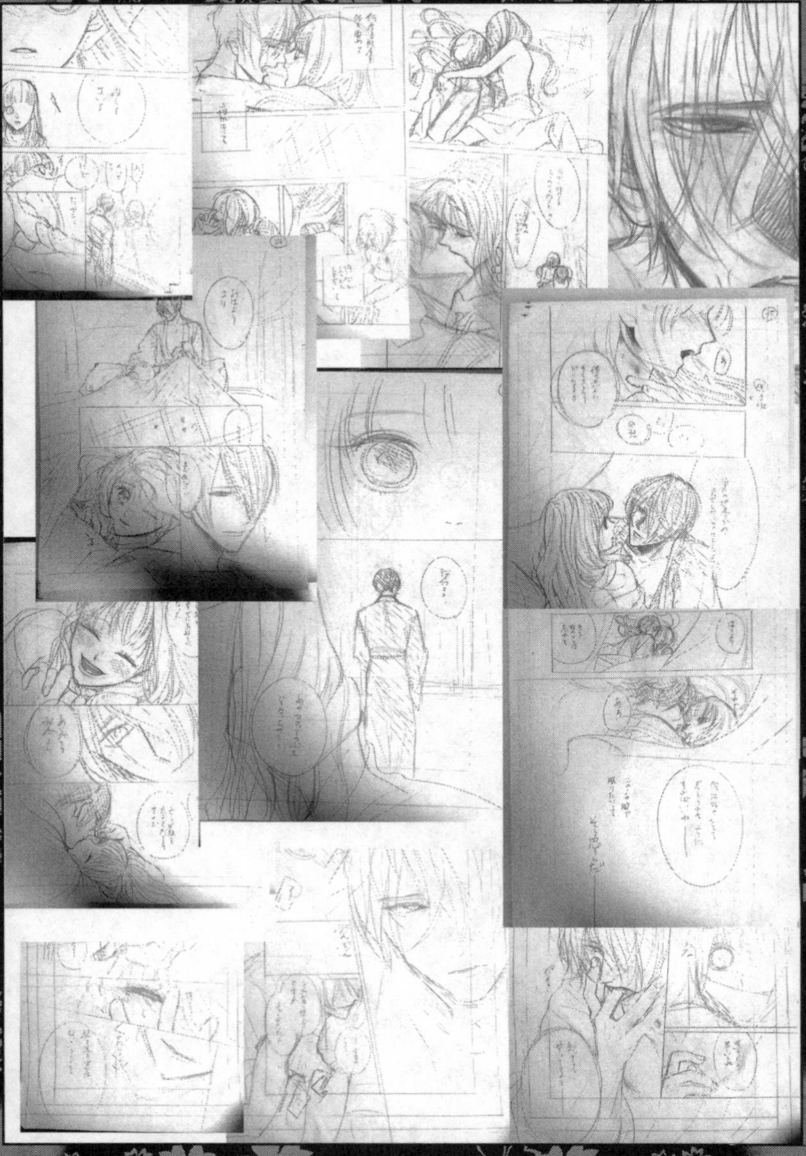

I'll keep sharing rough sketches from *Yakuza Lover* like this.

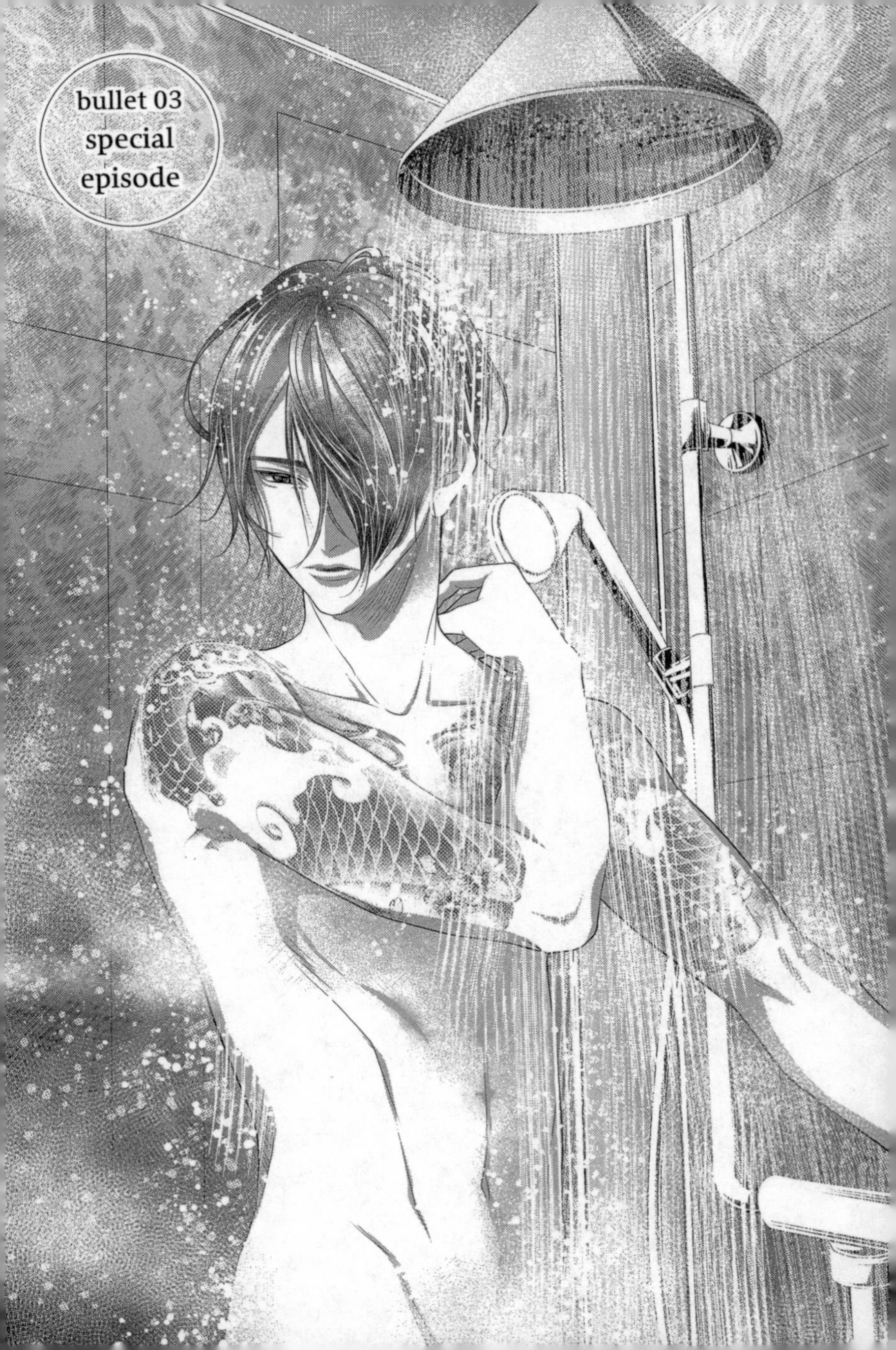
bullet 03
special
episode

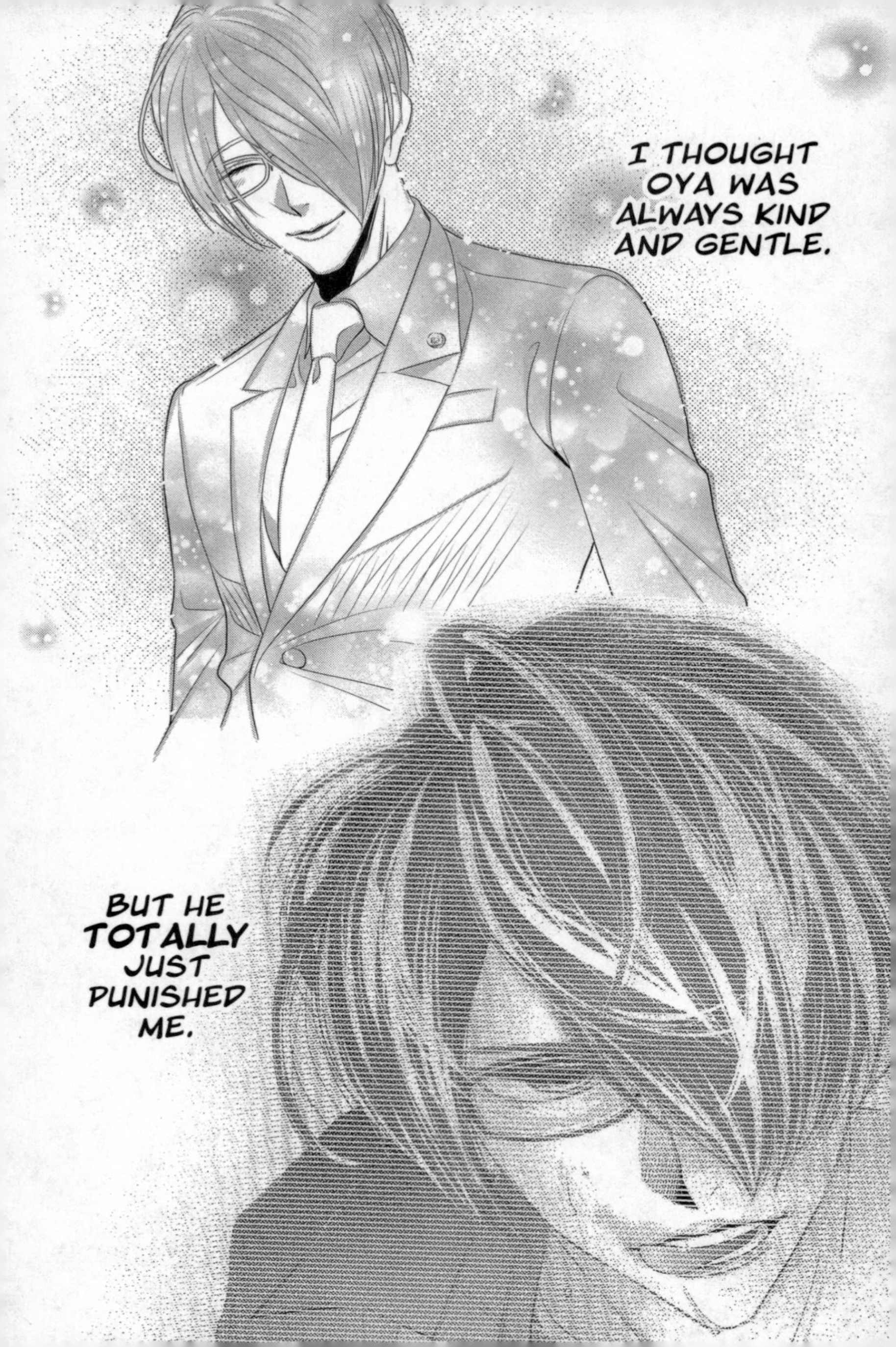
I THOUGHT OYA WAS ALWAYS KIND AND GENTLE.
BUT HE **TOTALLY** JUST PUNISHED ME.

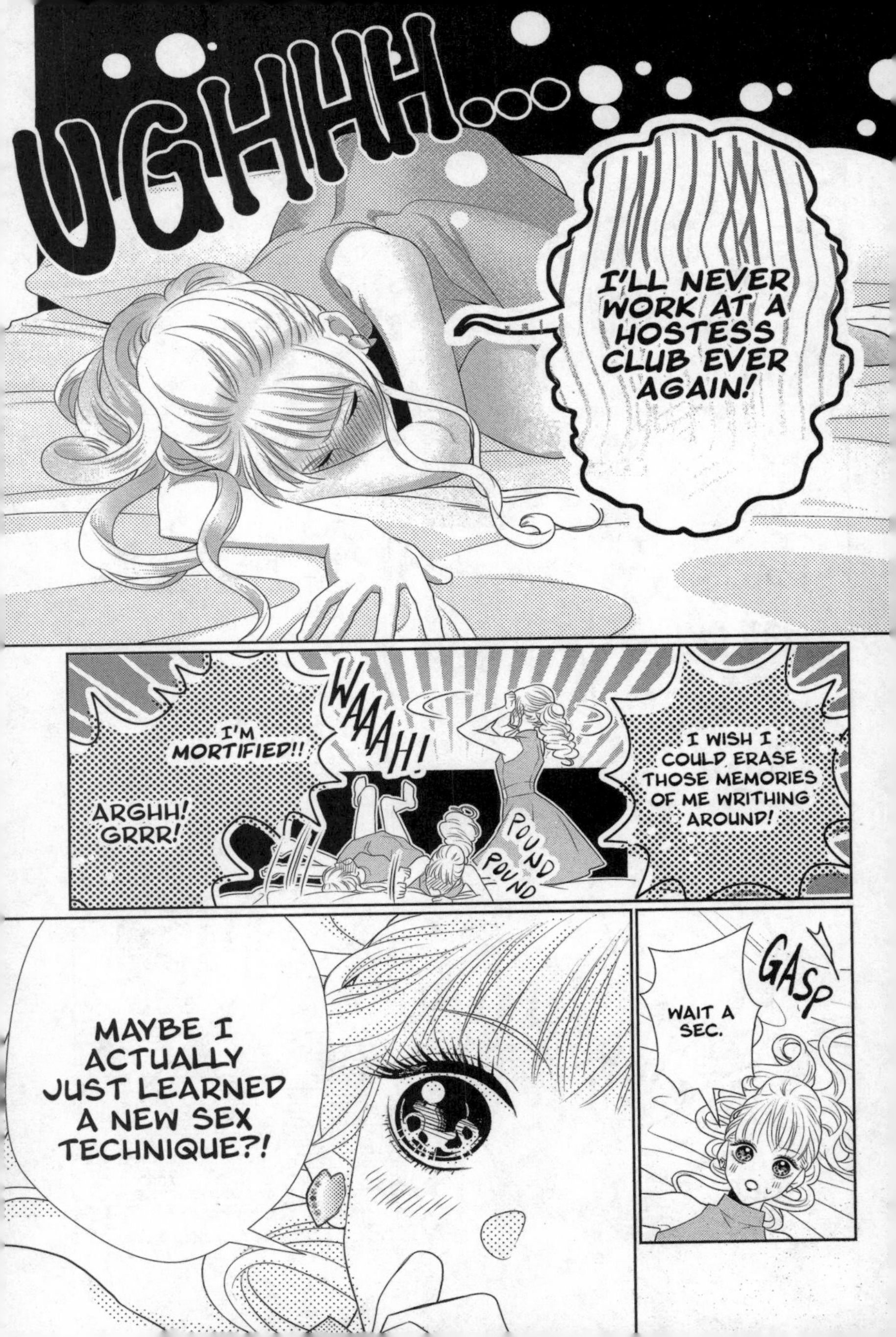
UGHHH...
I'LL NEVER WORK AT A HOSTESS CLUB EVER AGAIN!
I WISH I COULD ERASE THOSE MEMORIES OF ME WRITHING AROUND!
WAAAAH!
POUND POUND
I'M MORTIFIED!!
ARGHH! GRRR!
GASP
WAIT A SEC.
MAYBE I ACTUALLY JUST LEARNED A NEW SEX TECHNIQUE?!

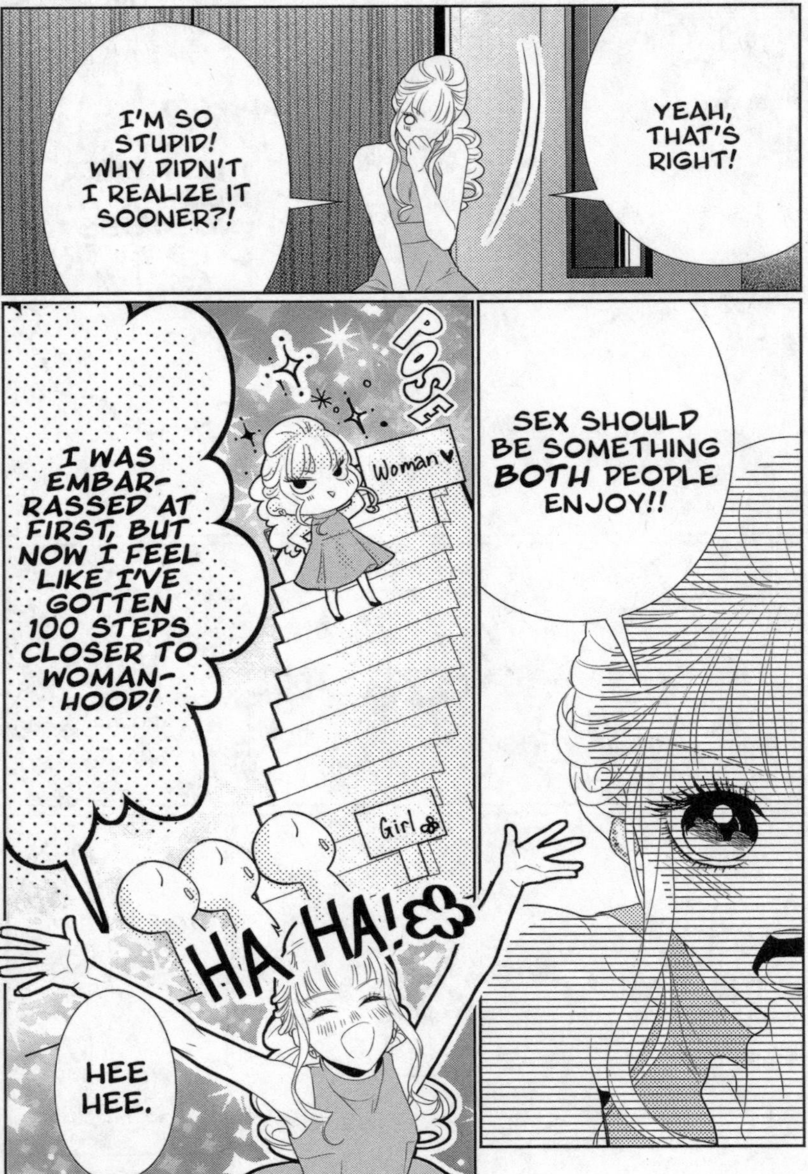
YEAH, THAT'S RIGHT!
I'M SO STUPID! WHY DIDN'T I REALIZE IT SOONER?!
SEX SHOULD BE SOMETHING BOTH PEOPLE ENJOY!!
POSE
Woman
I WAS EMBAR-RASSED AT FIRST, BUT NOW I FEEL LIKE I'VE GOTTEN 100 STEPS CLOSER TO WOMAN-HOOD!
Girl
HA HA!
HEE HEE.

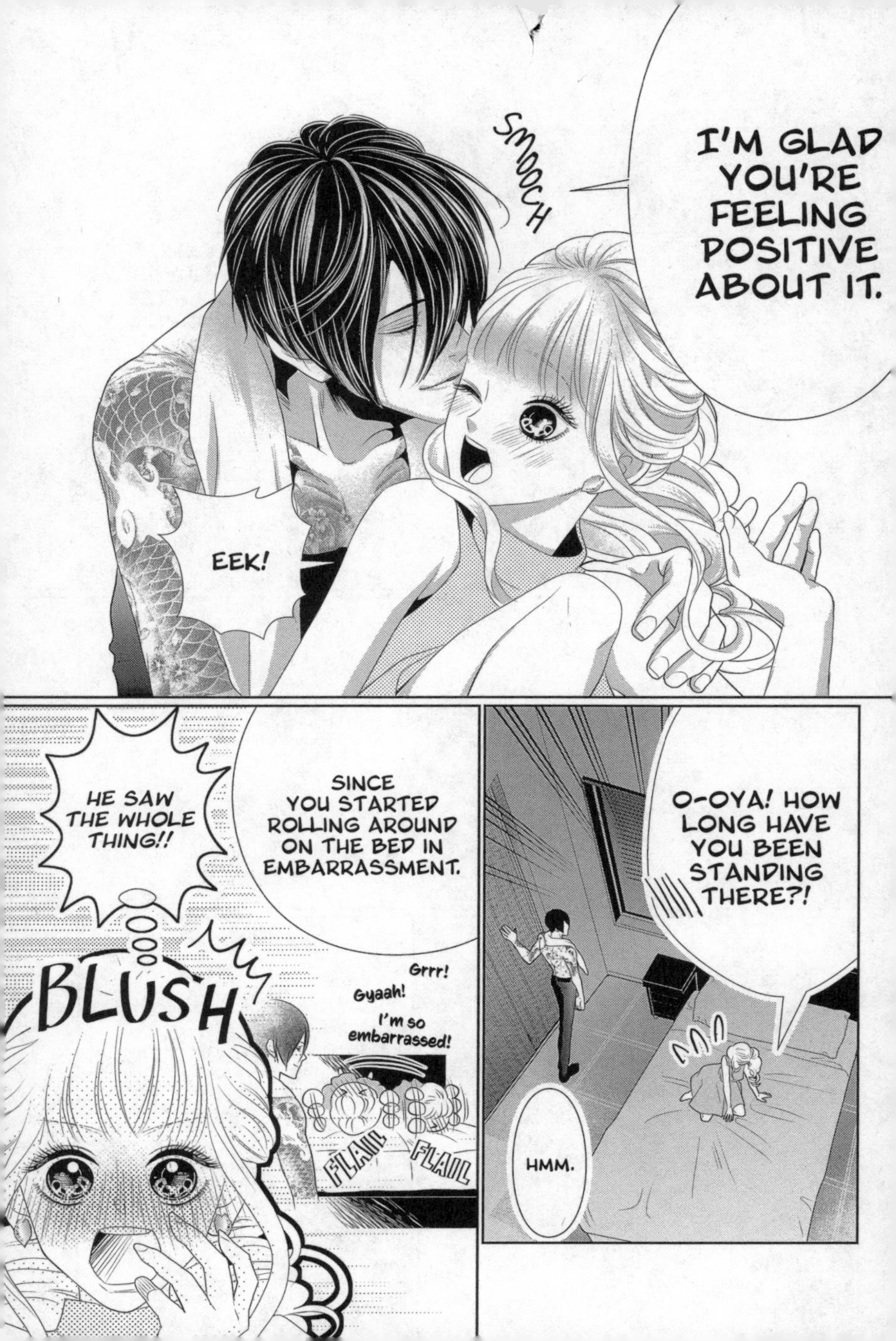
I'M GLAD YOU'RE FEELING POSITIVE ABOUT IT.
SMOOCH
EEK!
O-OYA! HOW LONG HAVE YOU BEEN STANDING THERE?!
HMM.
SINCE YOU STARTED ROLLING AROUND ON THE BED IN EMBARRASSMENT.
HE SAW THE WHOLE THING!!
Grrr!
Gyaah!
I'm so embarrassed!
FLAIL
FLAIL
BLUSH

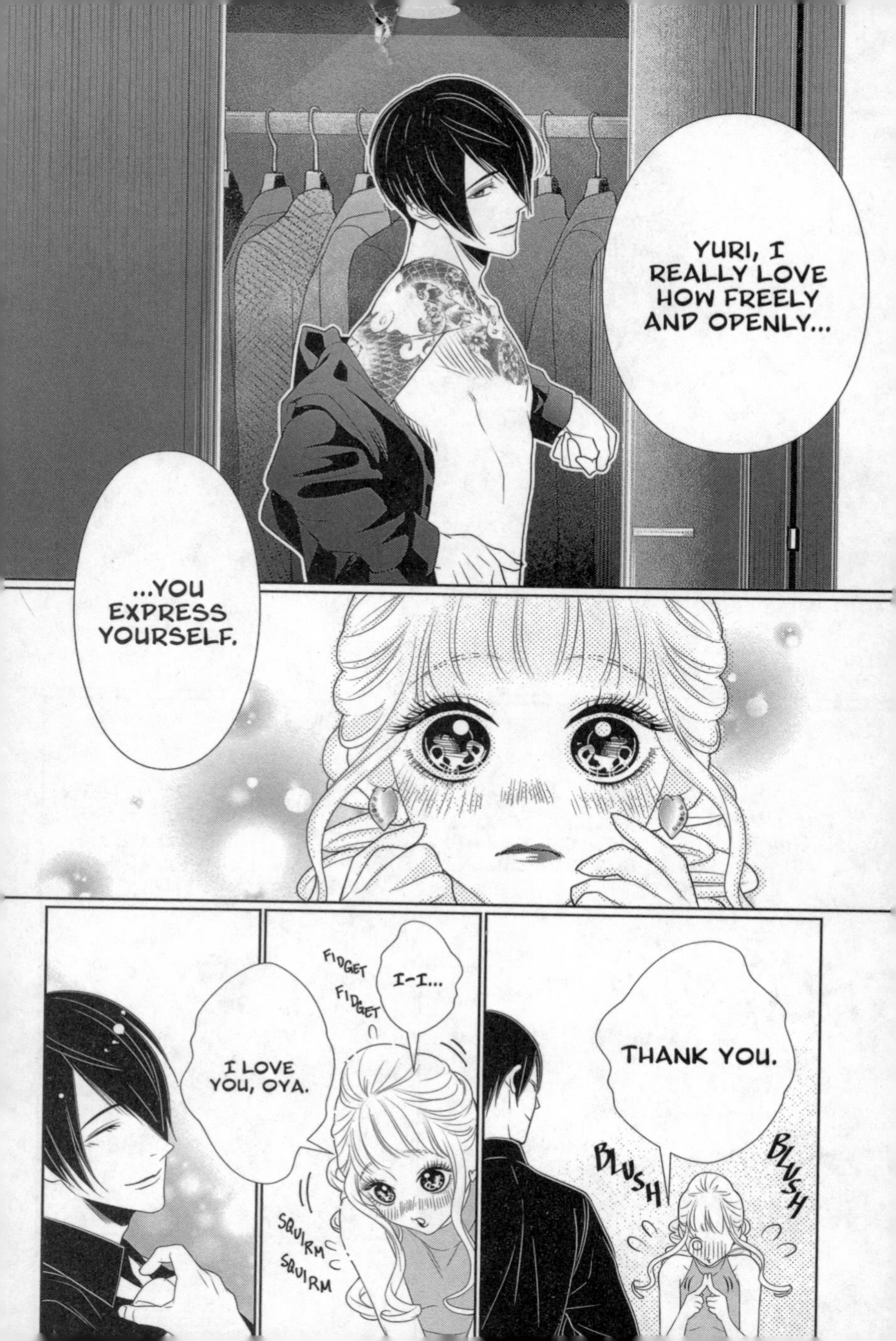
YURI, I REALLY LOVE HOW FREELY AND OPENLY...
...YOU EXPRESS YOURSELF.
THANK YOU.
BLUSH
BLUSH
FIDGET
FIDGET
I-I...
SQUIRM
SQUIRM
I LOVE YOU, OYA.

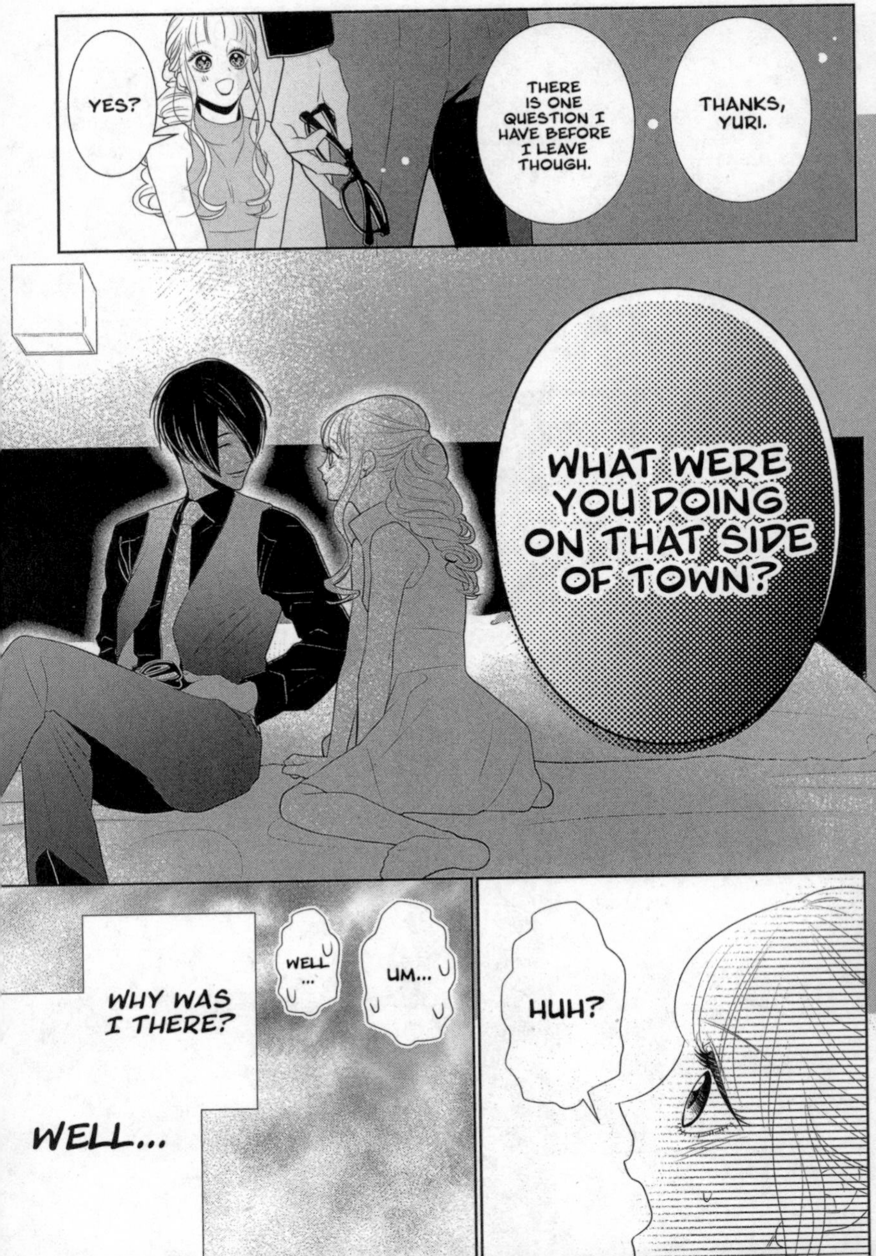
THANKS, YURI.
THERE IS ONE QUESTION I HAVE BEFORE I LEAVE THOUGH.
YES?
WHAT WERE YOU DOING ON THAT SIDE OF TOWN?
HUH?
UM...
WELL ...
WHY WAS I THERE?
WELL...

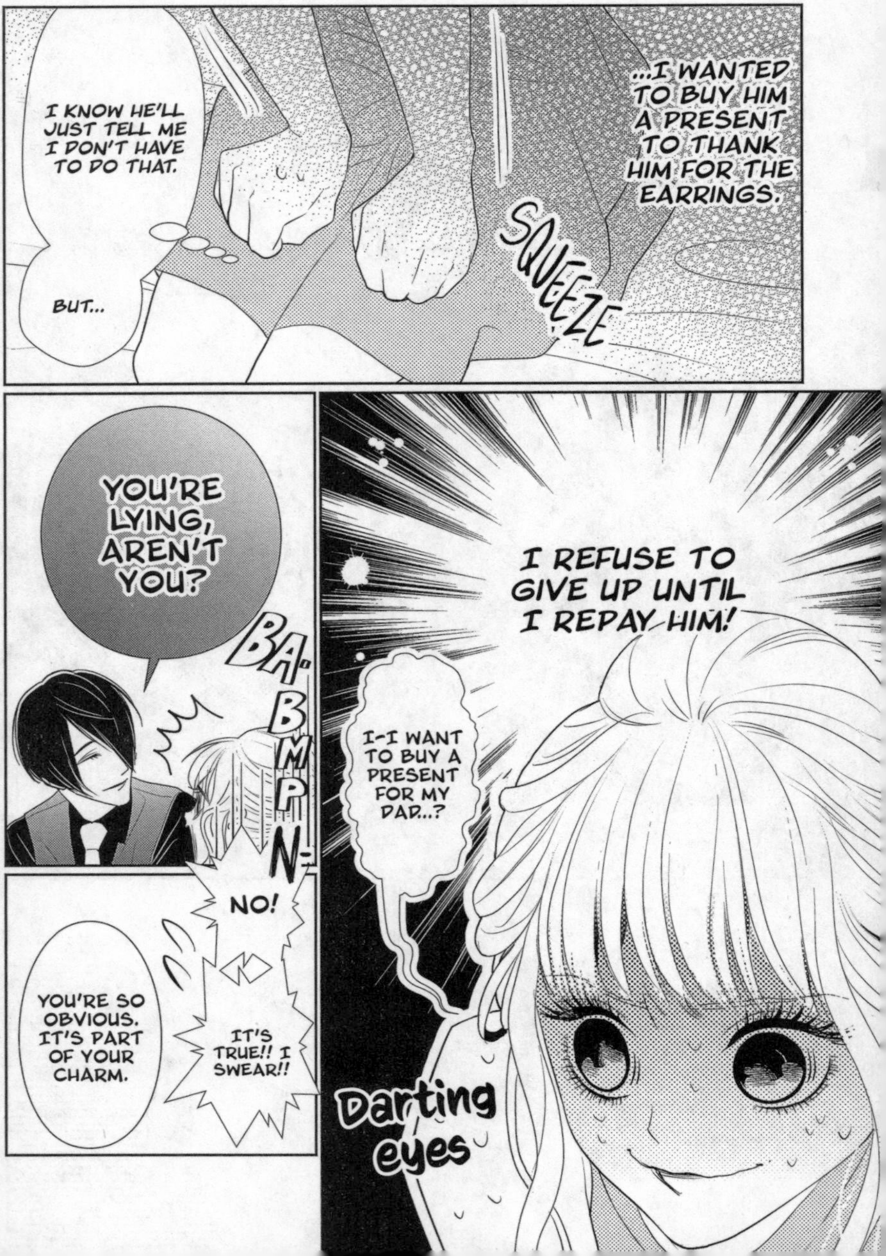
...I WANTED TO BUY HIM A PRESENT TO THANK HIM FOR THE EARRINGS.
SQUEEZE
I KNOW HE'LL JUST TELL ME I DON'T HAVE TO DO THAT.
BUT...
I REFUSE TO GIVE UP UNTIL I REPAY HIM!
I-I WANT TO BUY A PRESENT FOR MY DAD...?
Darting eyes
YOU'RE LYING, AREN'T YOU?
BA-BMPN-
NO!
IT'S TRUE!! I SWEAR!!
YOU'RE SO OBVIOUS. IT'S PART OF YOUR CHARM.

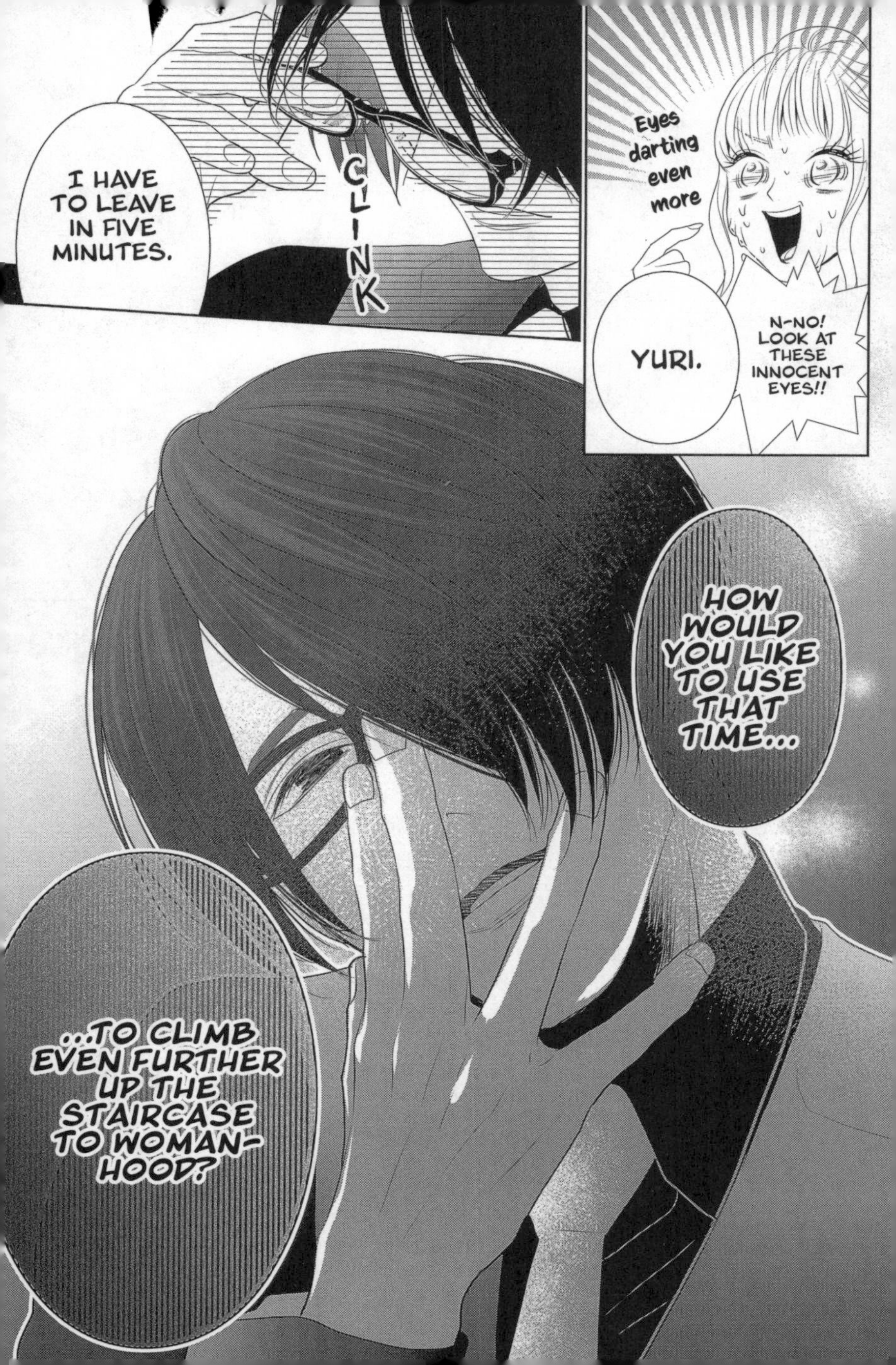

Eyes darting even more
N-NO! LOOK AT THESE INNOCENT EYES!!
YURI.
I HAVE TO LEAVE IN FIVE MINUTES.
CLINK
HOW WOULD YOU LIKE TO USE THAT TIME...
...TO CLIMB EVEN FURTHER UP THE STAIRCASE TO WOMAN-HOOD?

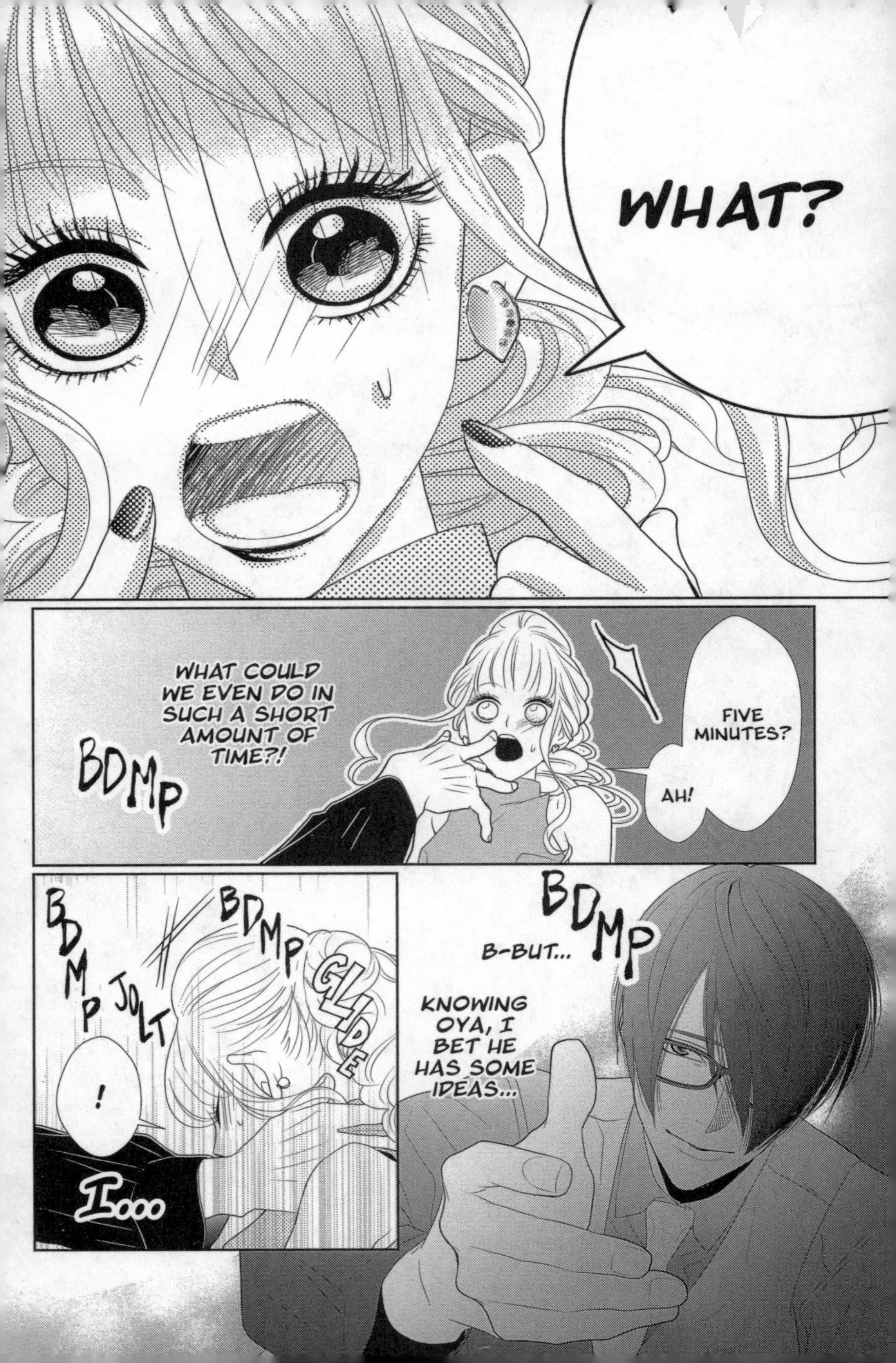
WHAT?
FIVE MINUTES?
AH!
WHAT COULD WE EVEN DO IN SUCH A SHORT AMOUNT OF TIME?!
BDMP
BDMP
B-BUT...
KNOWING OYA, I BET HE HAS SOME IDEAS...
GLIDE
BDMP
JOLT
BDMP
!
I...

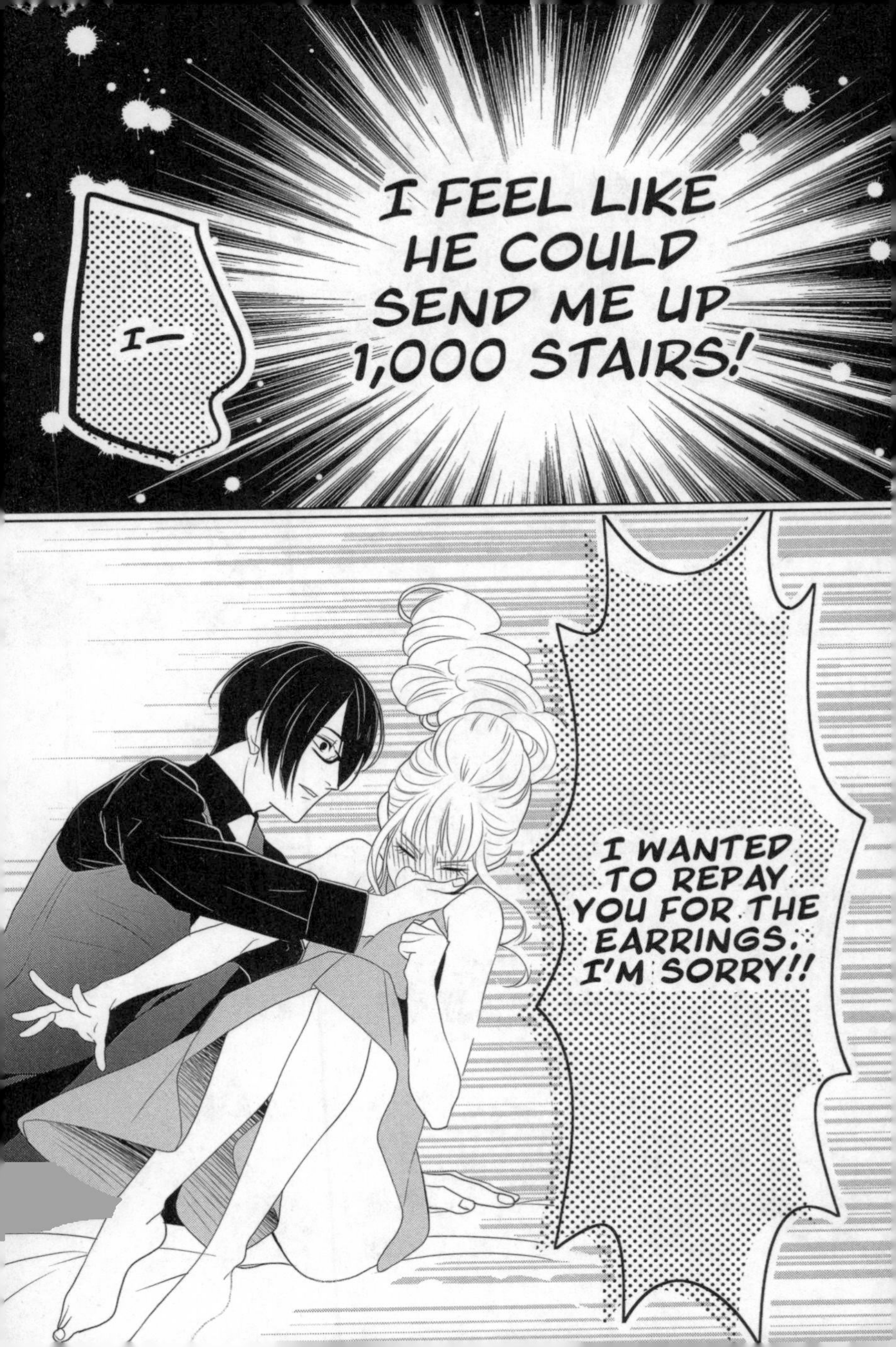
I FEEL LIKE HE COULD SEND ME UP 1,000 STAIRS!
I—
I WANTED TO REPAY YOU FOR THE EARRINGS. I'M SORRY!!

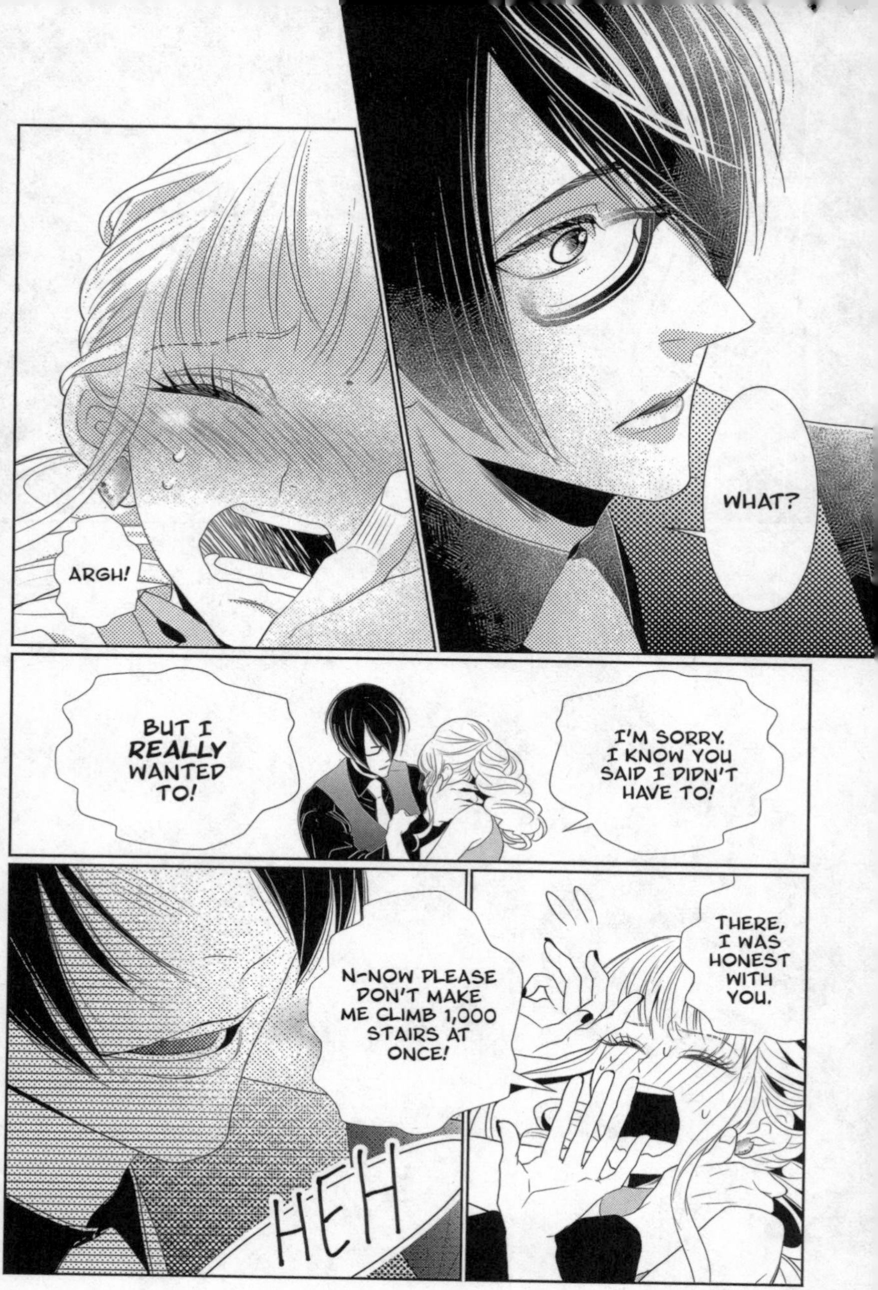
WHAT?
ARGH!
I'M SORRY. I KNOW YOU SAID I DIDN'T HAVE TO!
BUT I REALLY WANTED TO!
THERE, I WAS HONEST WITH YOU.
N-NOW PLEASE DON'T MAKE ME CLIMB 1,000 STAIRS AT ONCE!
HEH

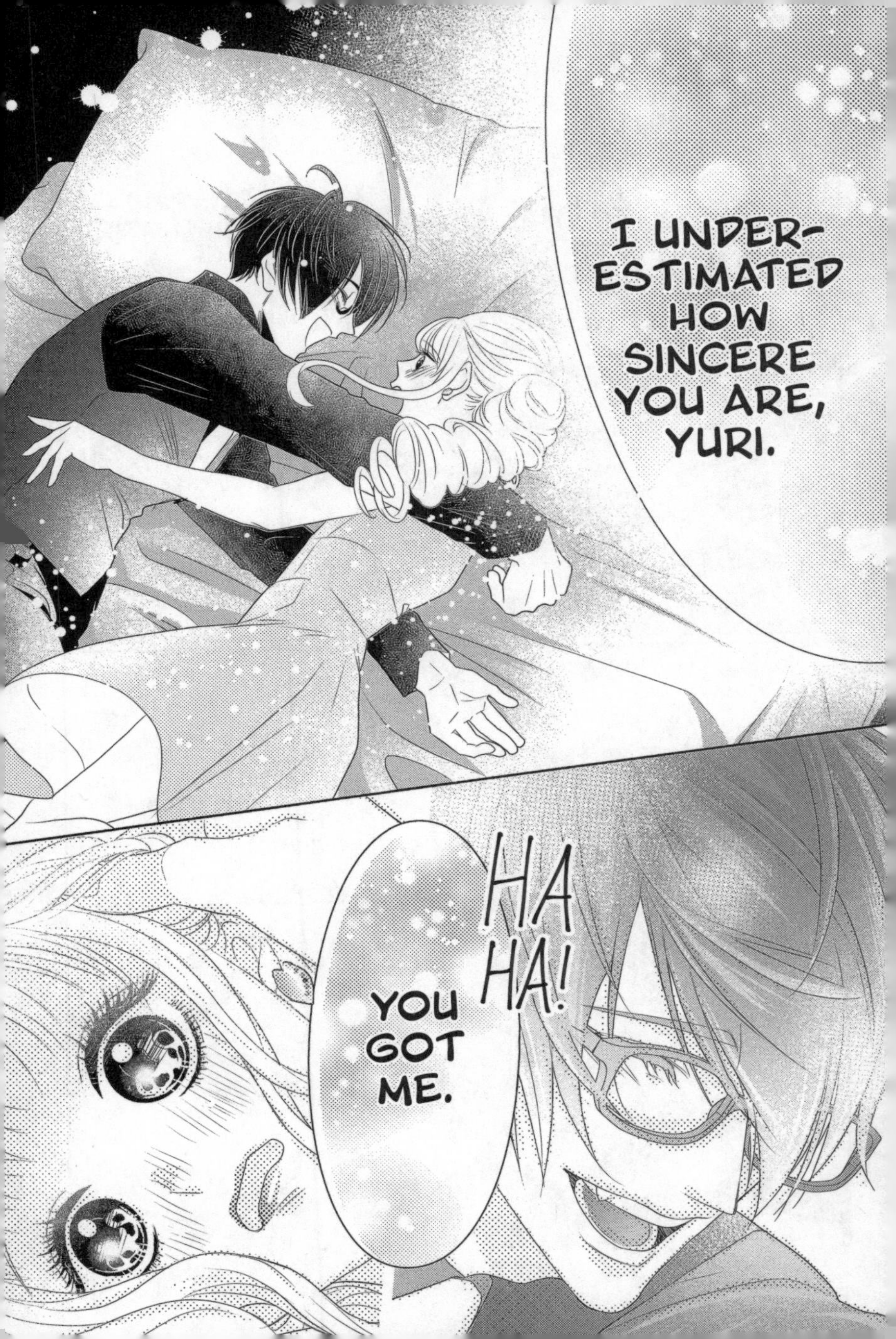
I UNDER-ESTIMATED HOW SINCERE YOU ARE, YURI.
HA HA!
YOU GOT ME.

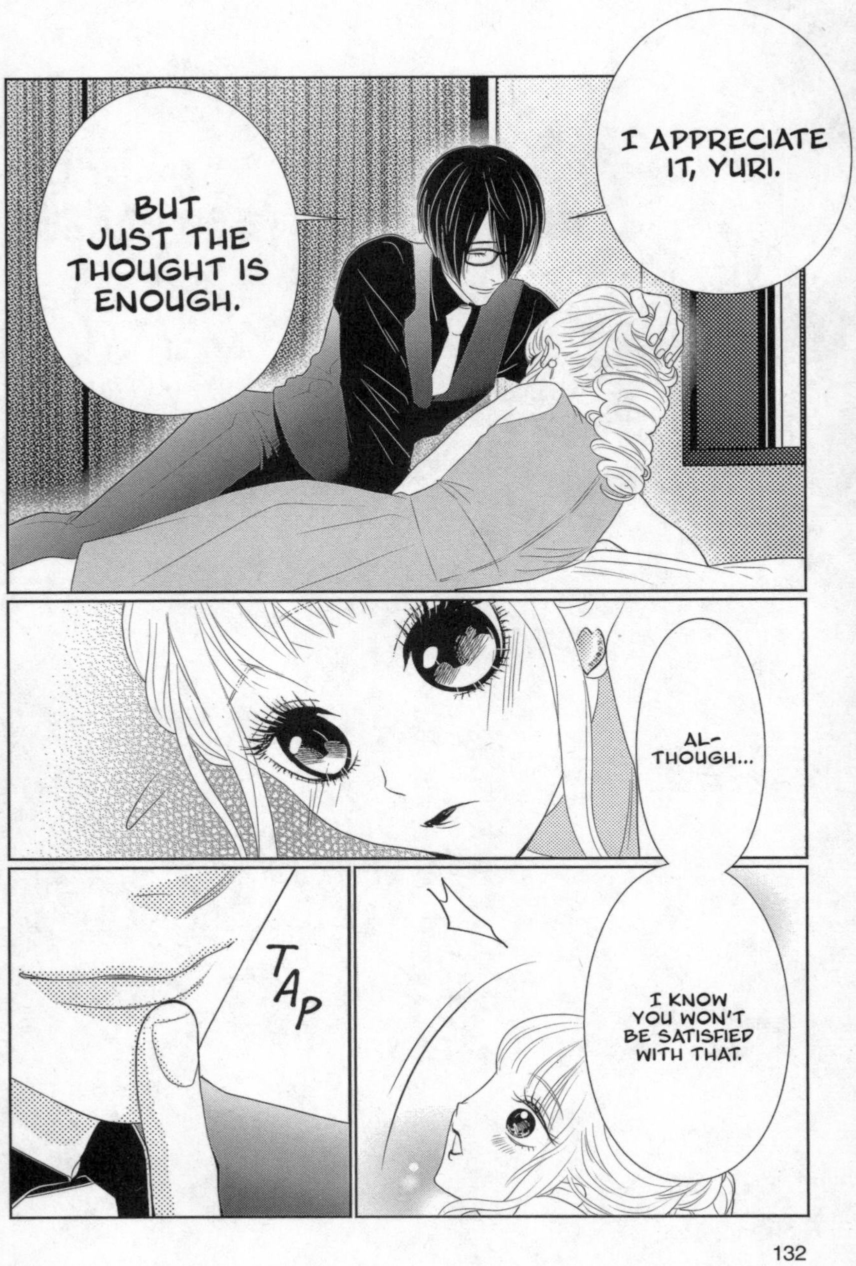
I APPRECIATE IT, YURI.
BUT JUST THE THOUGHT IS ENOUGH.
AL-THOUGH...
I KNOW YOU WON'T BE SATISFIED WITH THAT.
TAP

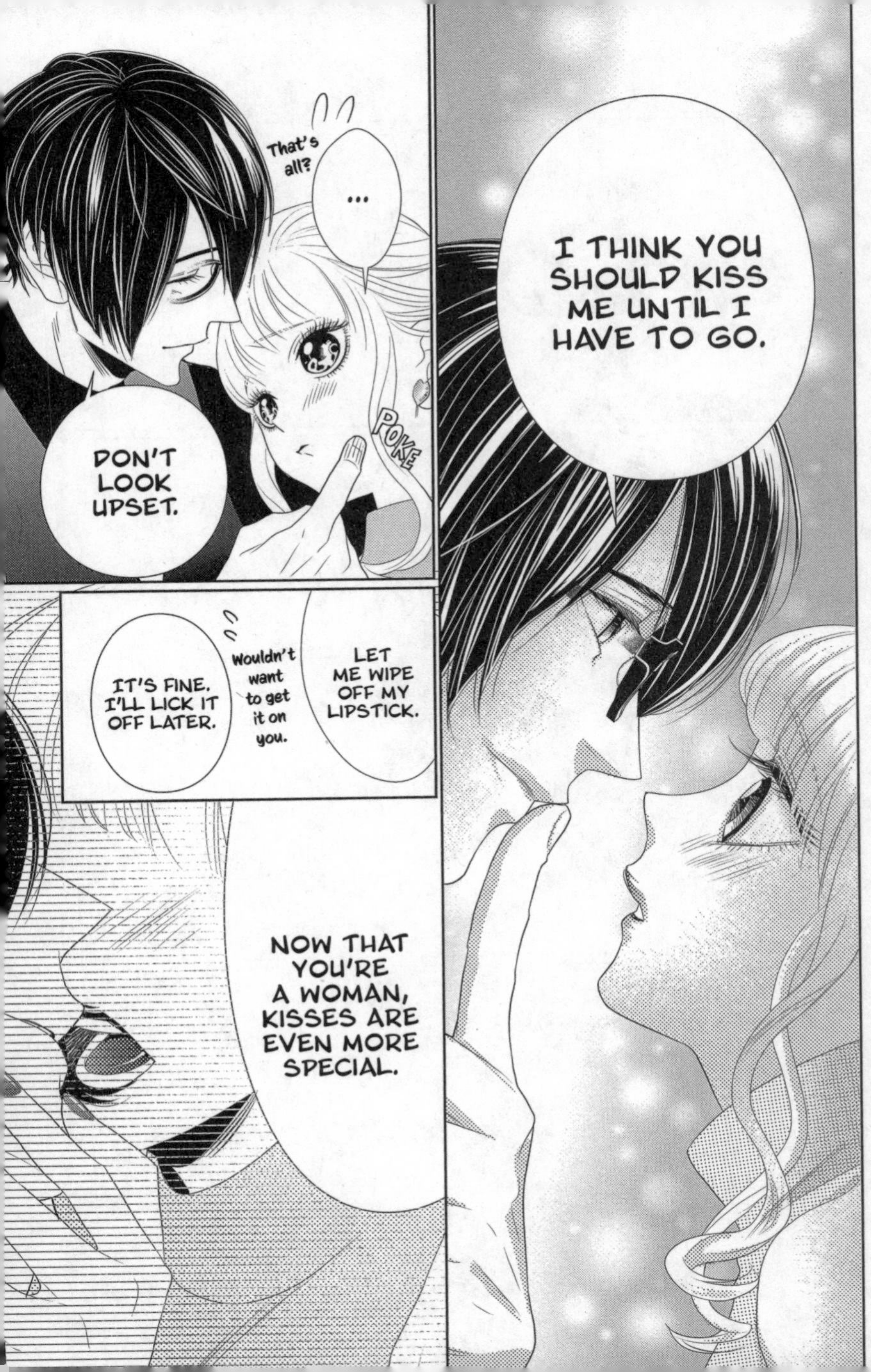
I THINK YOU SHOULD KISS ME UNTIL I HAVE TO GO.
That's all?
...
POKE
DON'T LOOK UPSET.
LET ME WIPE OFF MY LIPSTICK.
Wouldn't want to get it on you.
IT'S FINE. I'LL LICK IT OFF LATER.
NOW THAT YOU'RE A WOMAN, KISSES ARE EVEN MORE SPECIAL.

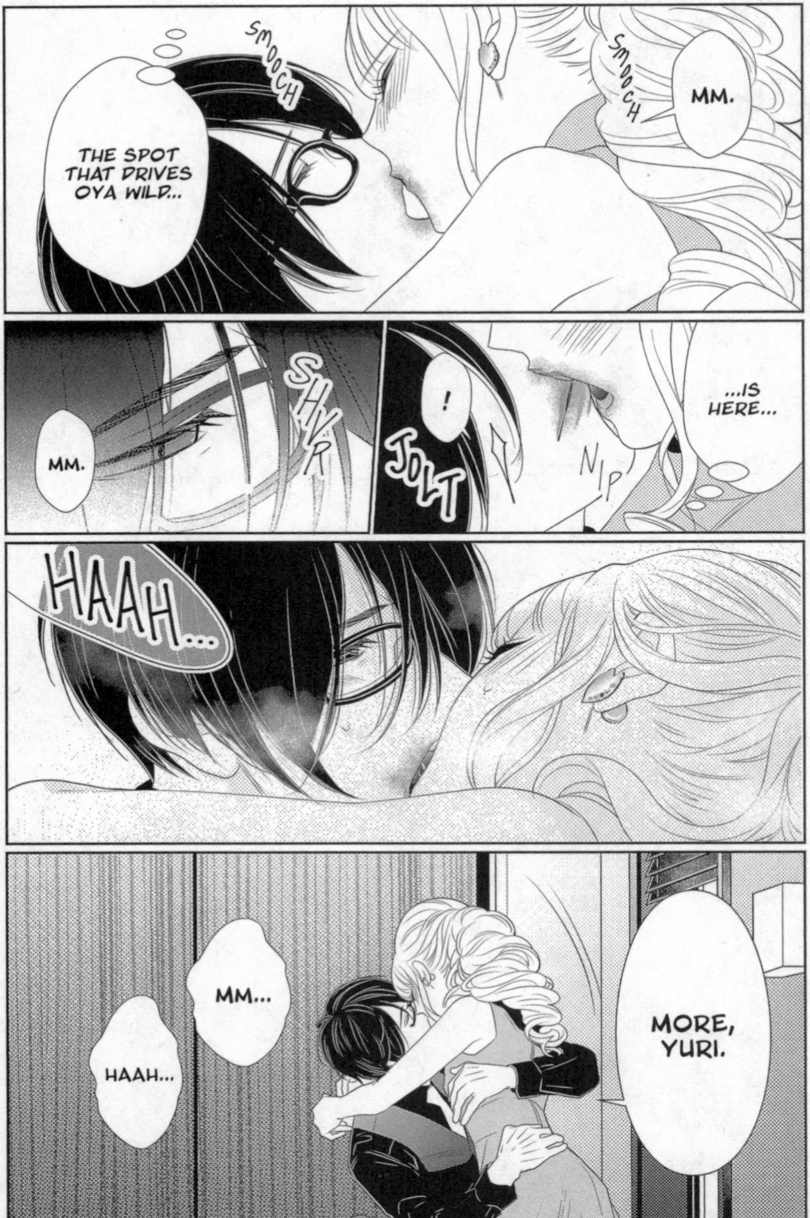
MM.
SMOOCH
SMOOCH
THE SPOT THAT DRIVES OYA WILD...
...IS HERE...
NIP
!
JOLT
SHVR
MM.
HAAH...
MORE, YURI.
MM...
HAAH...

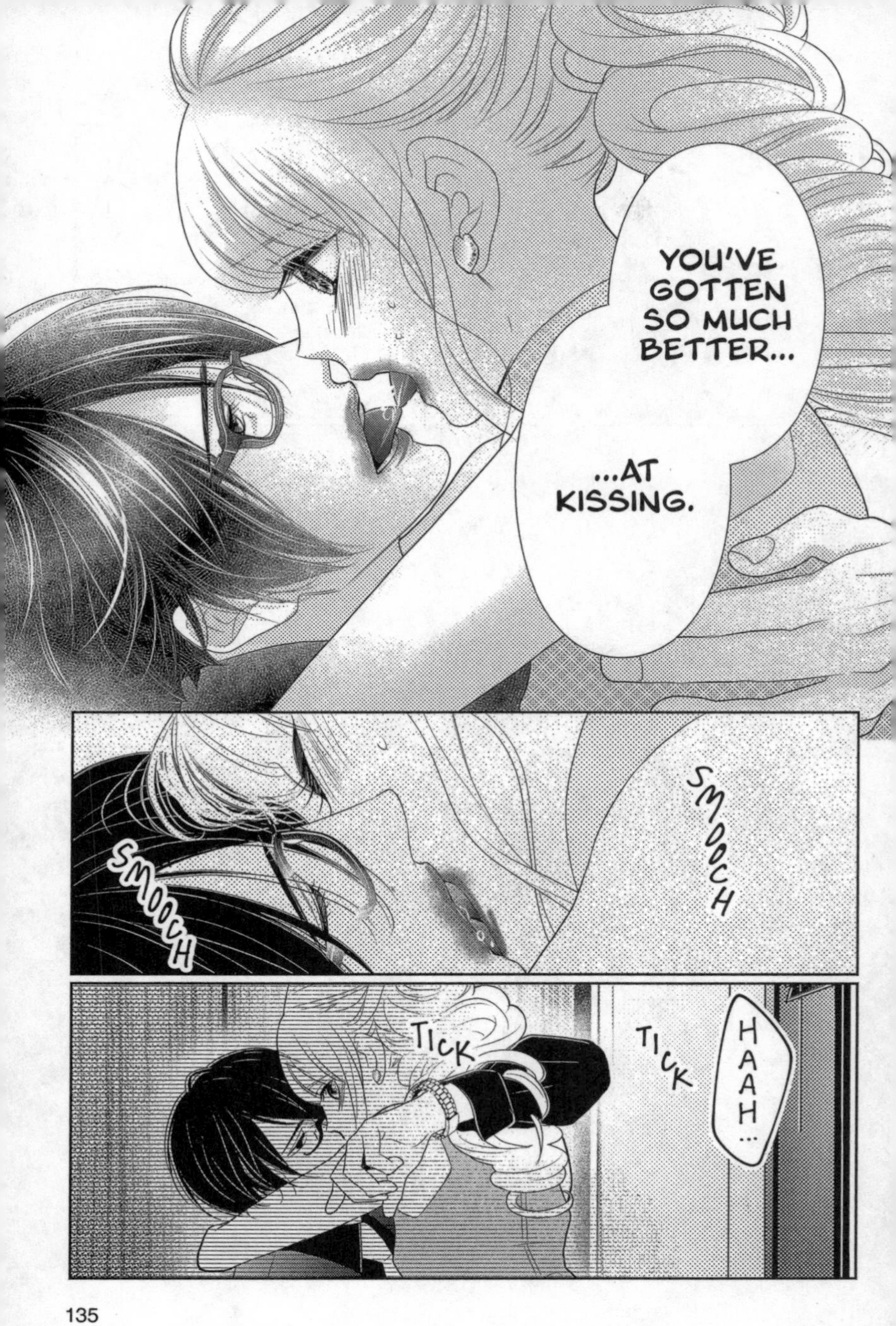
YOU'VE GOTTEN SO MUCH BETTER...
...AT KISSING.
SMOOCH
SMOOCH
HAAH...
TICK
TICK

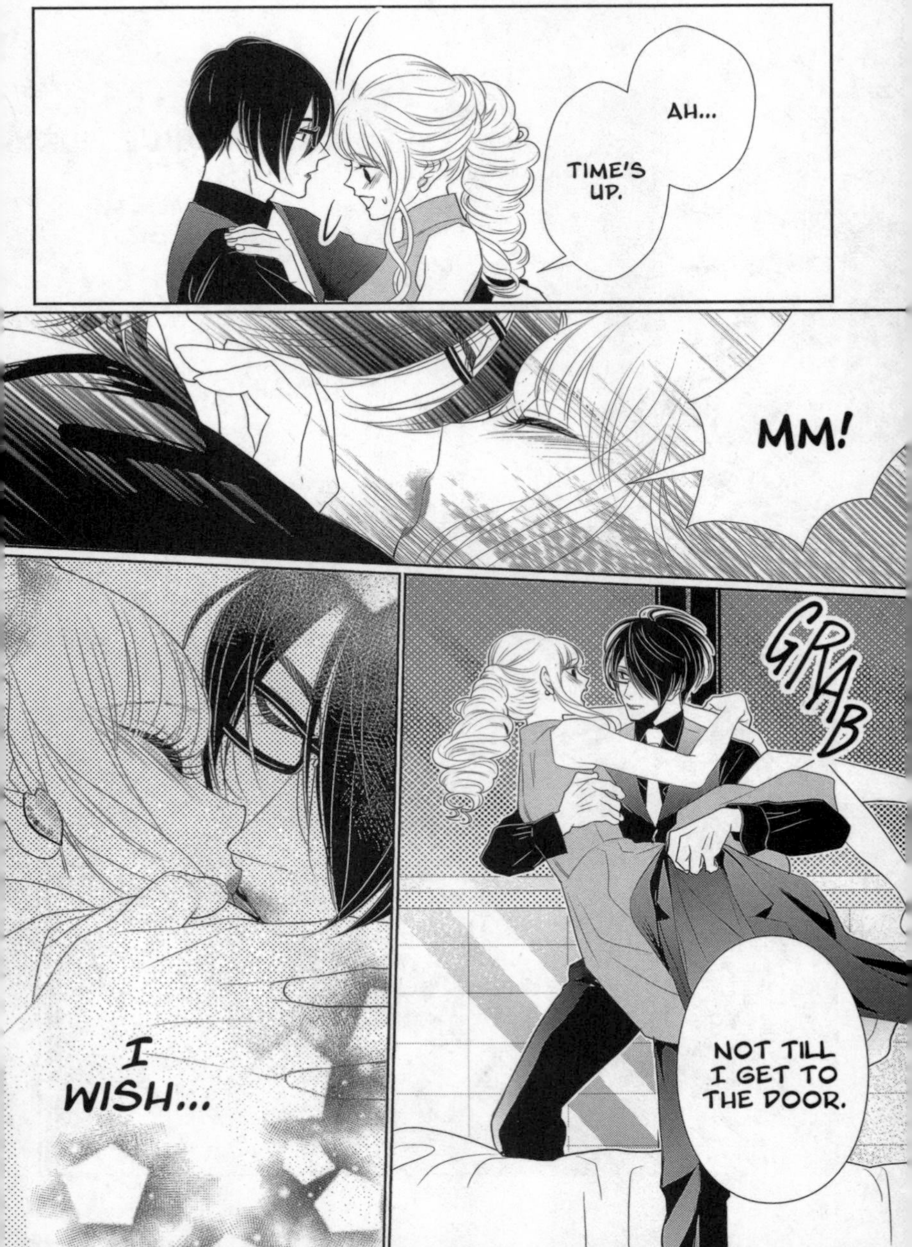
AH...
TIME'S UP.
MM!
GRAB
NOT TILL I GET TO THE DOOR.
I WISH...

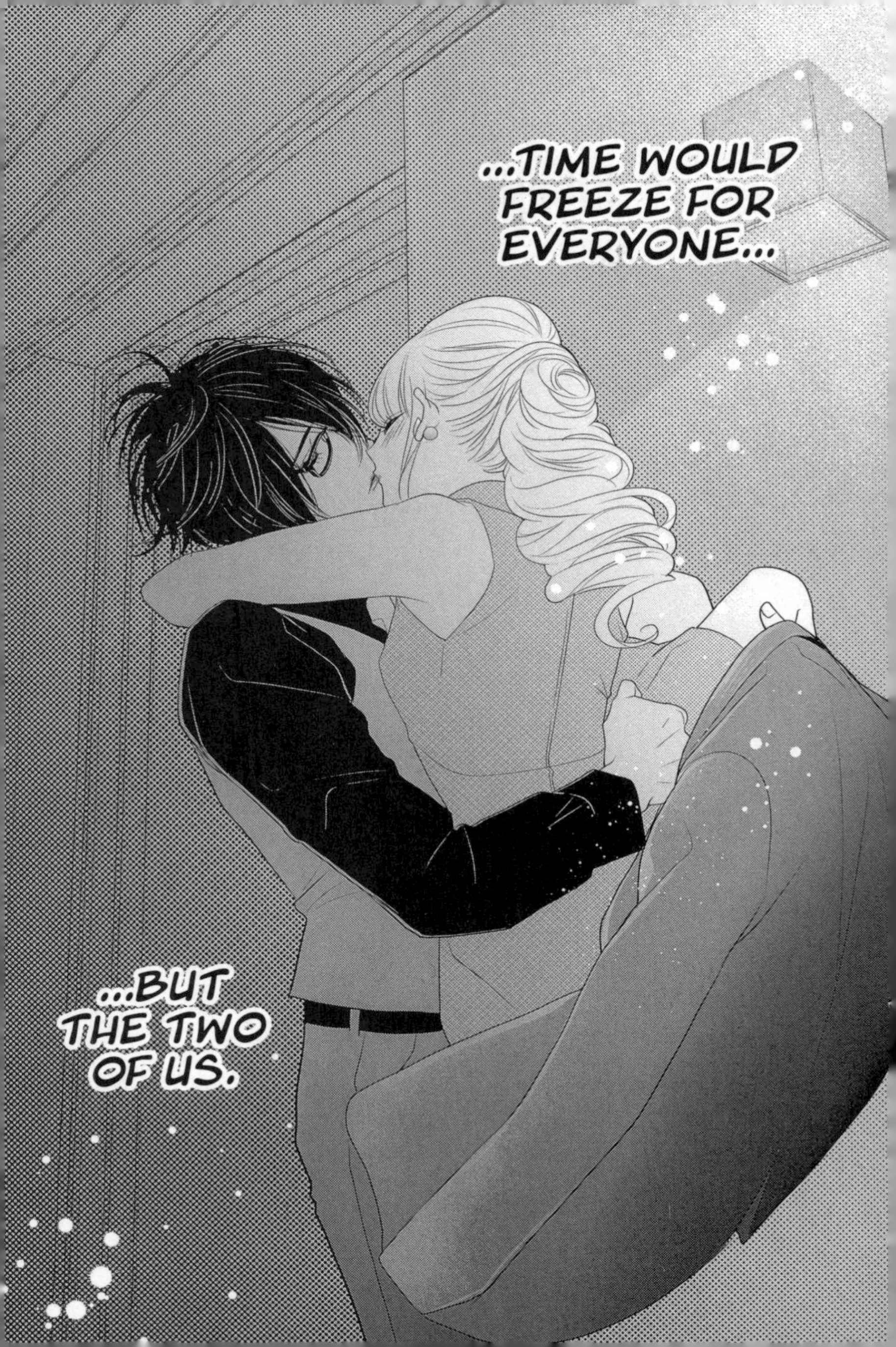
...TIME WOULD FREEZE FOR EVERYONE...
...BUT THE TWO OF US.

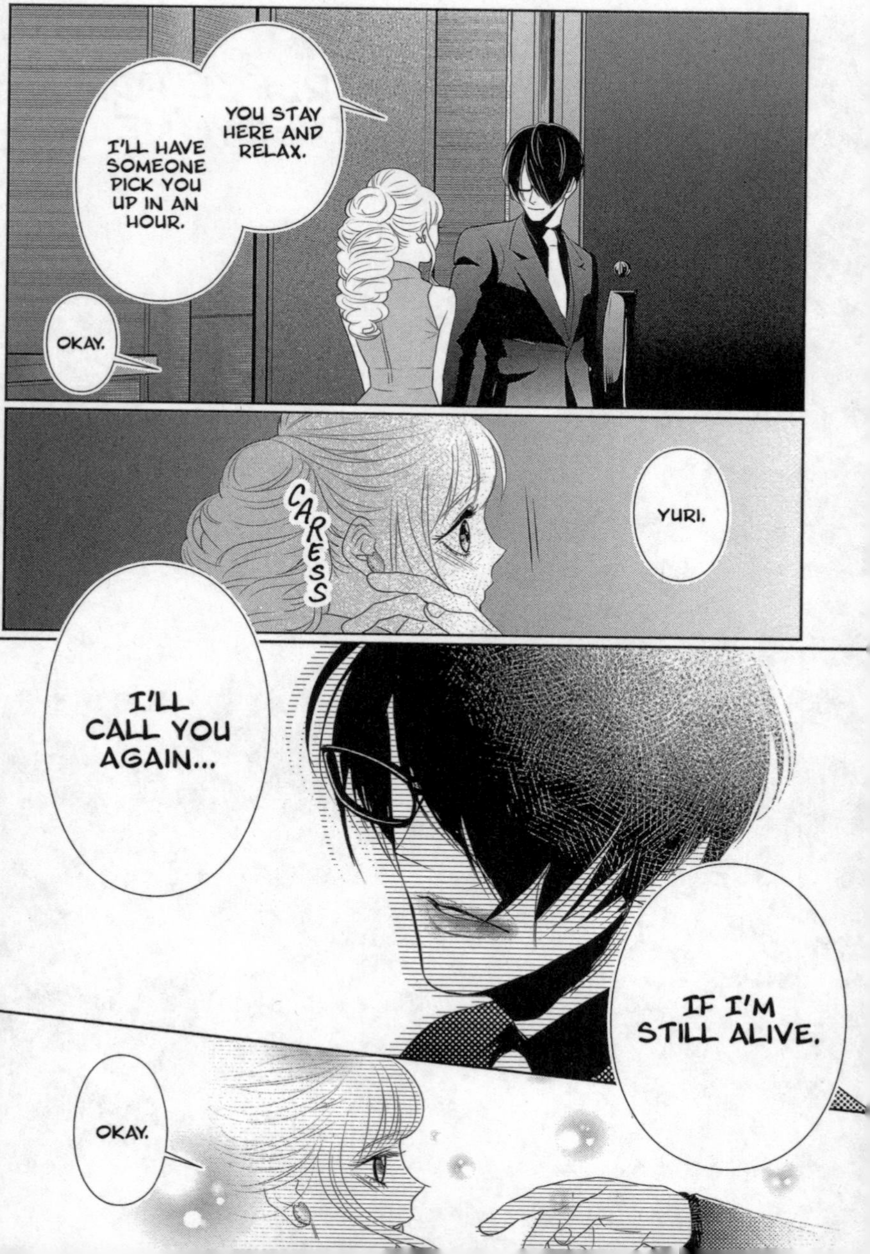
YOU STAY HERE AND RELAX.
I'LL HAVE SOMEONE PICK YOU UP IN AN HOUR.
OKAY.
YURI.
CARESS
I'LL CALL YOU AGAIN...
IF I'M STILL ALIVE.
OKAY.

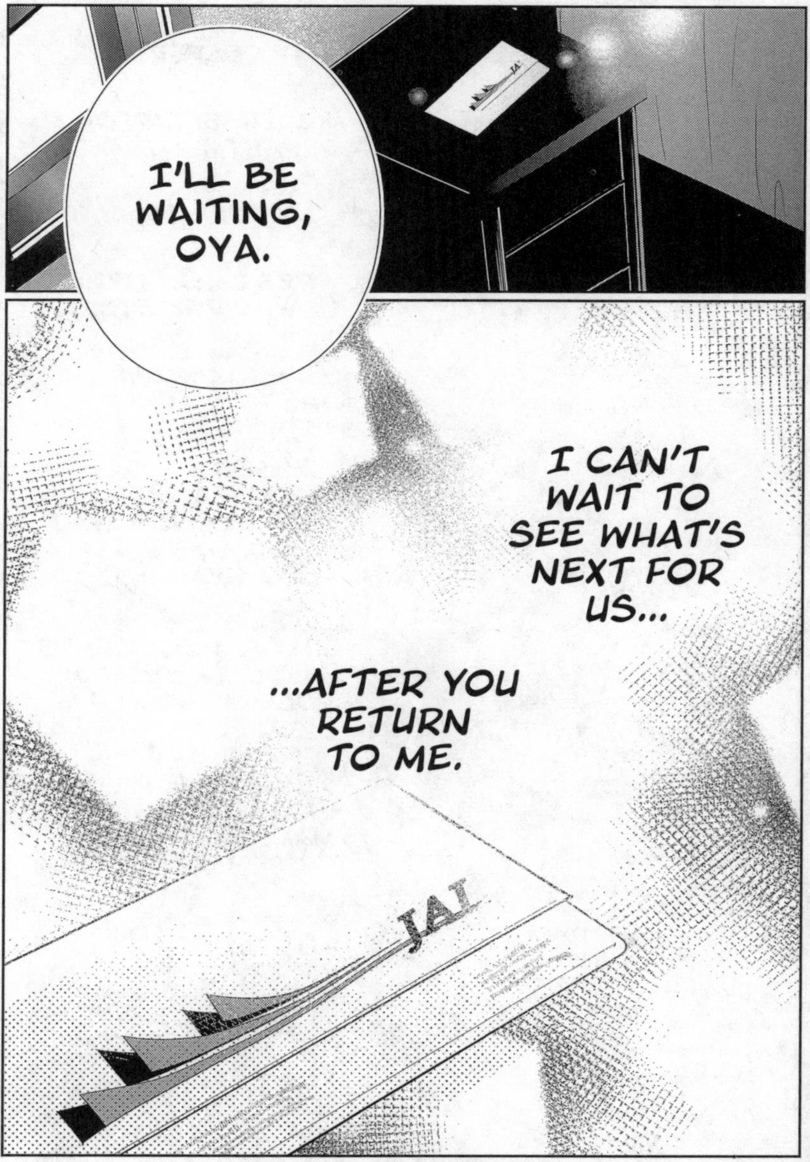
I'LL BE WAITING, OYA.
I CAN'T WAIT TO SEE WHAT'S NEXT FOR US...
...AFTER YOU RETURN TO ME.
JAL

bullet 03 special episode/end
Appeared in June 2019 issue of *Cheese!*

Special Thanks

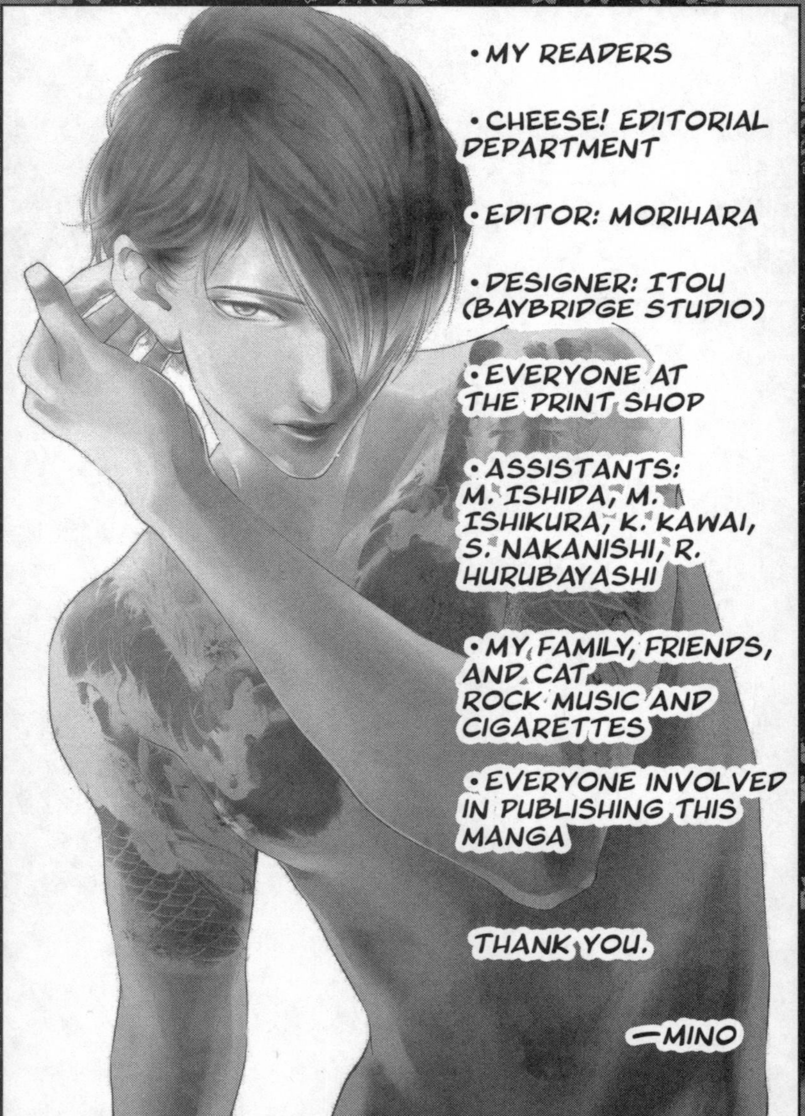

• MY READERS

• CHEESE! EDITORIAL DEPARTMENT

• EDITOR: MORIHARA

• DESIGNER: ITOU (BAYBRIDGE STUDIO)

• EVERYONE AT THE PRINT SHOP

• ASSISTANTS: M. ISHIDA, M. ISHIKURA, K. KAWAI, S. NAKANISHI, R. HURUBAYASHI

• MY FAMILY, FRIENDS, AND CAT
ROCK MUSIC AND CIGARETTES

• EVERYONE INVOLVED IN PUBLISHING THIS MANGA

THANK YOU.

—MINO

bullet 08
special episode

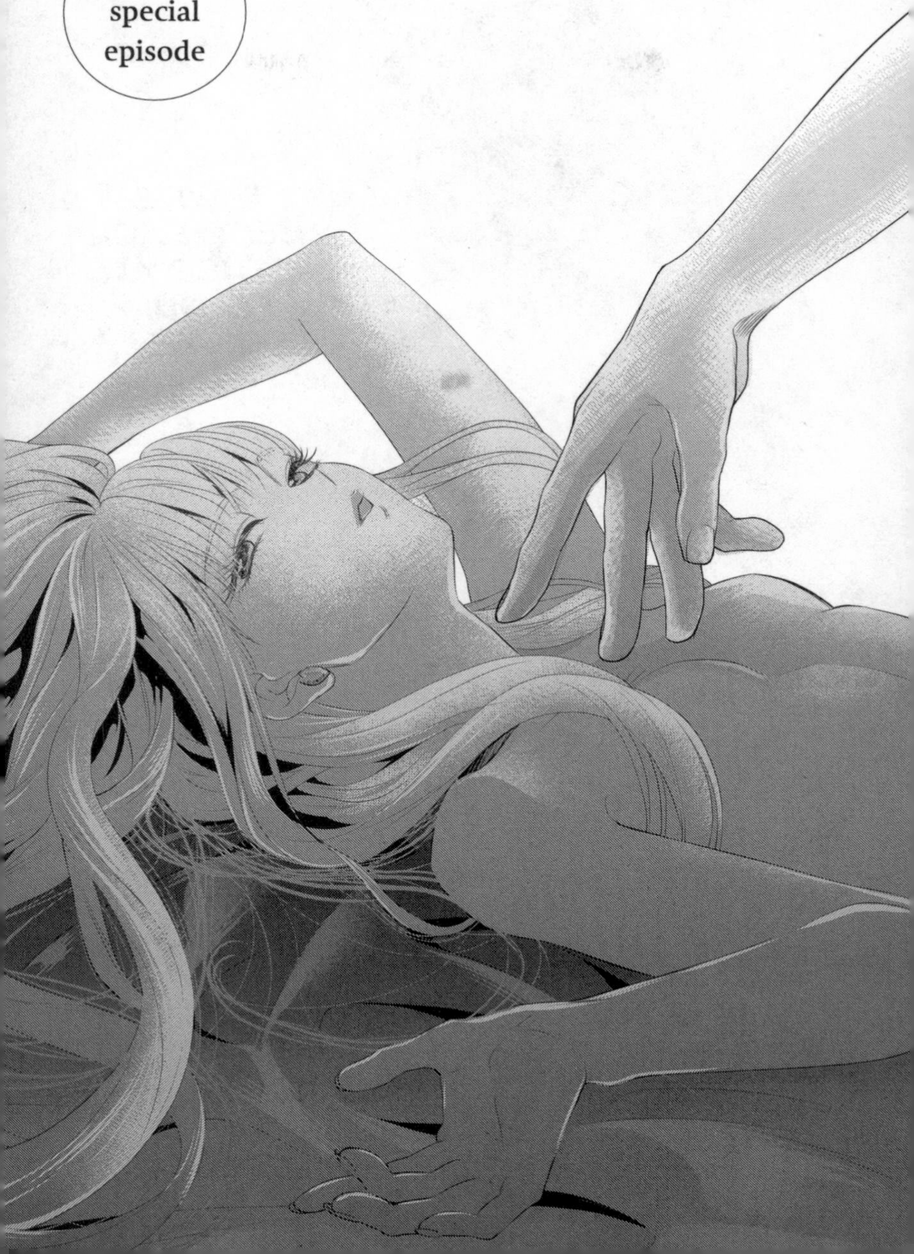

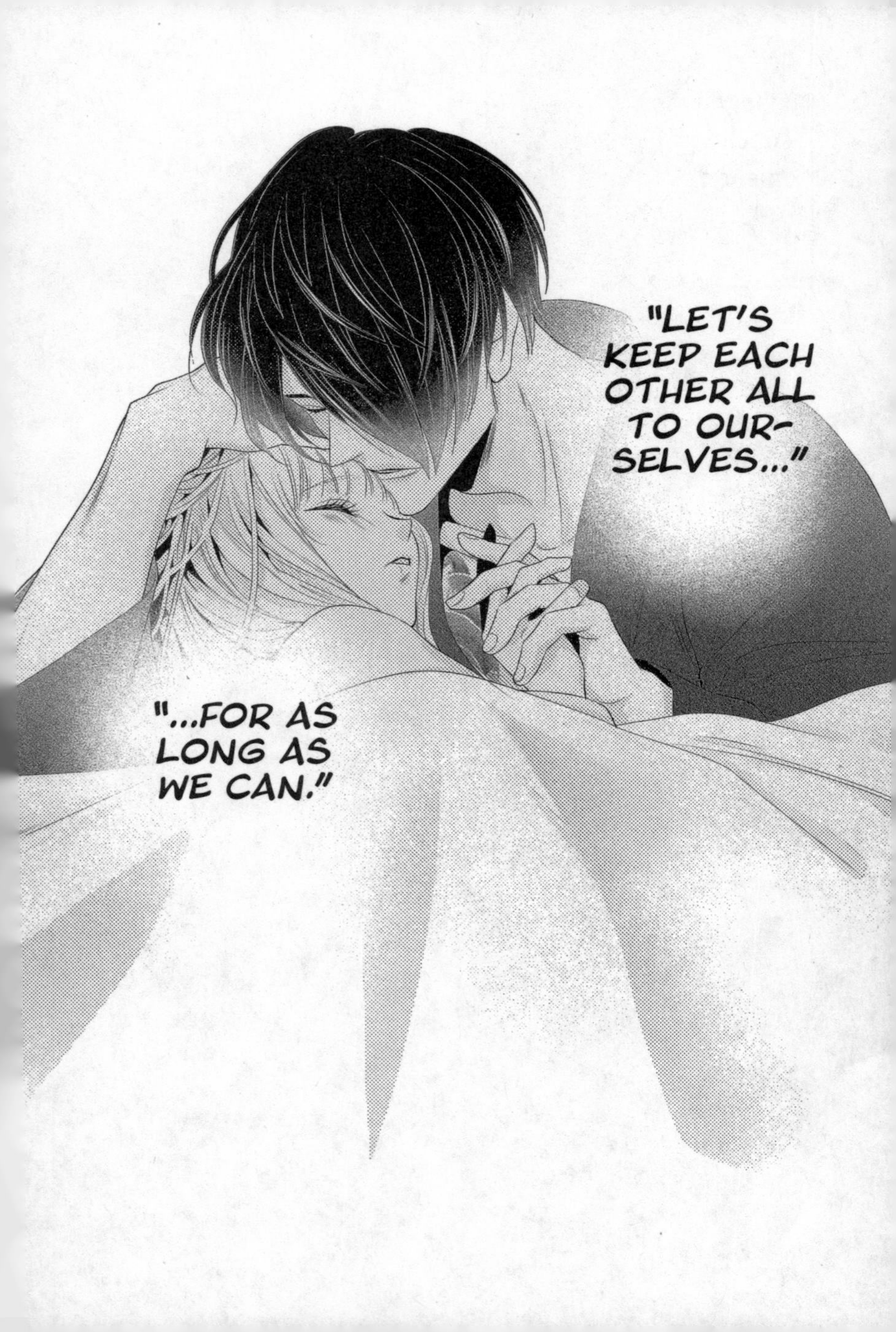
"LET'S KEEP EACH OTHER ALL TO OUR-SELVES..."
"...FOR AS LONG AS WE CAN."

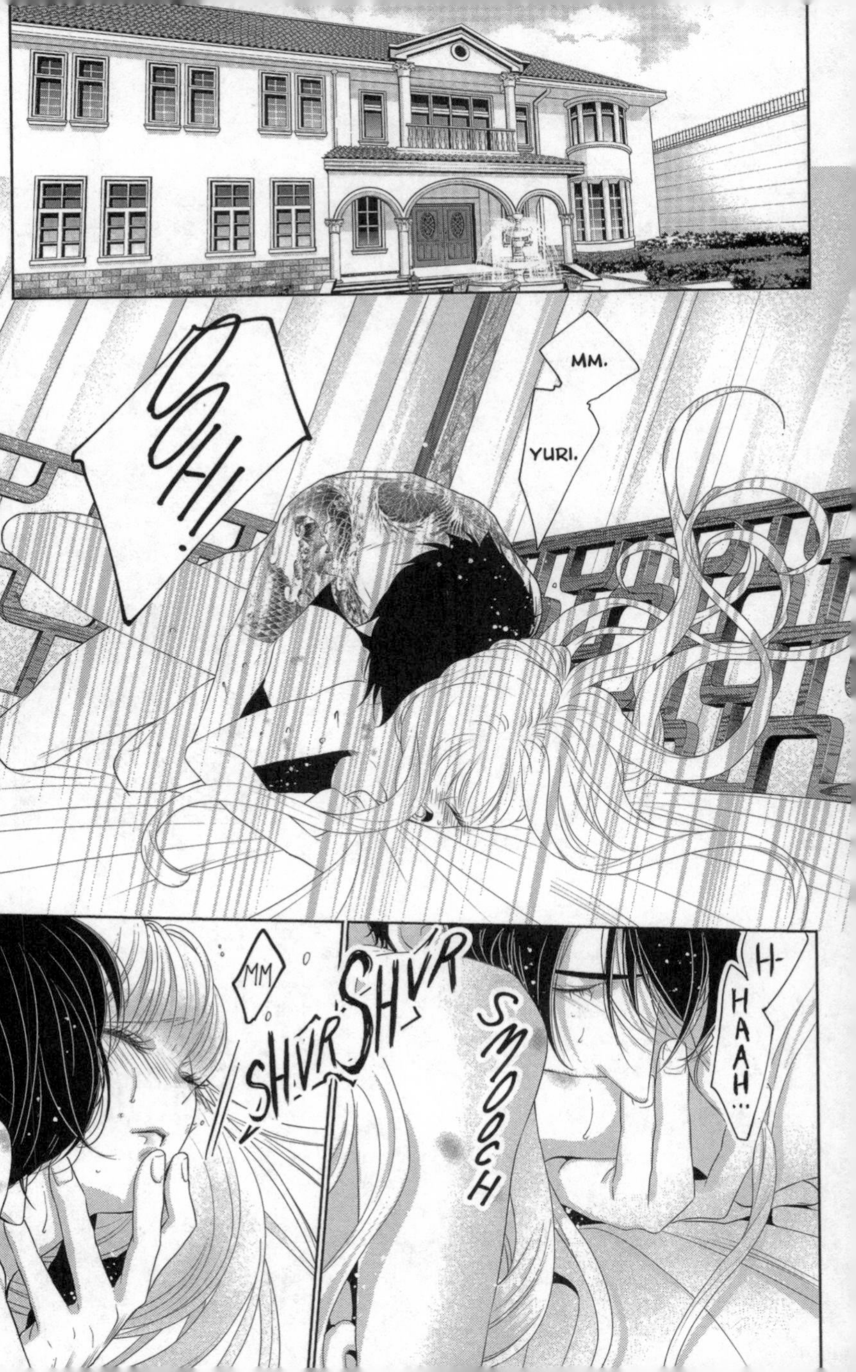
MM.
YURI.
OOH!!
H-HAAH...
SMOOOCH
SHVR SHVR
SHVR
MM

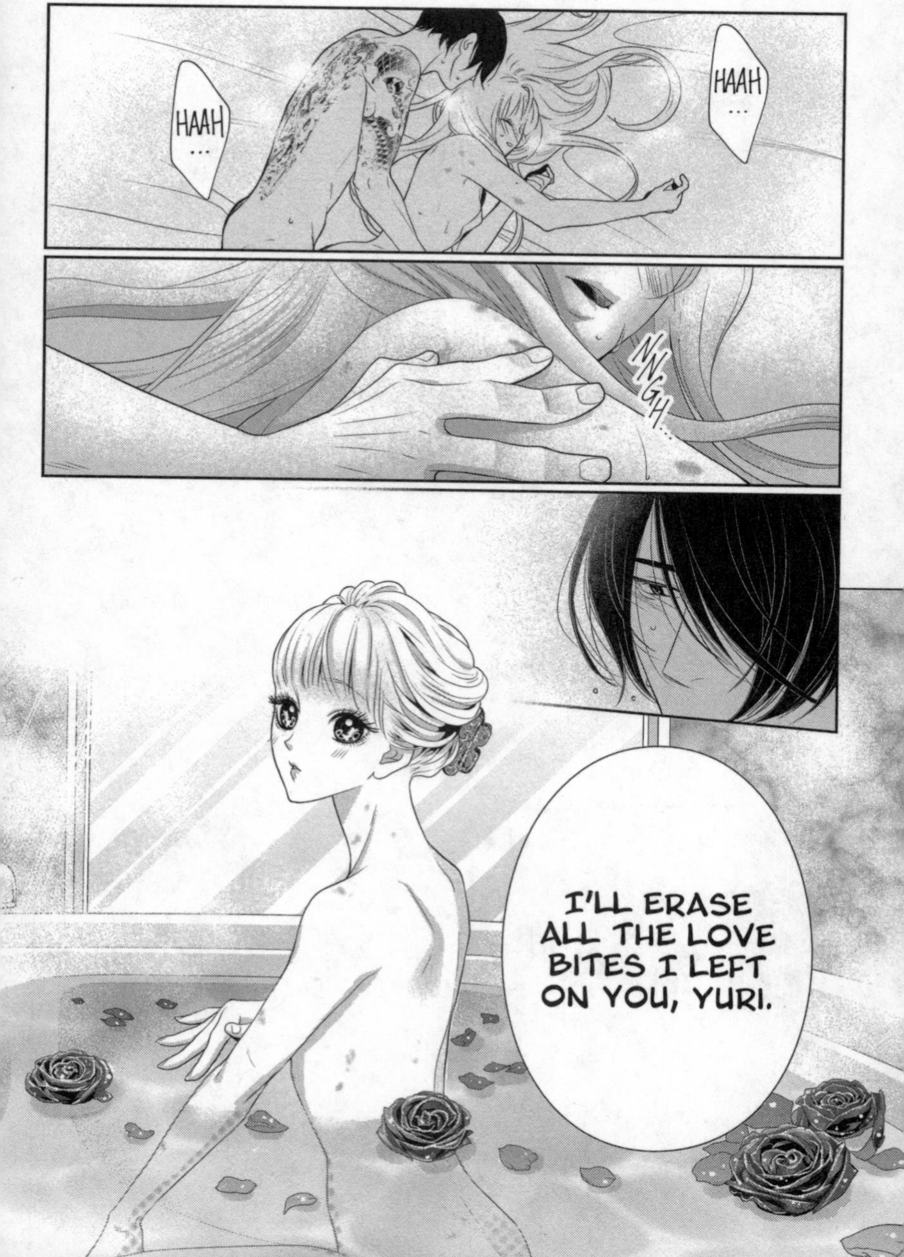
HAAH...
HAAH...
NNGH...
I'LL ERASE ALL THE LOVE BITES I LEFT ON YOU, YURI.

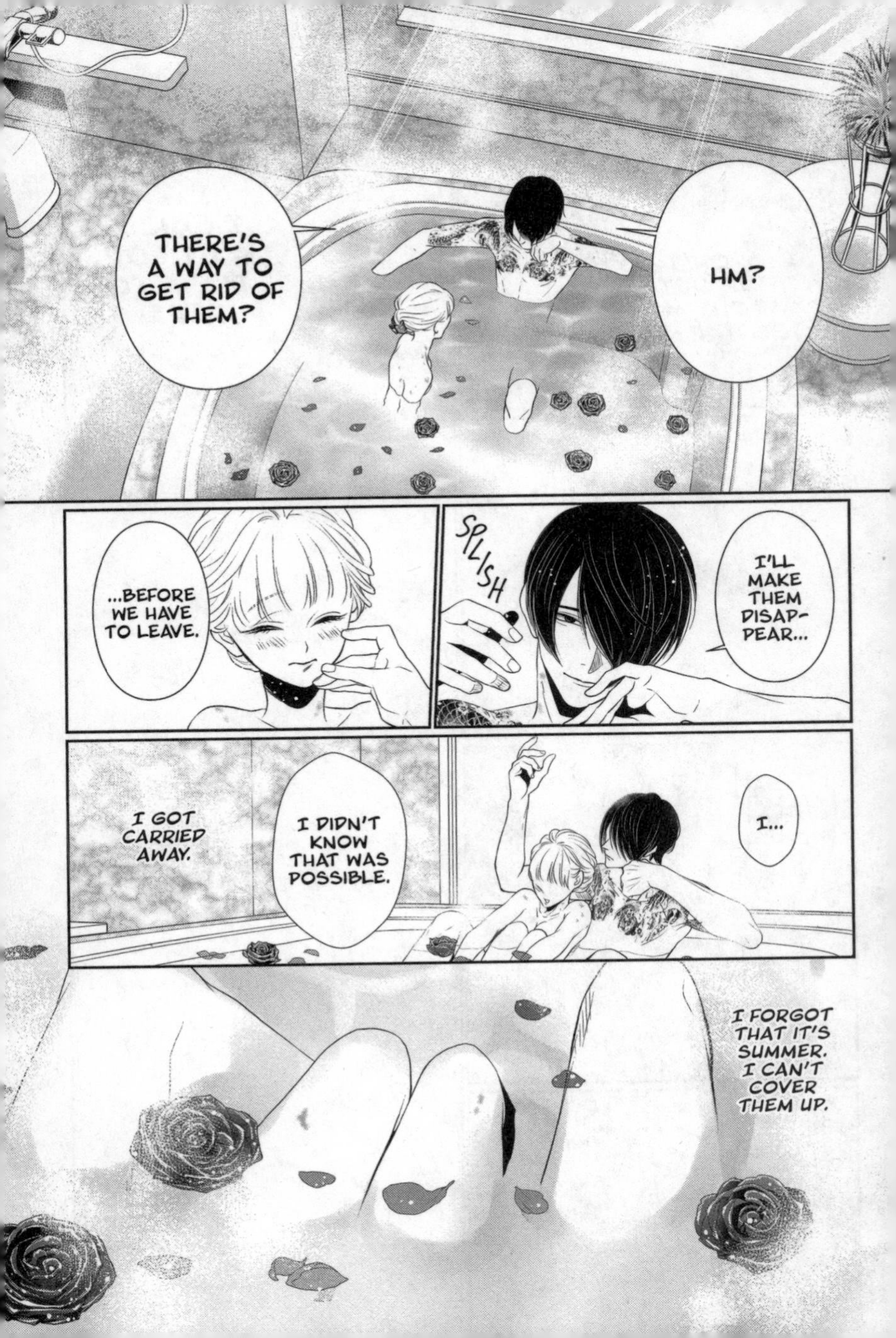
HM?
THERE'S A WAY TO GET RID OF THEM?
SPLISH
I'LL MAKE THEM DISAP-PEAR...
...BEFORE WE HAVE TO LEAVE.
I...
I DIDN'T KNOW THAT WAS POSSIBLE.
I GOT CARRIED AWAY.
I FORGOT THAT IT'S SUMMER. I CAN'T COVER THEM UP.

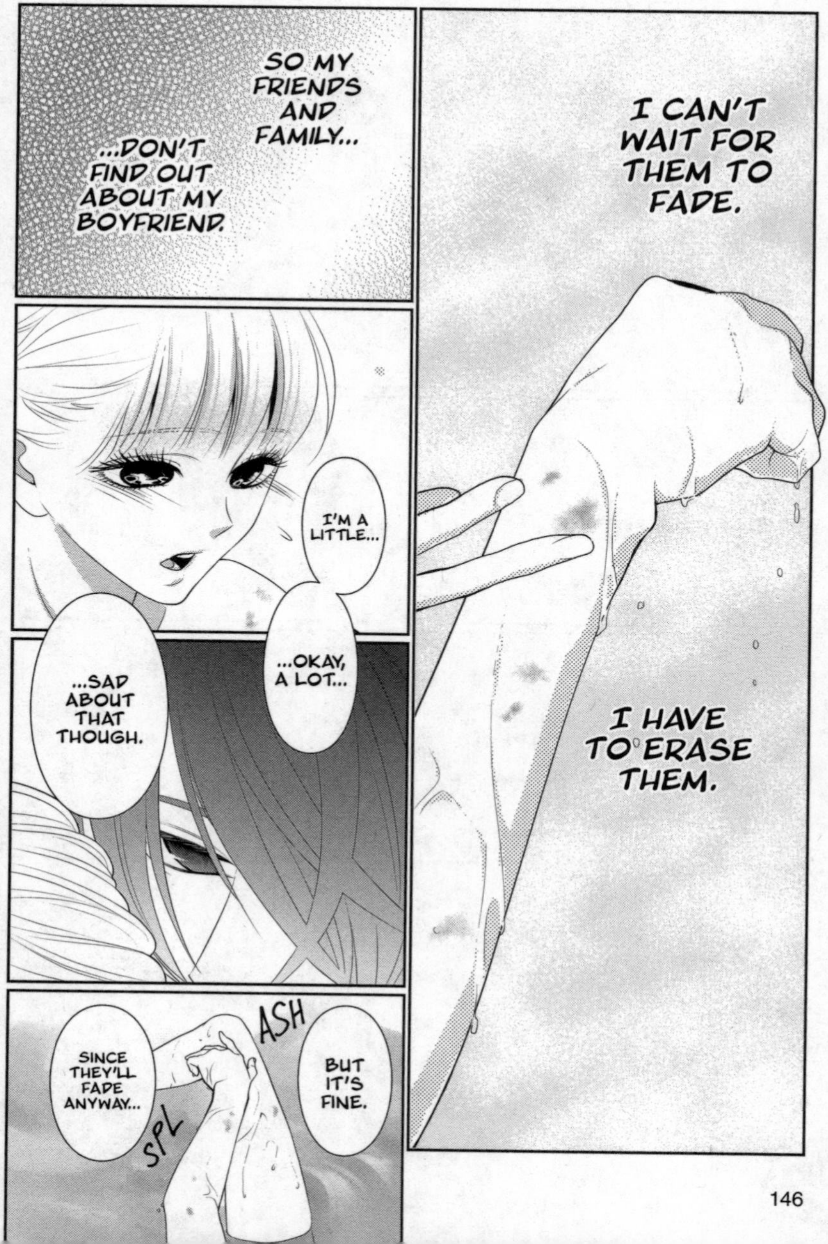
I CAN'T WAIT FOR THEM TO FADE.
I HAVE TO ERASE THEM.
SO MY FRIENDS AND FAMILY...
...DON'T FIND OUT ABOUT MY BOYFRIEND.
I'M A LITTLE...
...OKAY, A LOT...
...SAD ABOUT THAT THOUGH.
ASH
BUT IT'S FINE.
SINCE THEY'LL FADE ANYWAY...
SPL

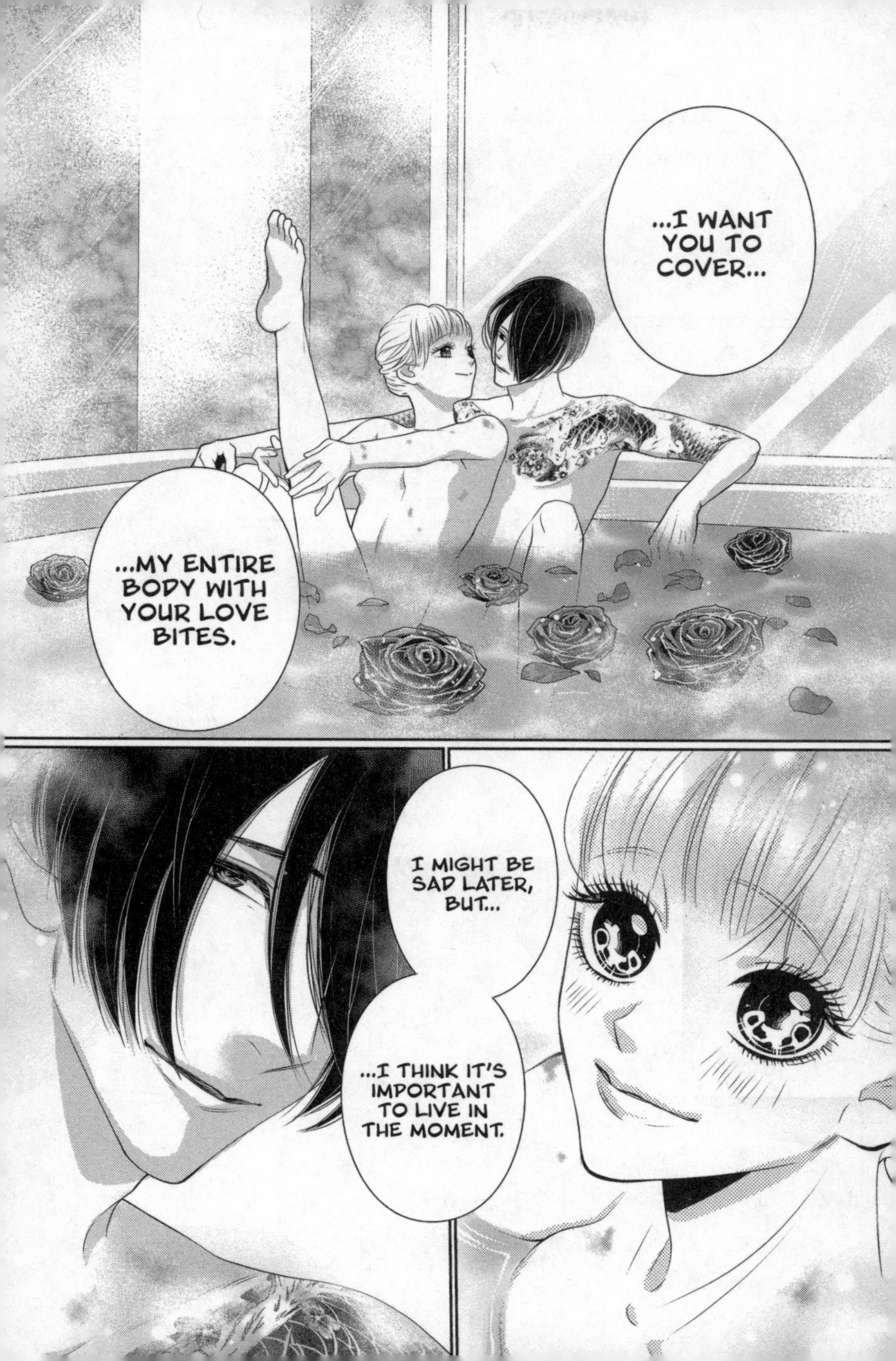
...I WANT YOU TO COVER...
...MY ENTIRE BODY WITH YOUR LOVE BITES.
I MIGHT BE SAD LATER, BUT...
...I THINK IT'S IMPORTANT TO LIVE IN THE MOMENT.

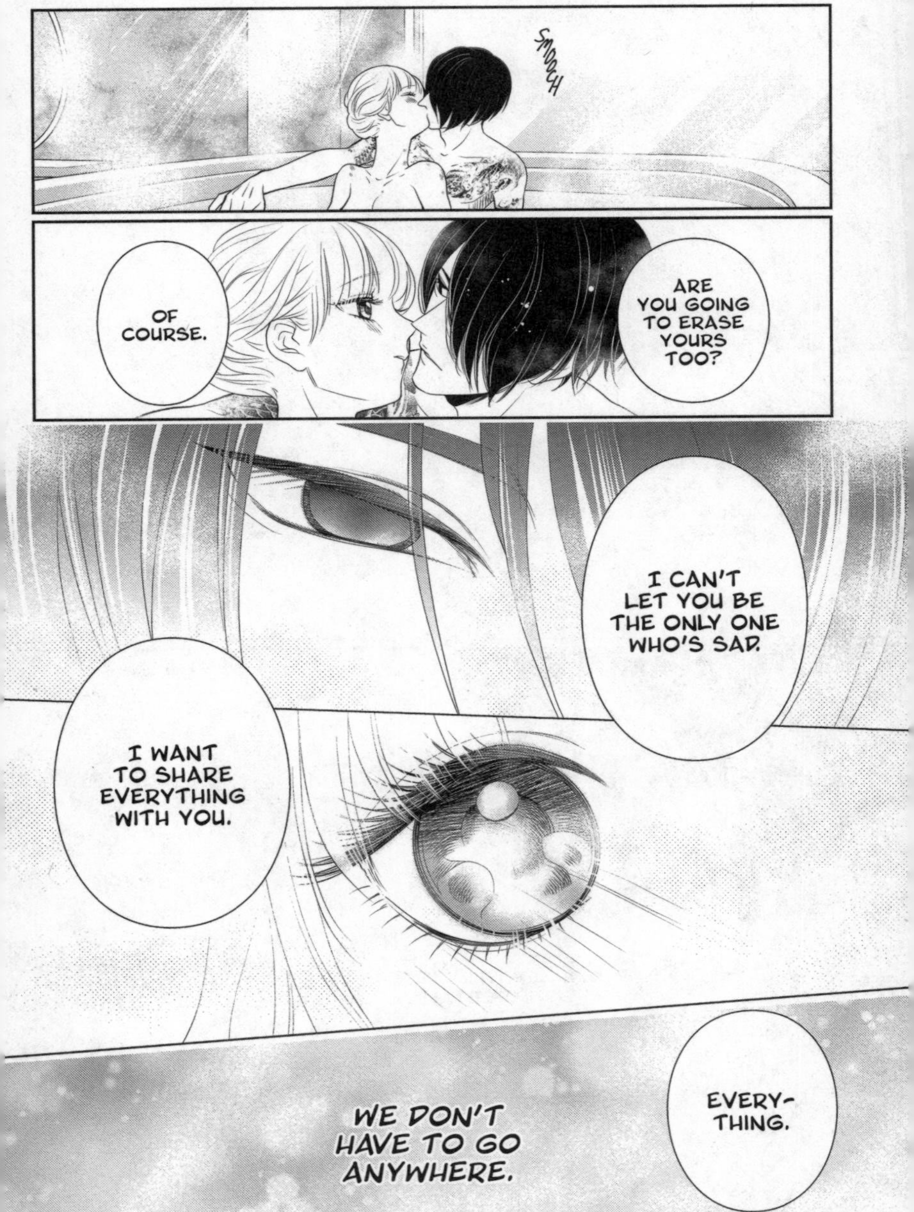
SMOOCH
ARE YOU GOING TO ERASE YOURS TOO?
OF COURSE.
I CAN'T LET YOU BE THE ONLY ONE WHO'S SAD.
I WANT TO SHARE EVERYTHING WITH YOU.
EVERY-THING.
WE DON'T HAVE TO GO ANYWHERE.

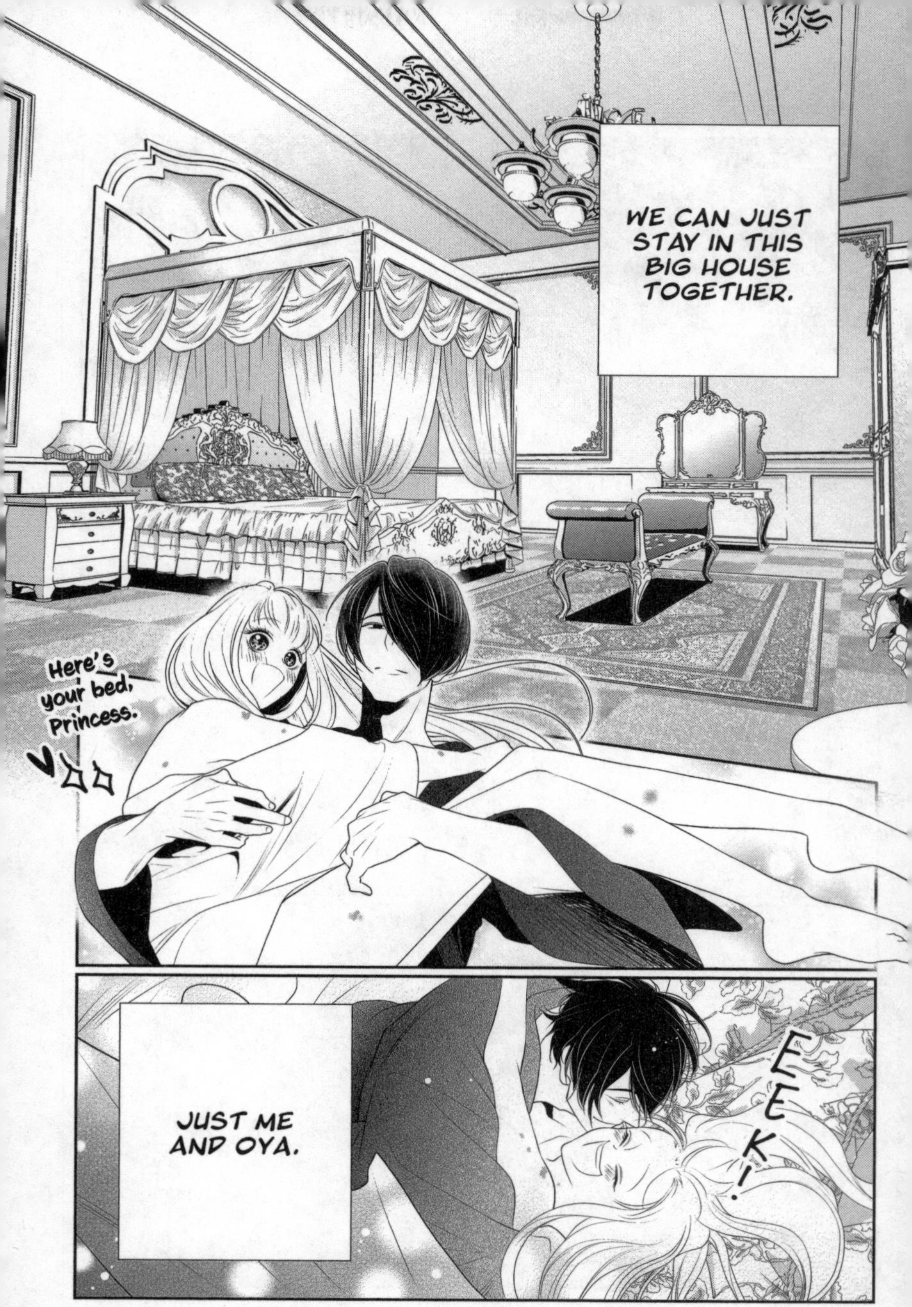
WE CAN JUST STAY IN THIS BIG HOUSE TOGETHER.
Here's your bed, Princess.
JUST ME AND OYA.
EEEK!

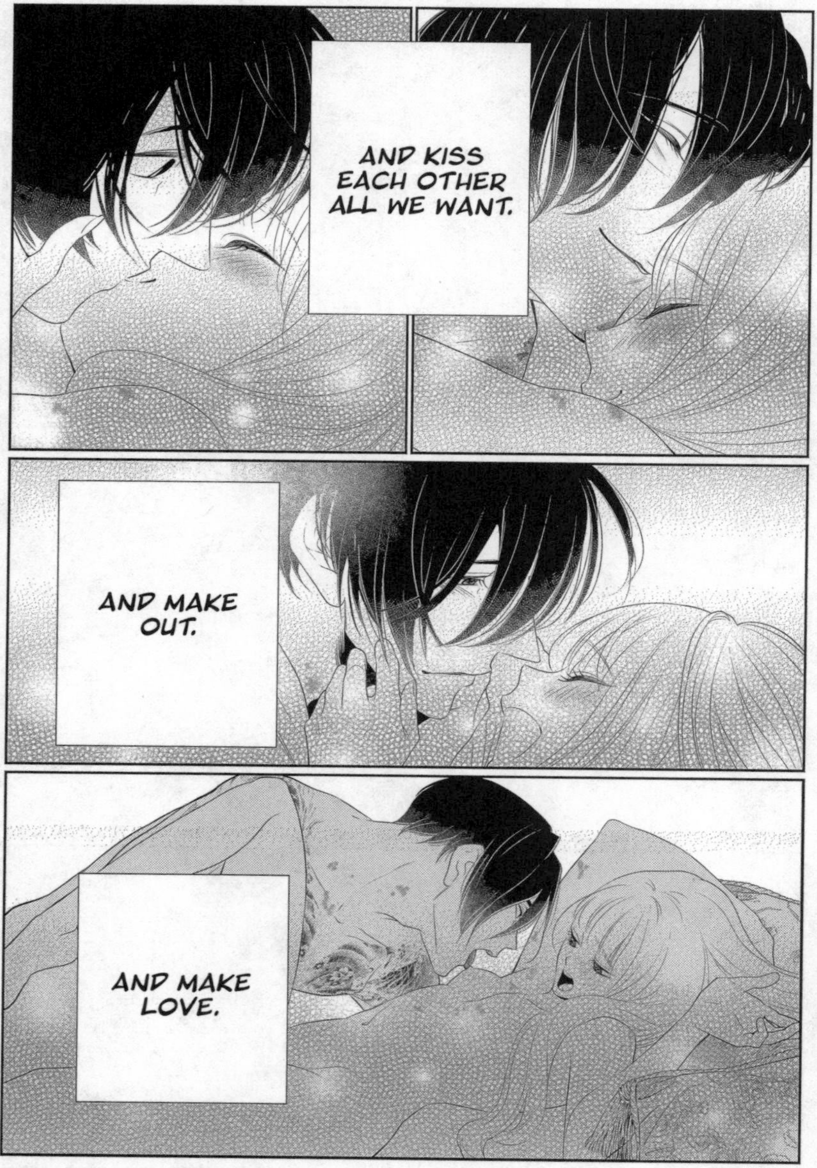
AND KISS EACH OTHER ALL WE WANT.
AND MAKE OUT.
AND MAKE LOVE.

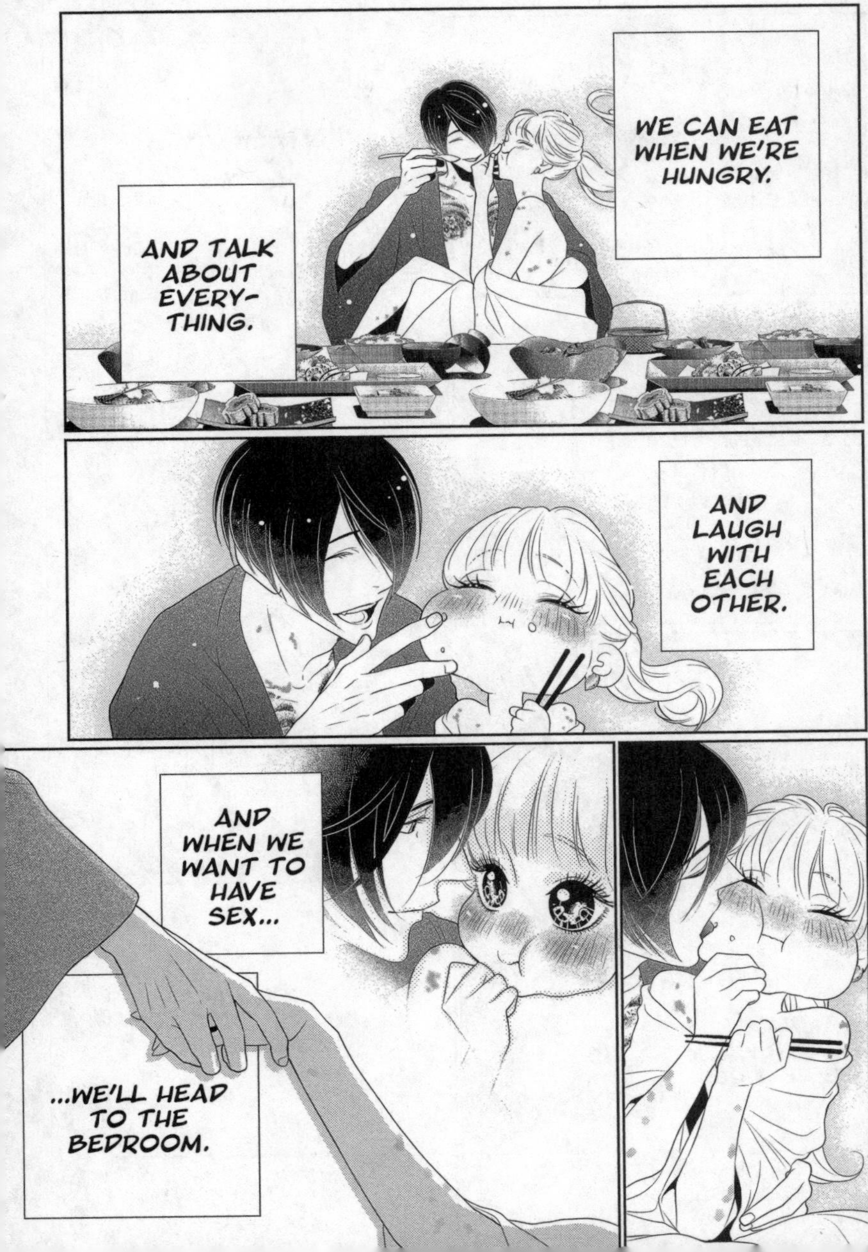
WE CAN EAT WHEN WE'RE HUNGRY.
AND TALK ABOUT EVERY-THING.
AND LAUGH WITH EACH OTHER.
AND WHEN WE WANT TO HAVE SEX...
...WE'LL HEAD TO THE BEDROOM.

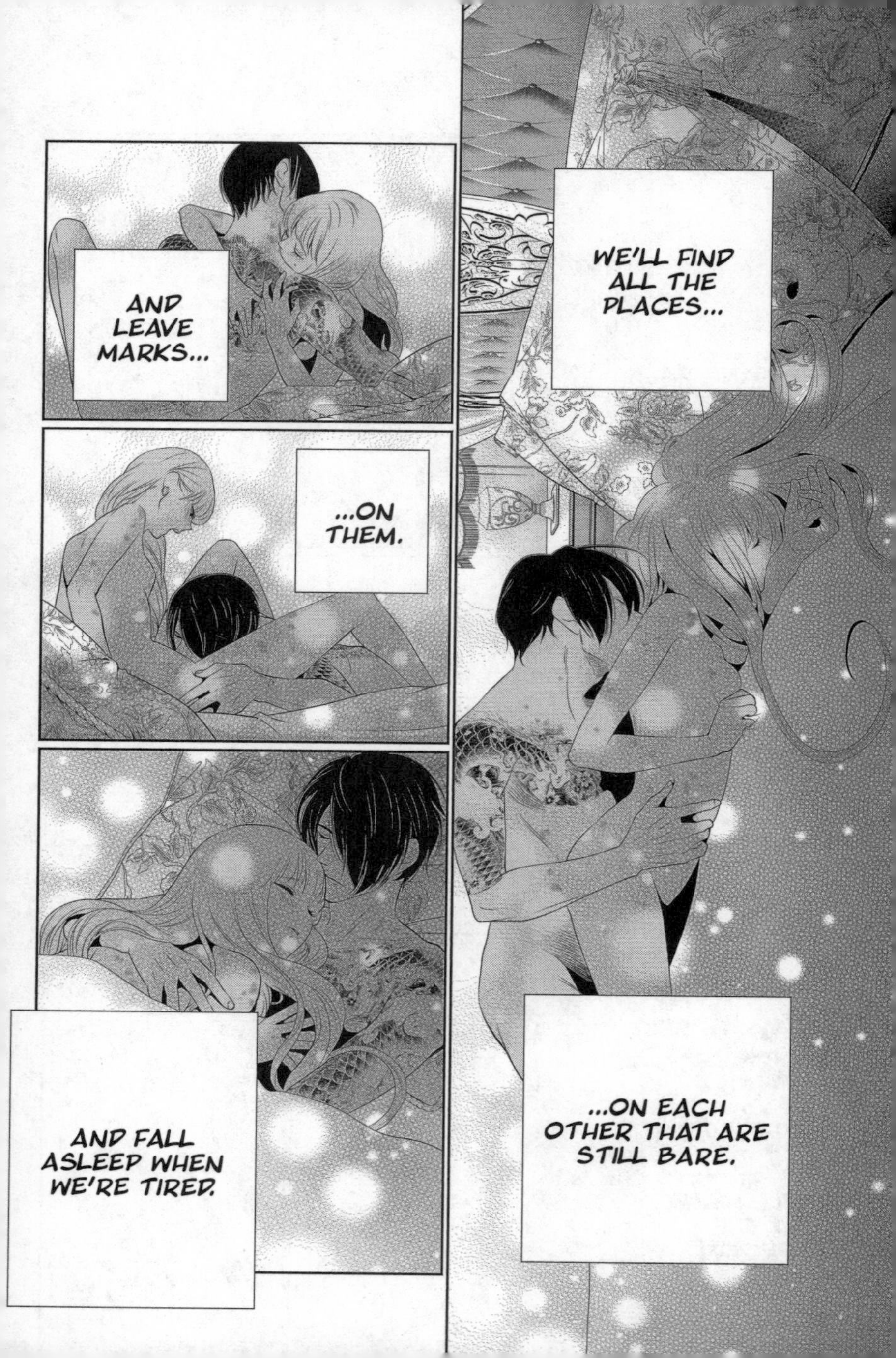
WE'LL FIND ALL THE PLACES...
...ON EACH OTHER THAT ARE STILL BARE.
AND LEAVE MARKS...
...ON THEM.
AND FALL ASLEEP WHEN WE'RE TIRED.

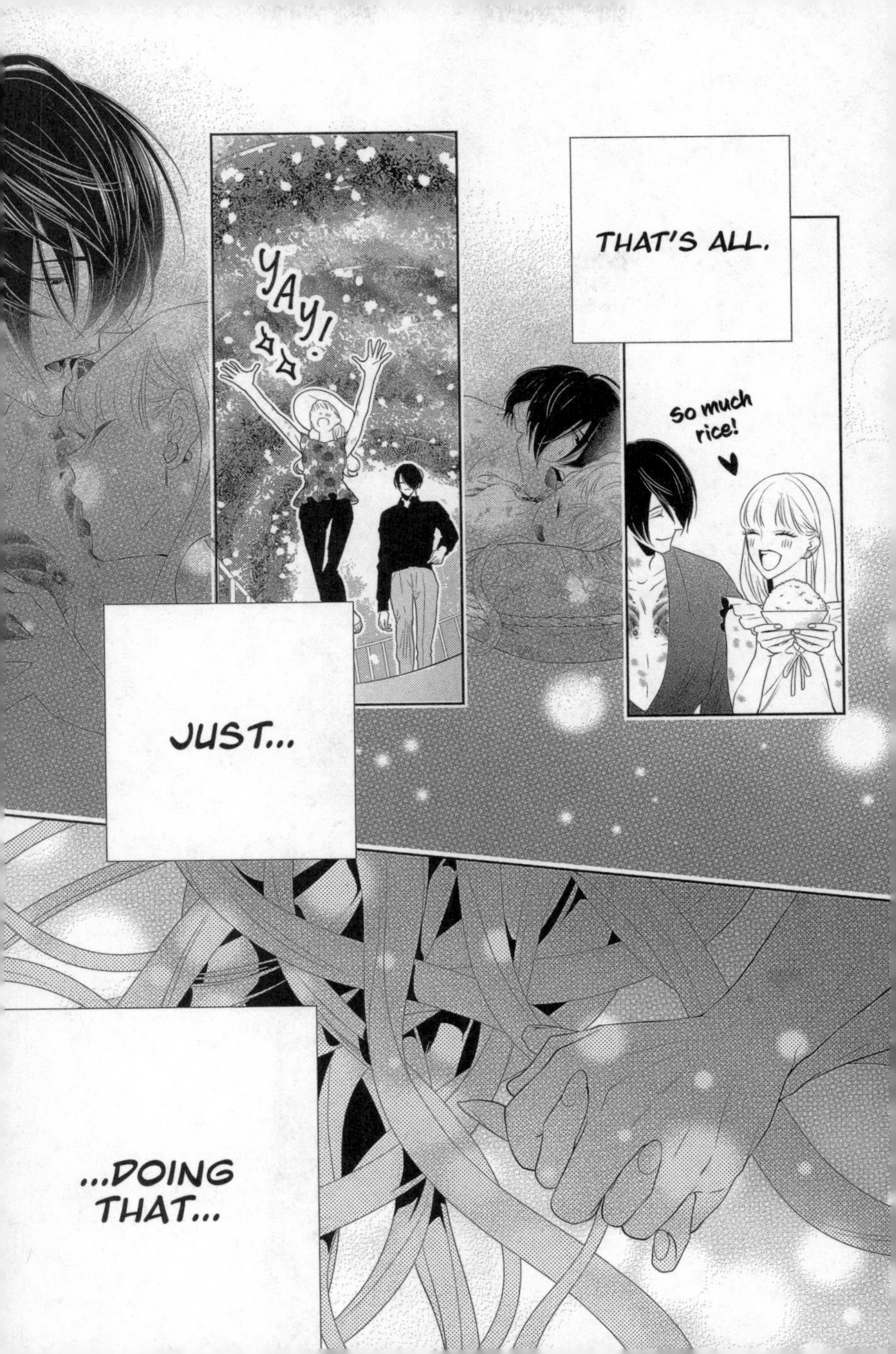
THAT'S ALL.
So much rice!
YAY!
JUST...
...DOING THAT...

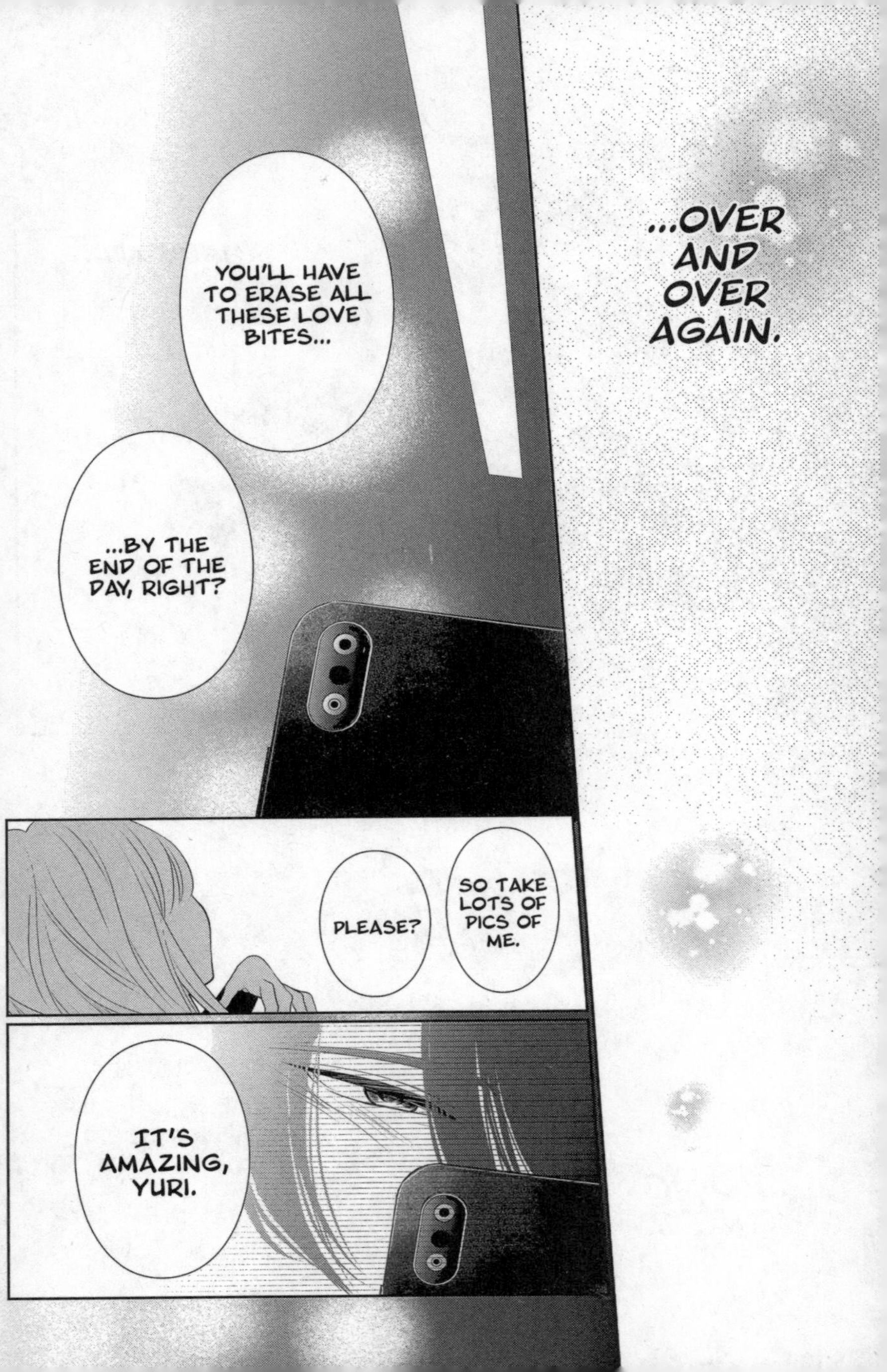
...OVER AND OVER AGAIN.
YOU'LL HAVE TO ERASE ALL THESE LOVE BITES...
...BY THE END OF THE DAY, RIGHT?
SO TAKE LOTS OF PICS OF ME.
PLEASE?
IT'S AMAZING, YURI.

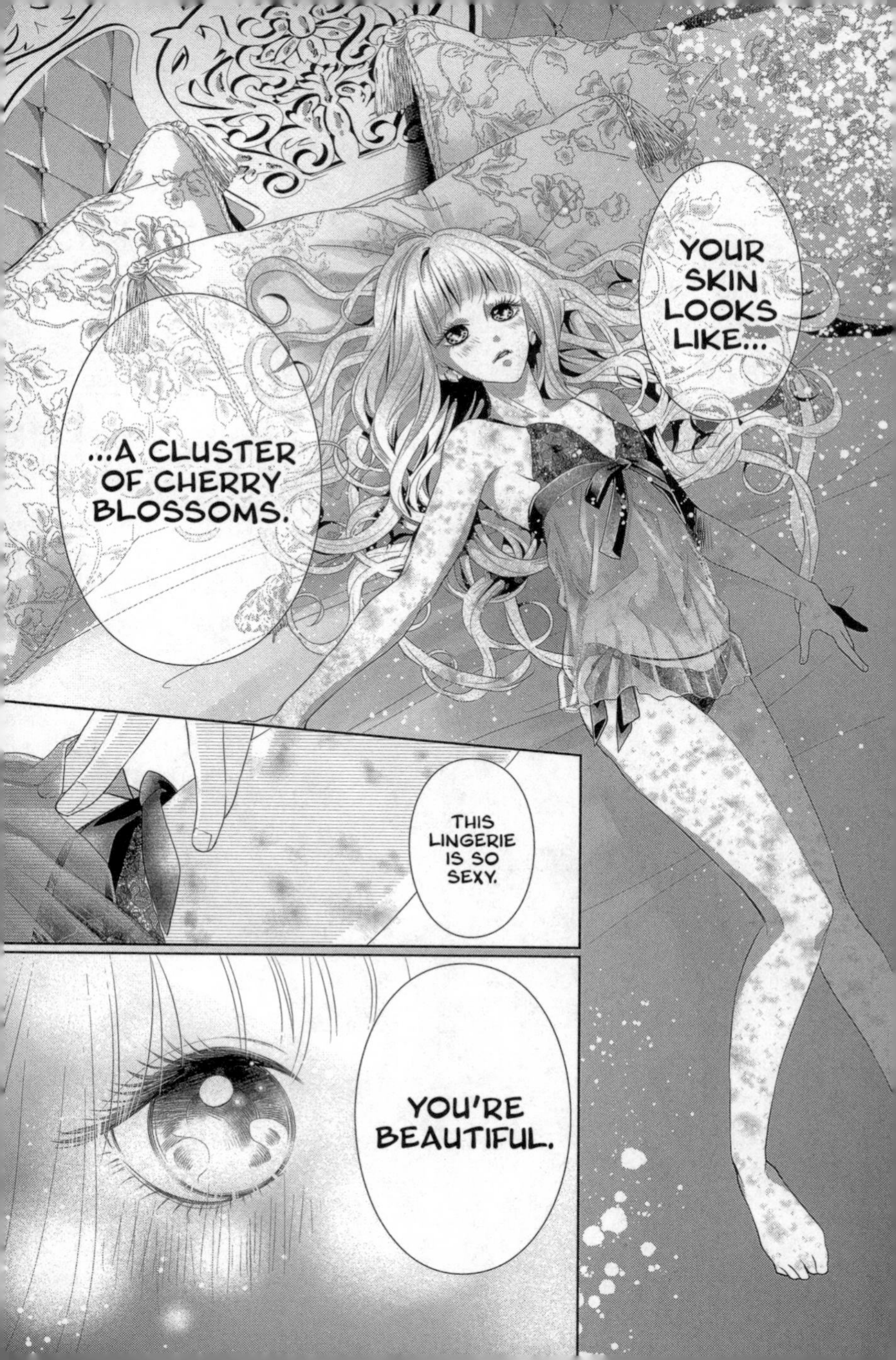
YOUR SKIN LOOKS LIKE...
...A CLUSTER OF CHERRY BLOSSOMS.
THIS LINGERIE IS SO SEXY.
YOU'RE BEAUTIFUL.

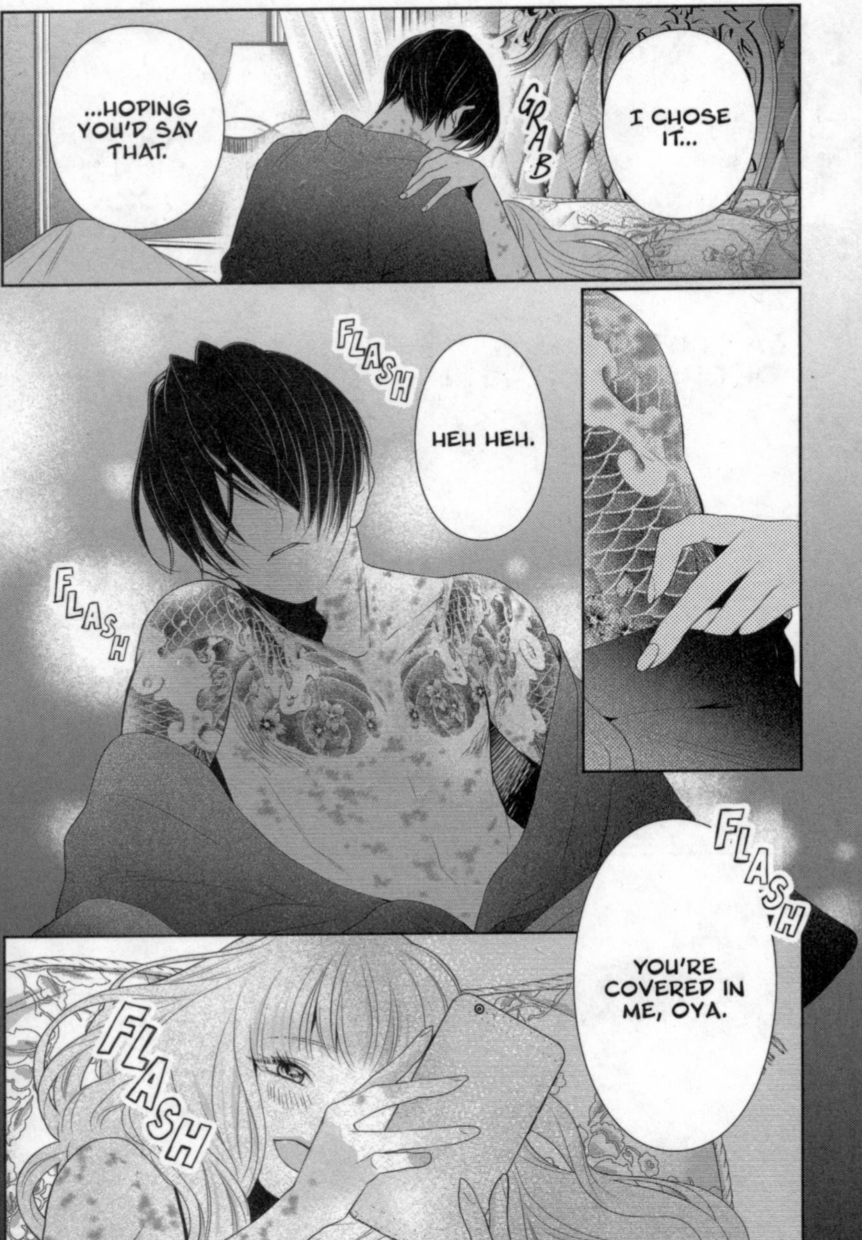
I CHOSE IT...
GRAB
...HOPING YOU'D SAY THAT.
FLASH
HEH HEH.
FLASH
FLASH
YOU'RE COVERED IN ME, OYA.
FLASH

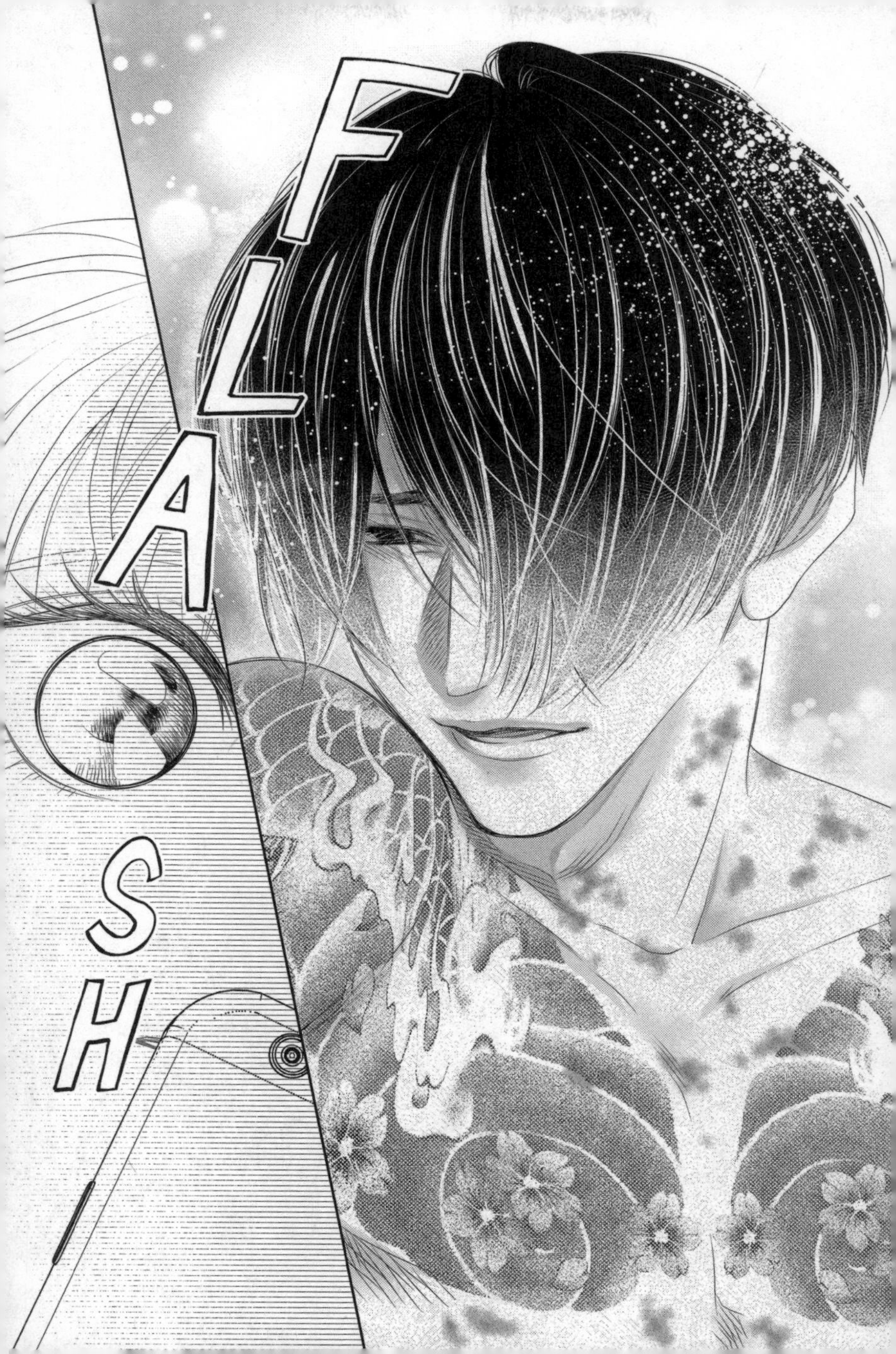
FLASH

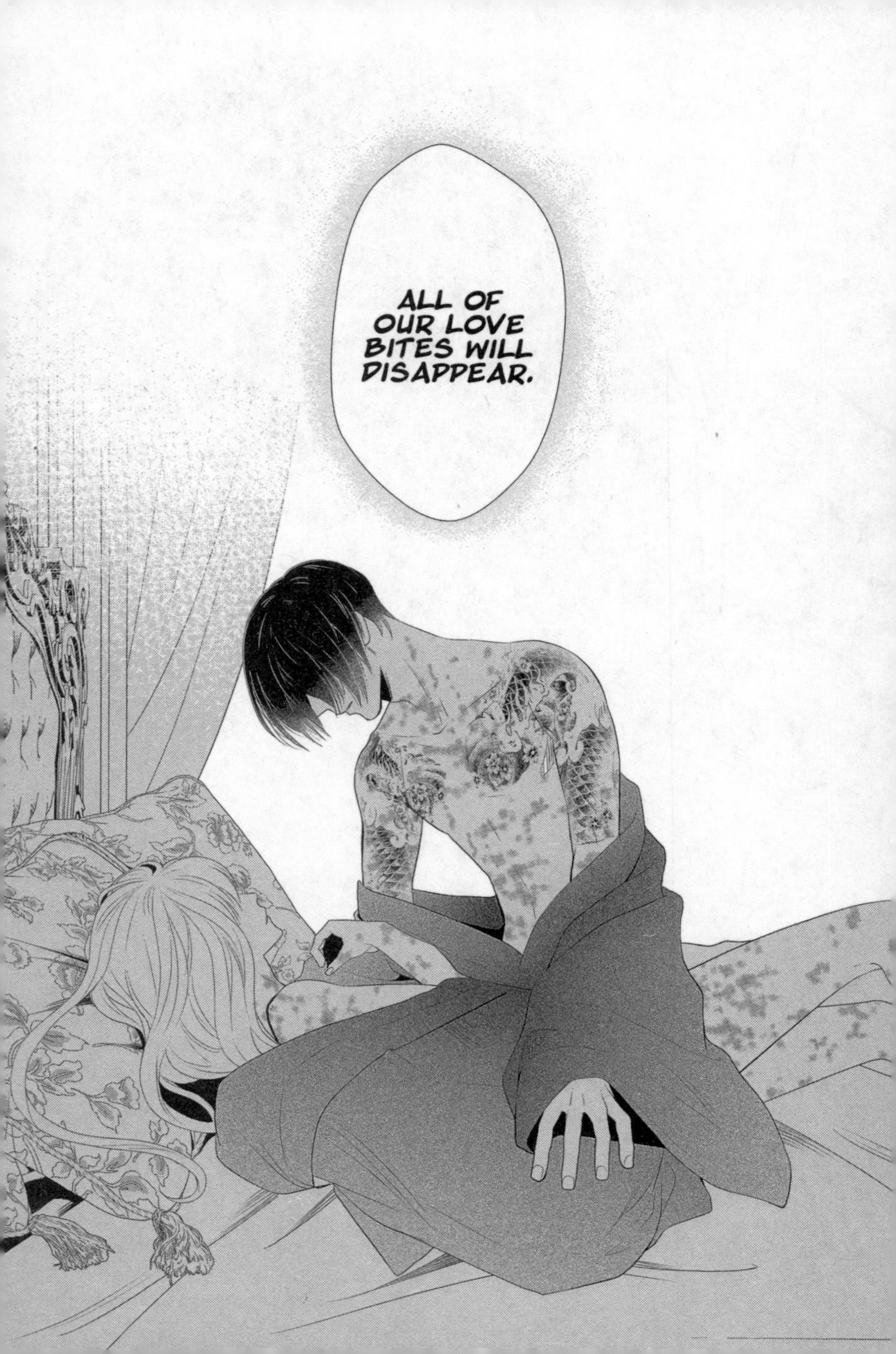
ALL OF OUR LOVE BITES WILL DISAPPEAR.

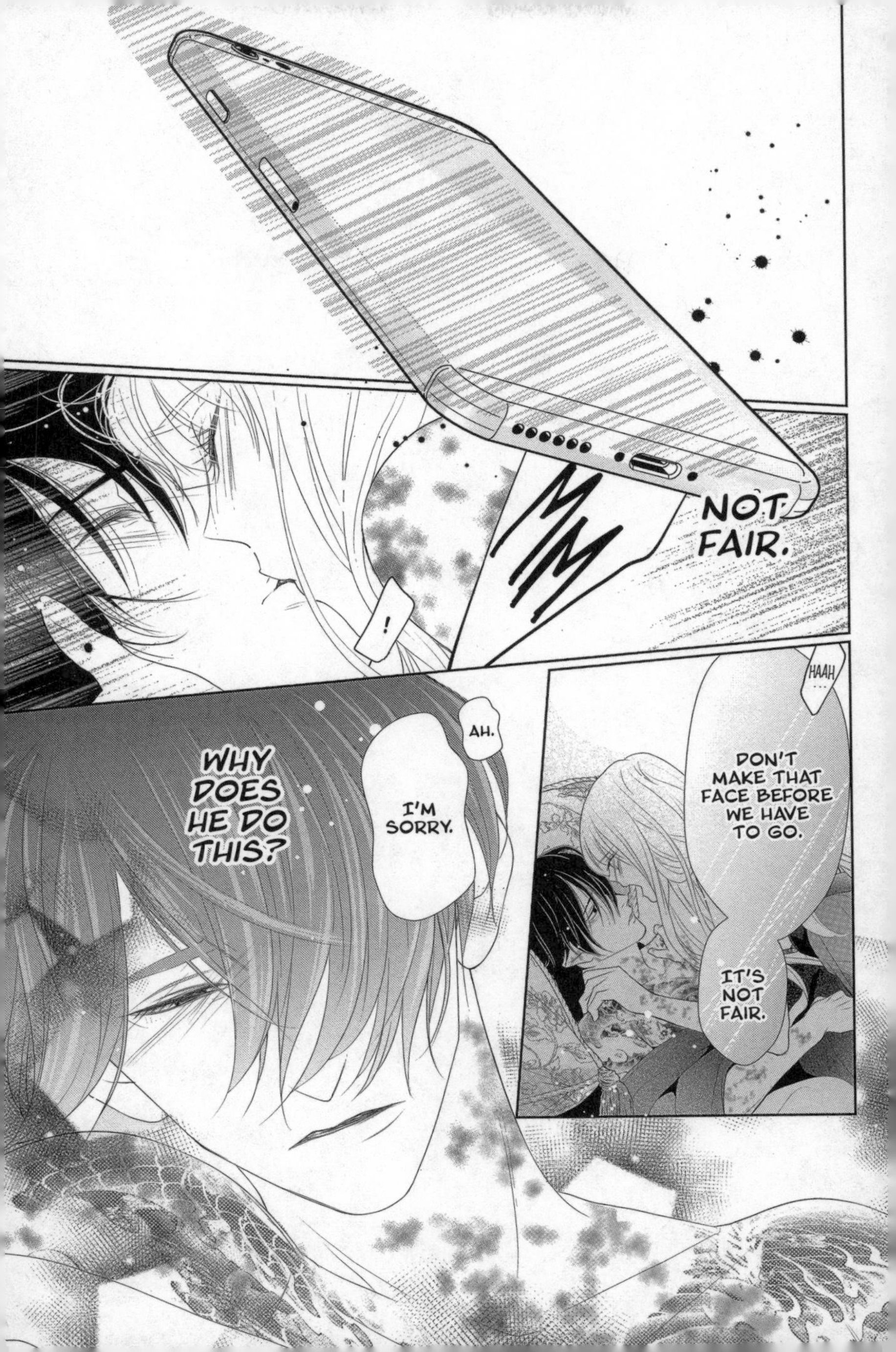
MM
NOT FAIR.
!
HAAH...
DON'T MAKE THAT FACE BEFORE WE HAVE TO GO.
IT'S NOT FAIR.
AH.
I'M SORRY.
WHY DOES HE DO THIS?

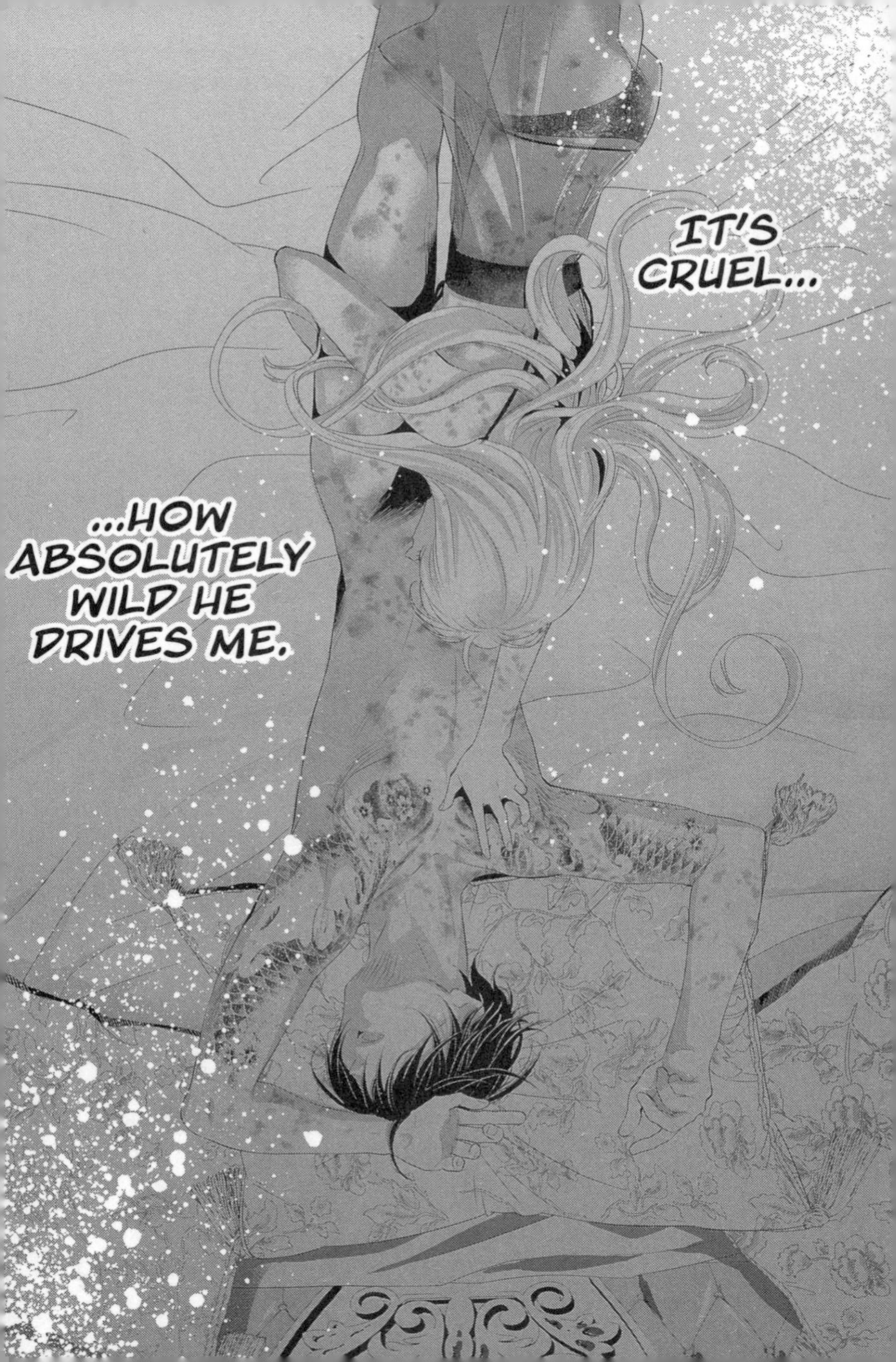
IT'S CRUEL...
...HOW ABSOLUTELY WILD HE DRIVES ME.

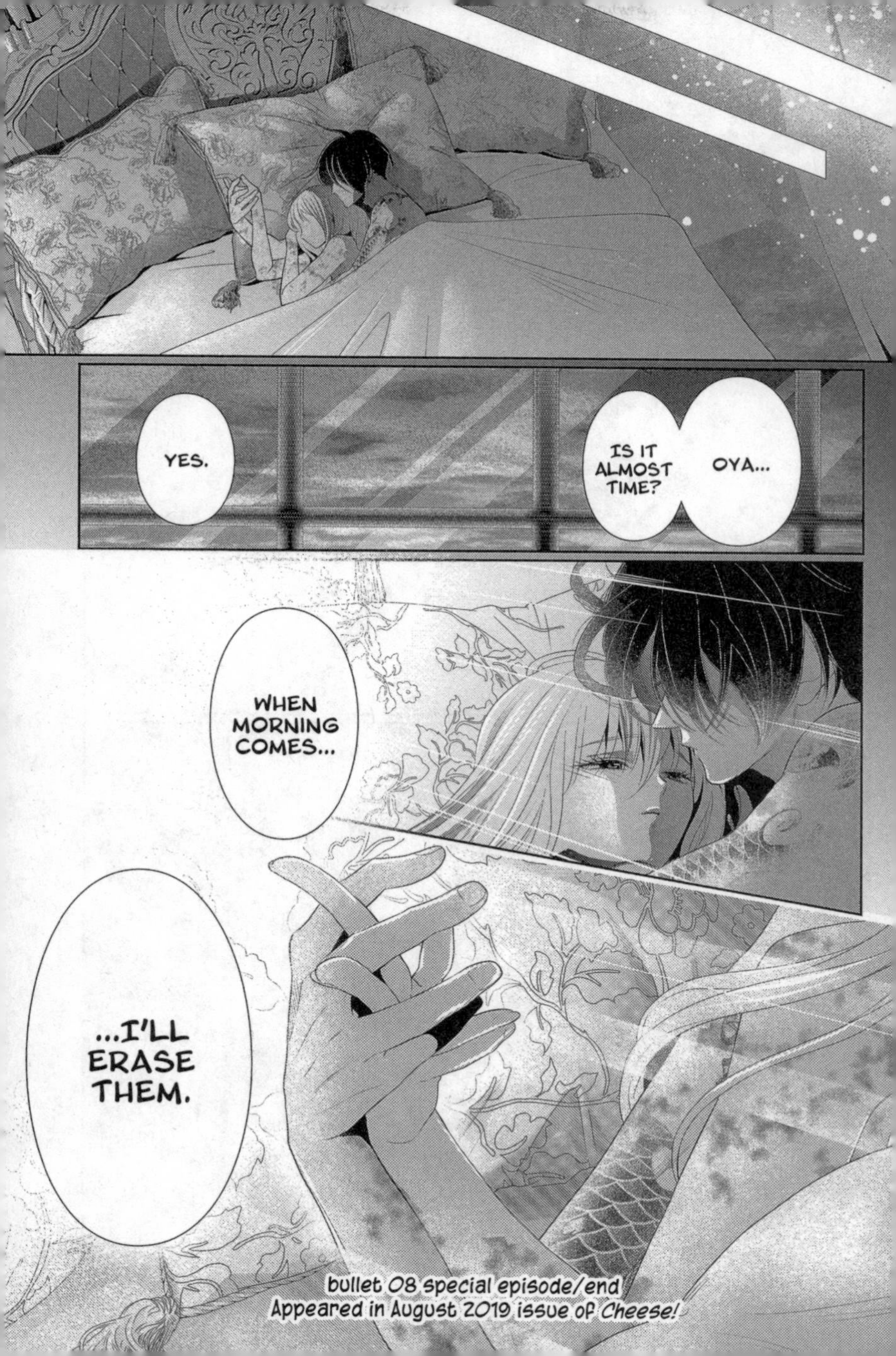
OYA...
IS IT ALMOST TIME?
YES.
WHEN MORNING COMES...
...I'LL ERASE THEM.

bullet 08 special episode/end
Appeared in August 2019 issue of *Cheese!*

bullet 09 secret scene: bonus Manga—Toshiomi Oya's Heart

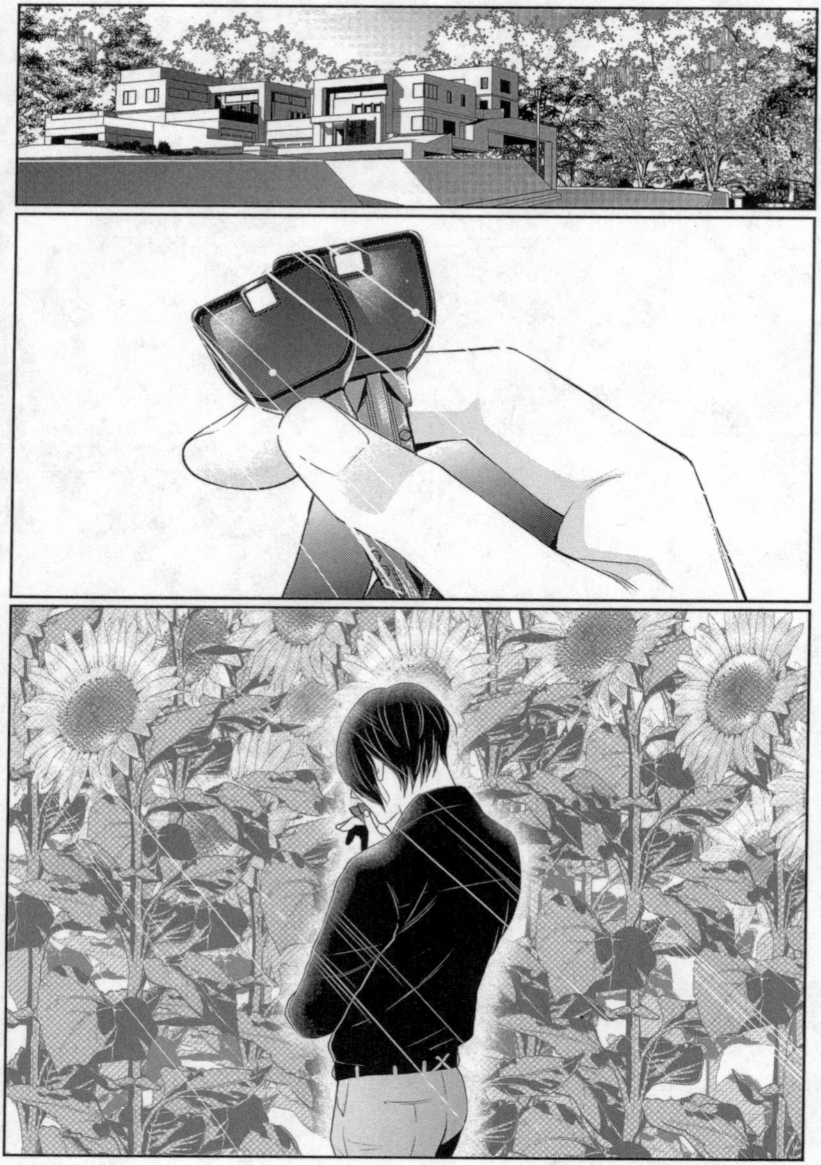

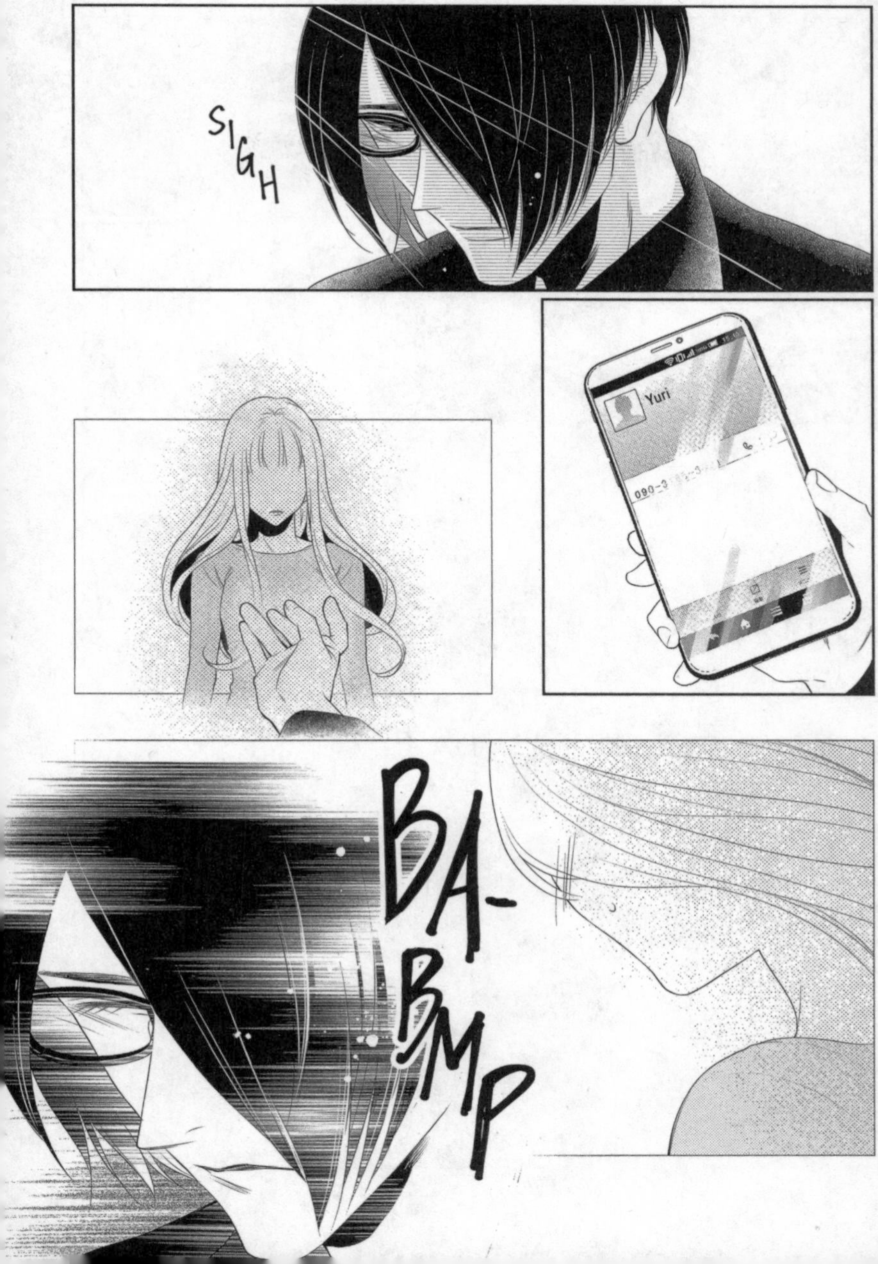
SIGH
Yuri
BA-BUMP

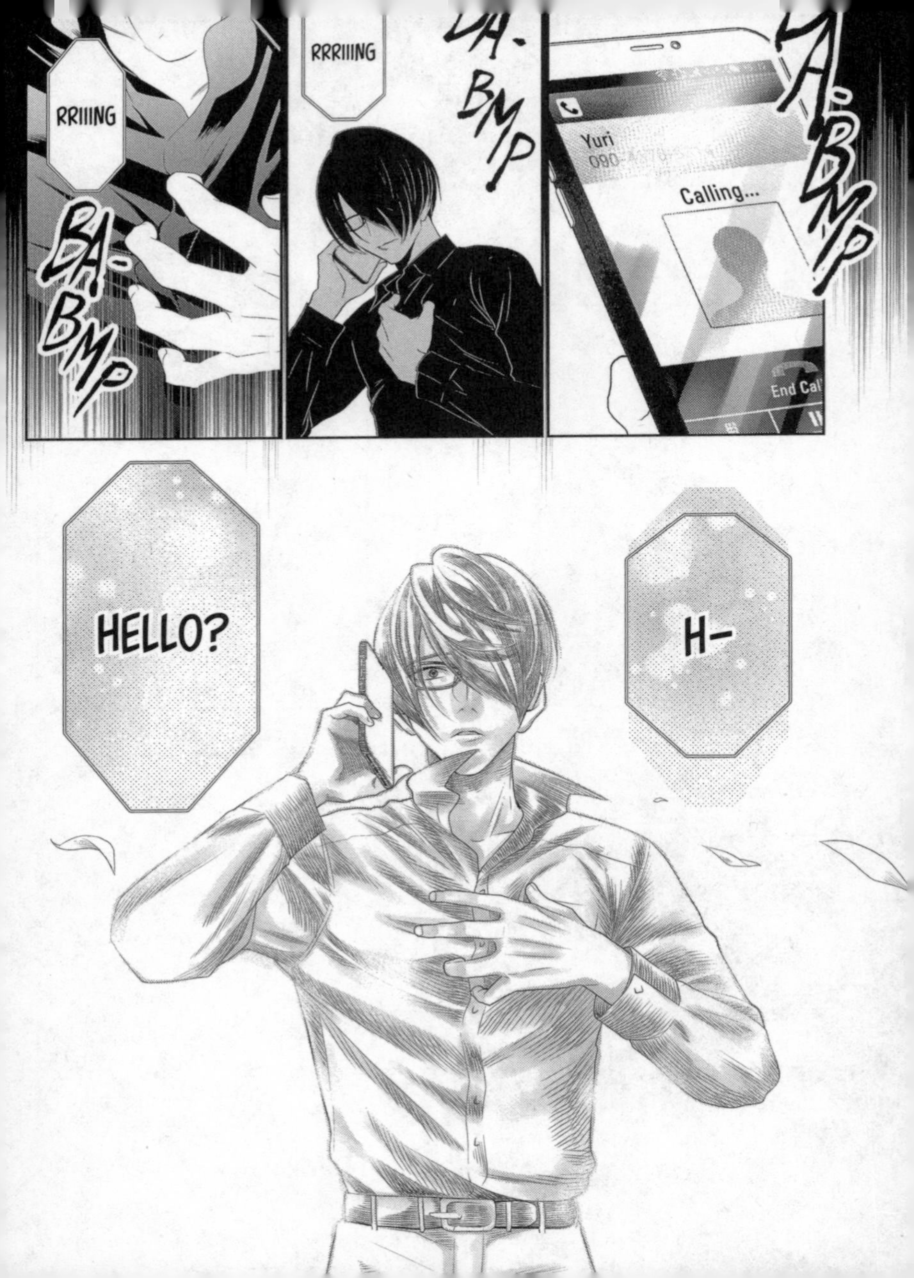

BA-BMP
Yuri
Calling...
RRRIIING
BA-BMP
RRIIING
BA-BMP
H-
HELLO?

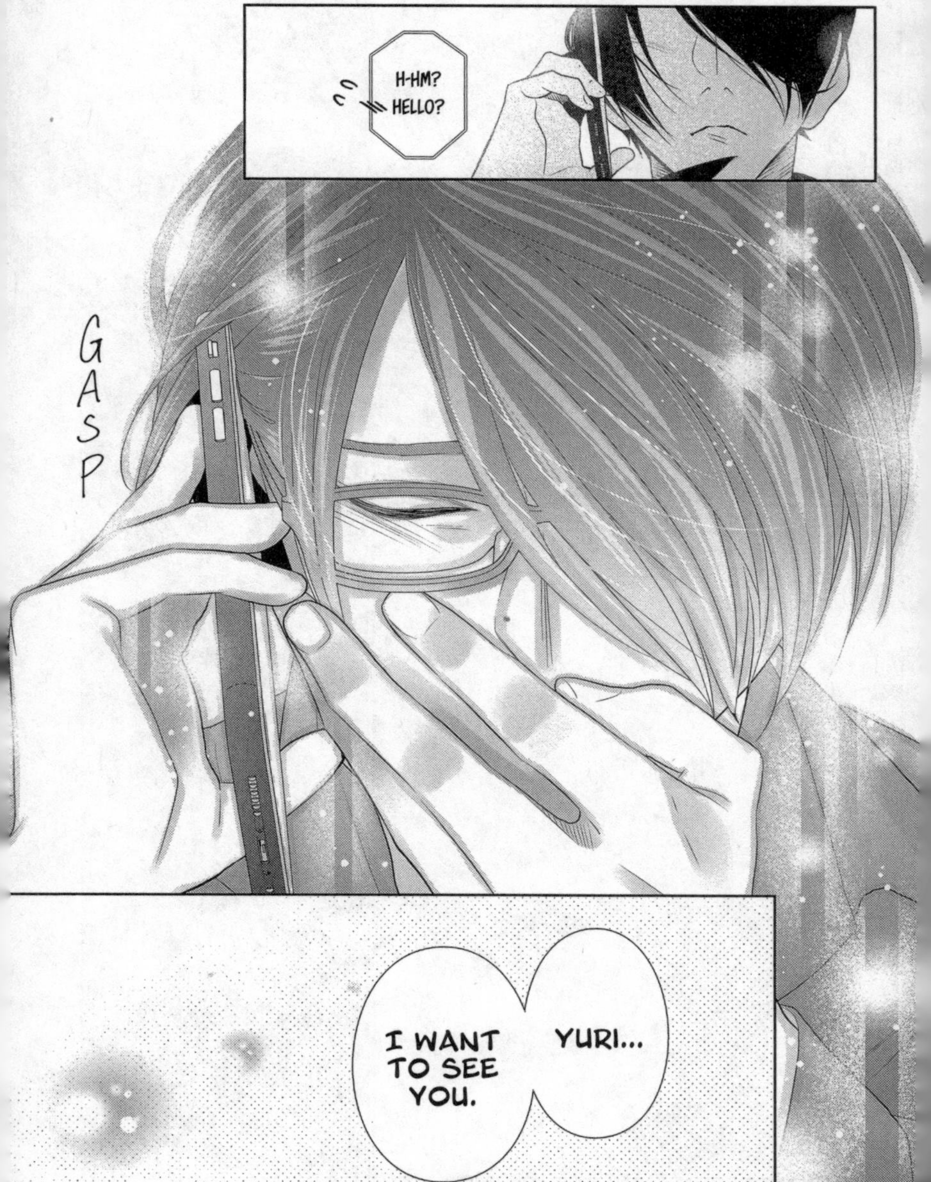
H-HM? HELLO?
GASP
YURI...
I WANT TO SEE YOU.

bullet 09 secret scene: bonus manga—Toshiomi Oya's Heart/end

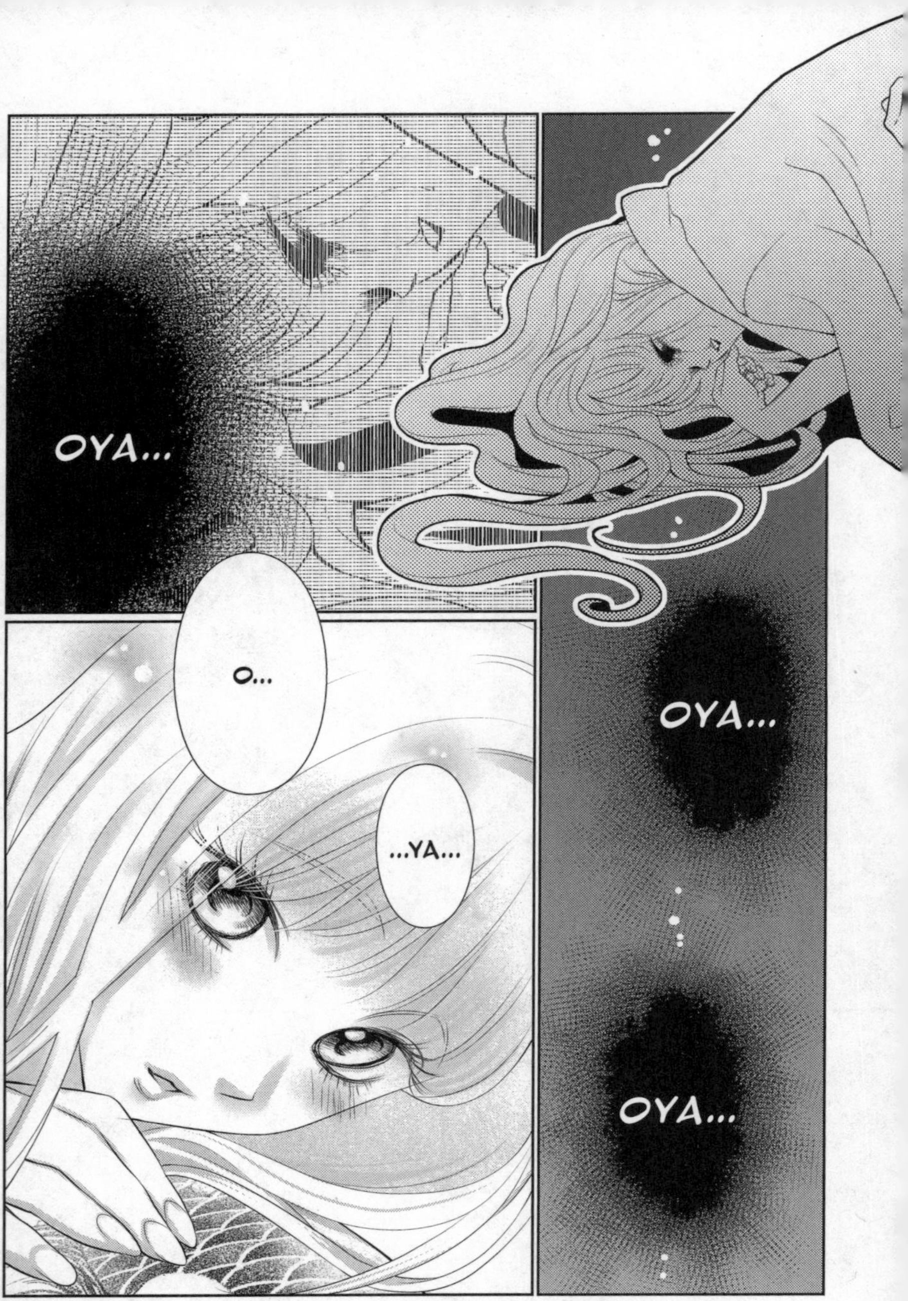
OYA...
OYA...
OYA...
O...
...YA...

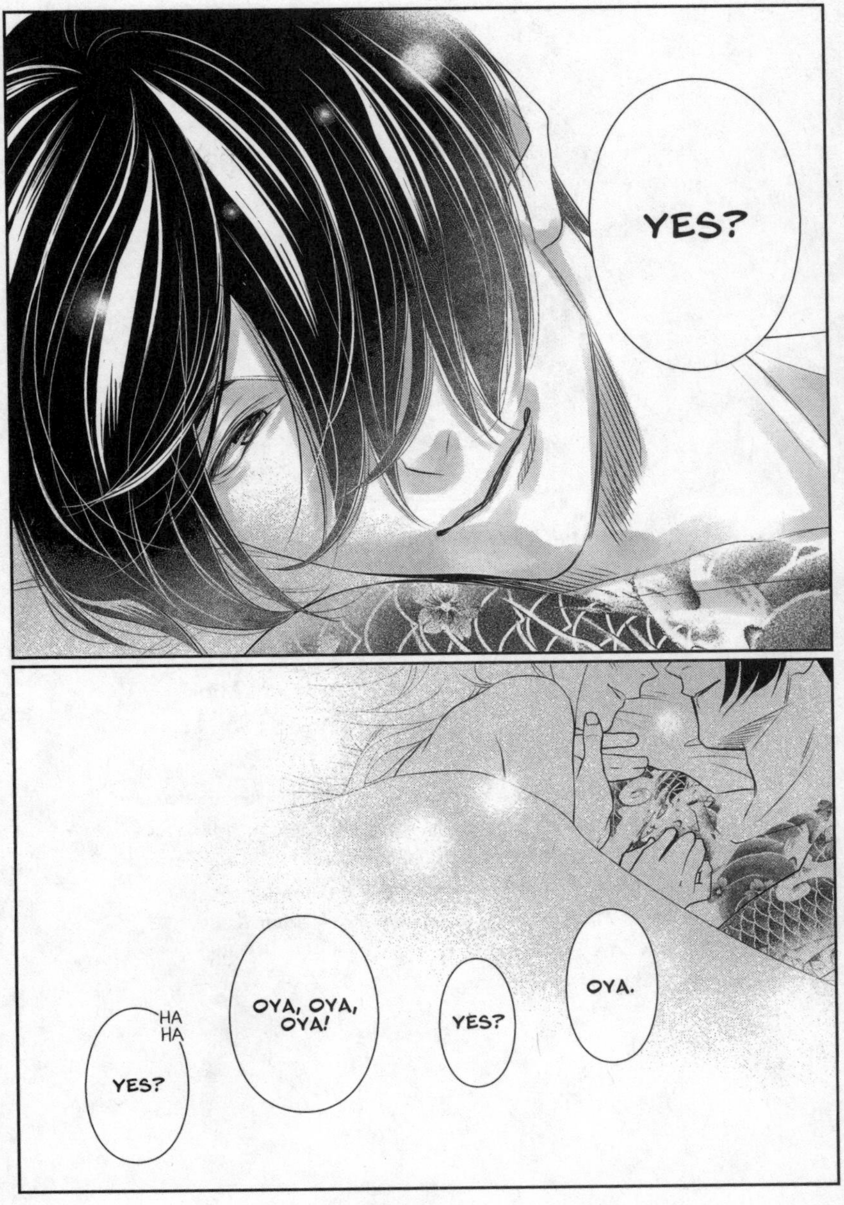
YES?
OYA.
YES?
OYA, OYA, OYA!
HA HA
YES?

YURI

Thank you so much for reading. I hope you enjoyed the final part of *Yakuza Lover*'s Shanghai story line and you continue to follow Yuri and Oya's foolish, growing romance.

—Nozomi Mino

Nozomi Mino was born on February 12 in Himeji, Hyogo Prefecture, in Japan, making her an Aquarius. She made her shojo manga debut in the May 2006 issue of *Cheese!* with "LOVE MANTEN" (Love Perfect Score). Since then, she has gone on to publish numerous works, including *Sweet Marriage*, *Wagamama Otoko wa Ichizu ni Koisuru* (Selfish Guys Love Hard), and *LOVE x PLACE.fam*. Her hobbies include going on drives and visiting cafes.

YAKUZA LOVER

Vol. 3
Shojo Beat Edition

STORY AND ART BY
Nozomi Mino

Translation: Andria Cheng
Touch-Up Art & Lettering: Michelle Pang
Design: Yukiko Whitley
Editor: Karla Clark

KOI TO DANGAN Vol. 3
by Nozomi MINO
© 2019 Nozomi MINO
All rights reserved.
Original Japanese edition published by SHOGAKUKAN.
English translation rights in the United States of America, Canada, the United
Kingdom, Ireland, Australia and New Zealand arranged with SHOGAKUKAN.

Printed in the U.S.A.

Published by VIZ Media, LLC
P.O. Box 77010
San Francisco, CA 94107

10 9 8 7 6 5 4 3 2 1
First printing, December 2021

viz.com

shojobeat.com

Everyone's Getting *Married*

STORY AND ART BY IZUMI MIYAZONO

Successful career woman Asuka Takanashi has an old-fashioned dream of getting married and becoming a housewife.

After her long-term boyfriend breaks up with her to pursue his own career goals, she encounters popular newscaster Ryu Nanami. Asuka and Ryu get along well, but the last thing he wants is to ever get married. This levelheaded pair who want the opposite things in life should never get involved, except...

 RATED M MATURE Shojo Beat
shojobeat.com

viz media
viz.com

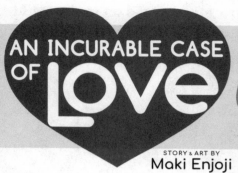

AN INCURABLE CASE OF LOVE

STORY & ART BY
Maki Enjoji

Nurse Nanase has striven to once again meet the prince of her dreams, so how is it he's become such an aggravating doctor?!

After witnessing a handsome and charming young doctor save a stranger's life five years ago, Nanase Sakura trained to become a nurse. But when she meets the doctor again and they start working together, she finds Kairi Tendo to be nothing like the man she imagined him to be!

VIZ

A smoldering tale of romance and revenge set in the world of the *New York Times* best seller *Dawn of the Arcana!*

THE
KING'S
Beast
麗

STORY & ART BY
Rei Toma

When they were children, Rangetsu's twin brother Sogetsu was ripped from her arms and sent to the palace to attend Prince Tenyou as a beast-servant, where he quickly fell victim to bloody dynastic intrigues. Now in a world that promises only bitterness, Rangetsu's one hope at avenging her brother is to disguise herself as a man and find a way into the palace!

RATED TEEN

VIZ

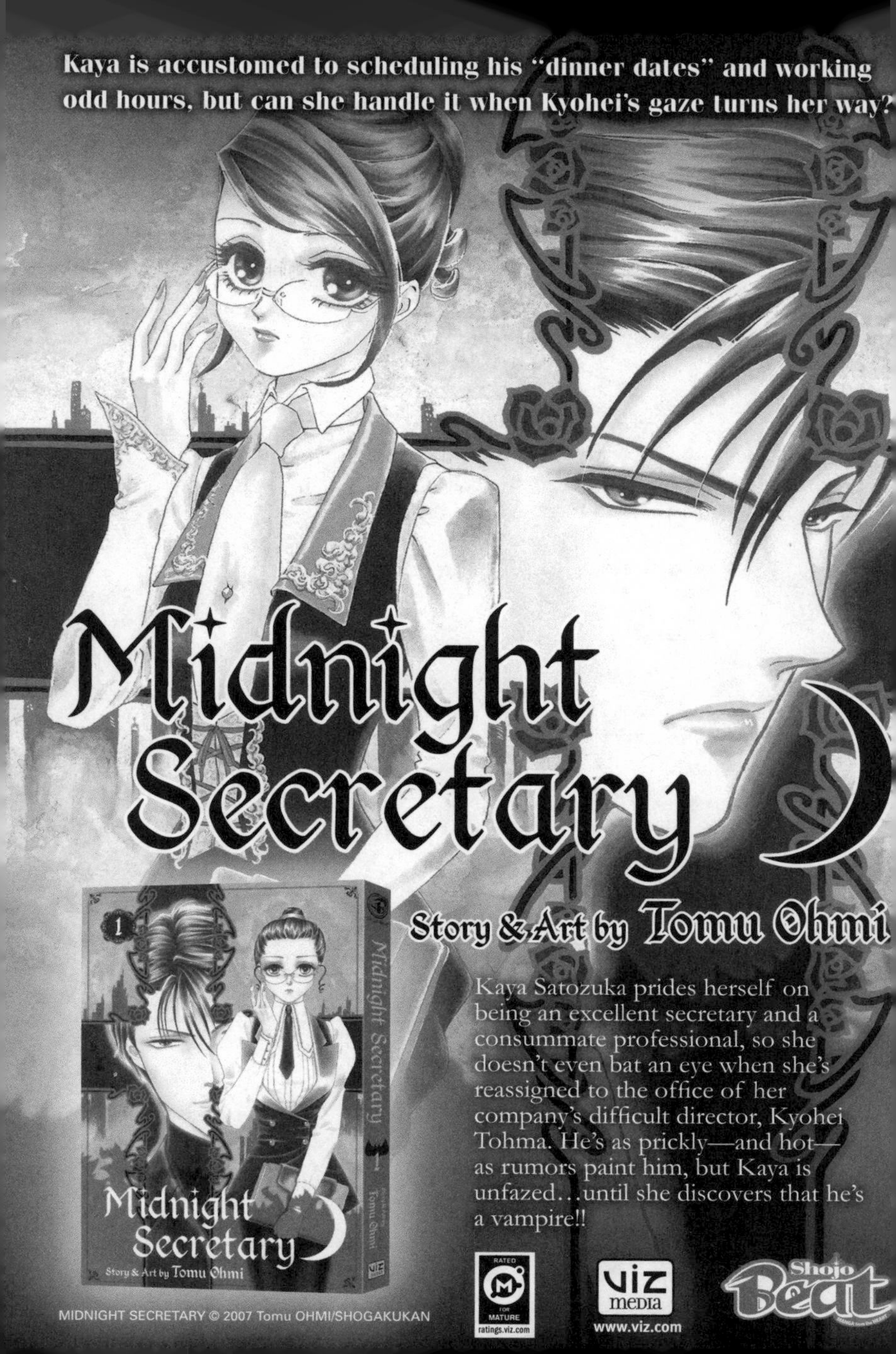

Kaya is accustomed to scheduling his "dinner dates" and working odd hours, but can she handle it when Kyohei's gaze turns her way?
Midnight Secretary
Story & Art by Tomu Ohmi
Kaya Satozuka prides herself on being an excellent secretary and a consummate professional, so she doesn't even bat an eye when she's reassigned to the office of her company's difficult director, Kyohei Tohma. He's as prickly—and hot—as rumors paint him, but Kaya is unfazed…until she discovers that he's a vampire!!
1
Midnight Secretary
Story & Art by Tomu Ohmi
MIDNIGHT SECRETARY © 2007 Tomu OHMI/SHOGAKUKAN
RATED
M
FOR MATURE
ratings.viz.com
VIZ media
www.viz.com
Shojo Beat

Revolutionary Girl UTENA

AFTER-the-REVOLUTION

Story and Art by **Chiho Saito** Original Concept by **Be-Papas**

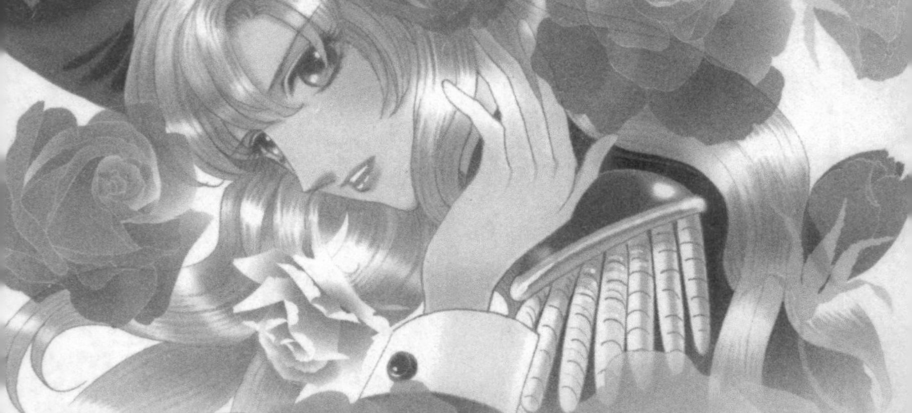

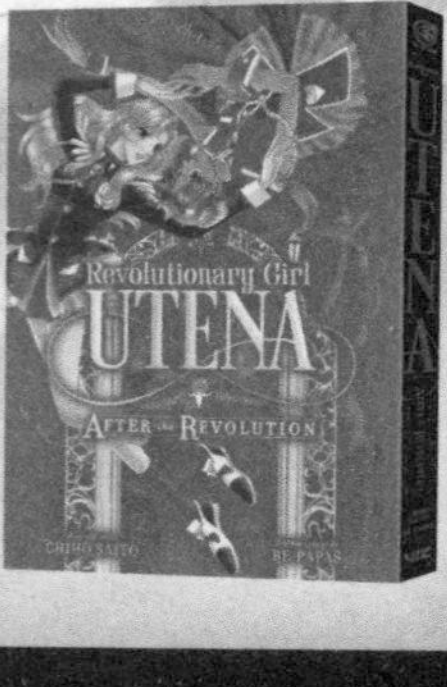
Revolutionary Girl
UTENA
AFTER the REVOLUTION
CHIHO SAITO
BE-PAPAS

Three short stories set after Utena's revolution!

Utena has saved Anthy by defeating Akio in the final duel, but in doing so she has vanished from the world. Now the student council members at Ohtori Academy find themselves in their own revolutions.